The Music of John Ireland

The Music of John Ireland

FIONA RICHARDS

Ashgate

Aldershot • Burlington USA • Singapore • Sydney

Published by
Ashgate Publishing Limited
Gower House
Croft Road
Aldershot
Hants GU11 3HR
England

Ashgate Publishing Company
131 Main Street
Burlington
Vermont 05401–5600
USA

Ashgate website: http://www.ashgate.com

British Library Cataloguing in Publication Data

Richards, Fiona.
    The Music of John Ireland.
    1. Ireland, John, 1879–1962—Criticism and interpretation.
    2. Music—Great Britain—20th century—History and criticism.
    I. Title.
    780.9'2

Library of Congress Control Number: 00–106479

ISBN 0 7546 0111 0

This book is printed on acid free paper

Edited and typeset in Times New Roman by Jane Wood.
Music examples set in Score by Stephen Ferre, New Notations, Saxmundham, Suffolk.

Printed and bound in Great Britain by MPG Books Ltd, Bodmin, Cornwall

Contents

List of figures

List of plates

Preface

I first started work on the music of John Ireland in 1993. The initial impetus was not only the music itself, but also the landscape of West Sussex, where I was living at the time. The beauty of this county – the exquisite village of Amberley, the wind-swept Rackham Banks, the mysterious grove of yews at Kingley Vale and the coast at Bosham – was and remains compelling. The discovery that Ireland was drawn to these same downland landscapes sparked a fascination for the man and his music. I therefore embarked on a PhD, with Professor Stephen Banfield as supervisor. As a starting-point, he suggested immersing myself in the works of E.M. Forster. As it turned out, this was exactly the stimulus I needed. Forster's places with potent yet elusive atmospheres, ancient burial mounds, prim eroticism and concealed emotions have parallels with Ireland's musical places. It is therefore to Stephen Banfield that I owe the most. Throughout my time working on this book, he has offered encouragement and criticism, and has always exuded enthusiasm for John Ireland and English music.

Several other people have had a significant input into this book. Martin Harlow has listened to and discussed Ireland's music at length, and has accompanied me on trips to Ireland's places: the Channel Islands, Chelsea, Dorset and West Sussex. I could not have completed this project without the assistance of Jane Taylor, of the John Ireland Trust. She has been generous with her time, and facilitated my work at the Trust: her knowledge of the extant biographical material has been invaluable. I must also thank Margaret and Peter Taylor, who have generously made their home available for my research, and who have contributed to the illustrations in this book. Jane Wood, at the Open University, has edited my work, tolerating numerous changes and revisions with patience and good grace. I am also very grateful to Caroline Cornish and Rachel Lynch at Ashgate Publishing for their work on the book.

The following people have either given interviews or have helped with the acquisition of material: Ken Adie, Timothy Adie, John Amis, Pat Blake, David Branson, the late Alan Bush, Geoffrey Bush, George Dannatt, David Dunhill, the late Ruth Dyson, Lewis Foreman, Sydney Hulke, Jonathan Hunt, Peter Hunt, Marcus Huxley, Caroline Ireland, Ben Johnson, Thea King, Lorna Konstam, Nigel Konstam, Janice Langley, the late Silvio Lenoir, Martin Le Page, Derek Longmire, the late Vivianne Longmire, Bonnie McClintock, Charles MacDonald, Mr and Mrs Miles, Revd Murray Millard, Alan Miller, Rita Miller, Lawrence Norcross, Rachel O'Higgins, Juliet Pannett, George Perkin, Bruce Phillips, Alan Rowlands, Colin Scott-Sutherland, Bill Strang, the late Kendall Taylor, Fred Tomlinson, Barbara Vincent, Brian White, Greg Woods. If there are others whom I have failed to mention, I can only apologize.

I wish to thank the following libraries and institutions for their assistance: Arundel Castle Trustees Limited, the British Library, Cambridge University Library, Chelsea Arts Club, Chelsea Library, Courtauld Institute, Deal Library, Dorset County Museum, General Register Office, Grenadier Guards, Holy Trinity Church, Chelsea, John Ireland Trust, Jersey Library, Leeds Grammar School, New Notations Computer Services, Priaulx Library Guernsey, Royal Academy of Music, Royal College of Music, St Luke's Church, Chelsea, La Société Jersiaise, Steyning Museum, Trafford Register Office, West Sussex Record Office, John Whybrow Photographers Ltd.

Finally, I am grateful to the Open University for time and money invested in the project: for periods of study leave and grants towards the production of music examples and editorial work.

Fiona Richards

Referencing systems

There are no footnotes in this book, and instead references appear in the text. When an edition of a book other than the first has been used, this has been cited, and details of earlier editions have been given in the bibliography. In the case of books and articles, the author's surname, the date and the page number(s) are given. For newspaper reviews, the source, date and page numbers where identifiable are included. Material drawn from the archive of St Luke's Church, Chelsea, has been labelled *St Luke's*, with dates and page numbers shown. Miscellaneous items are held at the John Ireland Trust. These are labelled *JIT*, 1, etc. All of these sources, which include record sleeve notes, periodical and newspaper entries and reviews, letters and conversations with the author, are listed more fully in the bibliography.

Ireland's correspondence has been used extensively. Details of the provenance of the letters are included in the bibliography. Where a letter is from Ireland, the recipient's initials and the date of the letter are given. Thus, EI: 11 April 1925 is a letter from Ireland to his sister Ethel. Where a letter is from a writer other than Ireland, both writer's and recipient's initials are recorded. Thus HL to GF: 17 June 1932 is a letter from Herbert Lambert to Gerald Finzi. The abbreviations of letter-writers and recipients are as follows:

AB (Adrian Boult)	HP (Helen Perkin)
AGM (Arthur Miller)	HR (Horace Randerson)
AM (Arthur Machen)	HRawlinson (Harold Rawlinson)
AR (Aidan Reynolds)	HRutland (Harold Rutland)
ARLG (Arthur Robert Lee Gardner)	HS (Herbert Sumsion)
CC (Clifford Curzon)	HW (Henry Wood)
CM (Charles Markes)	JB (Jocelyn Brooke)
Cramer (Cramer)	JI (John Ireland)
CSS (Colin Scott-Sutherland)	JL (John Longmire)
EC (Ernest Chapman)	KT (Kenneth Thompson)
EClark (Edward Clark)	KTaylor (Kendall Taylor)
EE (Edwin Evans)	KW (Kenneth Wright)
EI (Ethel Ireland)	LS (Linton Shields)
EL (Elizabeth Lutyens)	MB (Mary Bentley)
FT (Frederick Thurston)	MW (Marjorie Walde)
GB (Geoffrey Bush)	NB (Nancy Bush)
GD (George Dannatt)	NK (Norah Kirby)
GF (Gerald Finzi)	PG (Percy Grainger)
GP (George Parker)	PW (Paul Walde)
HB (Herbert Brown)	SI (Silvio Ireland)
HL (Herbert Lambert)	SN (Sydney Nicholson)

The original underlinings in Ireland's letters have been retained.

With the exception of well-known figures, the first names and dates of birth and death of composers and friends of Ireland have been given at their initial appearance. Where dates are not known, these have been omitted, for example in the case of violinist Bessie Smith. First names of poets and novelists have been given at their first appearance and, where known, their dates appear in the index. References to the musical works quoted in the text have been made by the use of bar numbers.

The list of works appears chronologically, so that periods of productivity and times of focus on particular genres or poets can be discerned. This list contains the following information: the title of the work, the date of composition and of any significant revisions, the scoring and, where relevant, the surname of the poet. The index of works lists pieces alphabetically. Song-cycles and groups of pieces are included as well as individual items.

Acknowledgements

For permission to reproduce copyright material, the author and publisher are most grateful to the following, a number of whom have generously made no charge.

Ken Adie (Plate 15 and material pertaining to Helen Perkin);

Boosey & Hawkes Music Publisher Ltd (Chap. 1, Exx. 2, 11–20; Chap. 2, Exx. 5–7, 10–11; Chap. 3, Exx. 5–10, 18; Chap. 4, Ex. 14; Chap. 5, Exx. 18–20, 22–26, Fig. 4; Chap. 7, Exx. 3–4, 6–7, 9, 10b, 11b, 12–16; Chap. 8, Exx. 1–4, 11);

Chap. 6, Ex. 1b reproduced by permission of Boosey & Hawkes Music Publisher Ltd. © Copyright 1905 by Adolph Fürstner. US Copyright renewed. Copyright assigned 1943 to Hawkes & Son (London) Ltd. (a Boosey & Hawkes Company) for the world excluding Germany, Italy, Portugal and the former territories of the USSR (excluding Estonia, Latvia and Lithuania);

The British Library (Chap. 3, Figs 1–2: British Library shelf marks 012627g5 and 12298.k.5);

The Syndics of Cambridge University Library (Plates 5 and 6: Add. 9473);

Canal + Image UK (Plate 17);

Chelsea Arts Club: by kind permission of the Trustees and Chairman of the Chelsea Arts Club (Plate 14);

The Conway Library, Courtauld Institute of Art (Chap. 2, Fig. 1; Chap. 9, Fig. 3);

George Dannatt (information gleaned from interviews with Charles Markes and material acquired from Adrian Boult);

David Dunhill (Plate 13);

EMI Music: © 1959 B. Feldman & Co. Ltd (trading as H. Freeman & Co.) EMI Music Publishing Ltd, London WC2H 0EA. Reproduced by permission of International Music Publications Ltd. (Chap. 4, Exx. 10–11a);

AM Heath (extracts from the writings of Jocelyn Brooke);

The John Ireland Trust (Plates 1–4, 7–12, 18–20; Chap. 1, Exx. 1, 6; Chap. 2, Exx. 4, 9; Chap. 3, Exx. 14–16; Chap. 4, Exx. 1, 3, 9a, 11b, 13; Chap. 5, Exx. 1a–b, 14–17, Fig. 3; Chap. 6, Exx. 1a, 10–13a; Chap. 7, Exx. 8, 10a, 11a, Fig. 2; Chap. 8, Ex. 10; Chap. 9, Fig. 2);

Patricia Kapp (Introduction, Fig. 0.1);

Kent Arts and Libraries (Chap. 7, Fig. 3);

St Mary the Virgin, Shipley, West Sussex (Fig. 9.4);

Robin Millard (Chap. 2, Fig. 3);

Music Sales Ltd (Chap. 2, Ex. 3; Chap. 5, Ex. 1b; Chap. 6, Exx. 10–13a; Chap. 8, Ex. 10b; Chap. 9, Exx. 1–3);

© Oxford University Press 1928. Extract reproduced by permission. Licence no. 05132 (Chap. 3, Ex. 11; Chap. 6, Exx. 6–8, 13b; Chap. 8, Ex. 9);

Janet Machen Pollock (letters from Arthur Machen to John Ireland);

Alan Rowlands (Chap. 4, Ex. 1);

The Royal Borough of Kensington and Chelsea Libraries and Arts Service (Chap. 2, Fig. 2; Chap. 5, Fig. 1);

Royal College of Music (Chap. 1, Fig. 1);

St Luke's Church, Chelsea (Chap. 2, material quoted from archive material);

Schott (Chap. 3, Exx. 14–16; Chap. 4, Ex. 1a; Chap. 8, Exx. 10a, c, d);

Colin Scott-Sutherland (Chap. 4, Fig. 1);

The Society of Authors, London as the literary representative of the Estate of A.E. Housman (extracts from Housman poems);

Stainer & Bell Ltd, London, England (Chap. 1, Exx. 3–10; Chap. 2, Exx. 1–2; Chap. 3. Exx. 1–4, 12–13, 17; Chap. 4, Exx. 2, 4–8, 9b, 12, 15; Chap. 5, Exx. 1c, 2–13; Chap. 6, Exx. 2–5, 14–16; Chap. 7, Exx. 1–2, 5, Fig. 1; Chap. 8, Exx. 5–8, Chap. 9, Fig. 1);

The Executors of the Sylvia Townsend Warner Estate and Chatto & Windus as publisher (extracts from Townsend Warner, *Lolly Willowes* and *The Diaries of Sylvia Townsend Warner*);

West Sussex Record ref. W.S.R.O. PM. 394 (Chap. 3, Fig. 3): Ordnance Survey, 1 inch to 1 mile (1:10,560); 'Popular Edition', sheet 133; published 1920, reprint of 1931 (enlarged detail).

Every effort has been made to contact all copyright holders of material cited in the book. Where attempts to trace holders have been unsuccessful, sincere apologies are offered.

Introduction

Aspects of John Ireland

The death of the composer John Ireland in 1962 at the age of 82 prompted a wave of tributes, which alluded mainly to his gift for writing for the piano, his love of nature and his rigorous craftsmanship. It is evident from these obituaries that it is difficult to place Ireland. Though not born early enough to be part of the fabric of the British Musical Renaissance, he did not belong to a modernist generation. He was himself aware of this problem of 'belonging', writing in 1925: 'People of the older school regard me as a revolutionary, while the rising generation look on me as an old fogey, so one pleases nobody but oneself' (EI: 11 April 1925). Several of the obituaries commented on this, *The Times* noting that he 'never went out of his way to court popularity' and 'held himself apart from the English musical renaissance' (*The Times*, 13 June 1962: 12). The *Manchester Guardian* described him as 'a composer moreover of highly independent mind' (*Manchester Guardian*, 13 June 1962: 2). A few years later, writing in 1969, William Mann, at that time music critic for *The Times*, made similar observations on Ireland's separateness:

> During his working life he was, among his composing British contemporaries, something of a loner: not a folksongite, nor a Bright Young Thing, in musical language closer to Debussy and Stravinsky than to any British composers, except perhaps his consciously Irish professor Stanford and the cosmopolitan Delius. These influences were subsumed quite deeply so that Ireland's music always sounded idiosyncratic.
>
> (Mann, 1969: 9)

Ireland's music is highly personal, both because it is nearly always tied to a specific event or place or person in his life, but also because of its individual musical qualities. His music is an expression of a state of mind. There is a sombre side and a rapturous side, intensity and utter gaiety: he could produce lightweight, charming pieces, but also music that was darkly oppressive. 'His music was never written in any sense for the big battalions and will remain the preserve of the poetically-inclined' (*Daily Telegraph*, 13 June 1962).

Ireland the man was as elusive as the music. He was a collector of beautiful furniture and works of art, but for long periods chose to live in what were essentially bedsits. He was Romantic in spirit, but in later life utterly unromantic in his short, squat appearance and domestic obsessions. John Ireland was a public figure with a very private face. Herbert Lambert, a fellow musician who was friendly with him in the 1930s, wrote of him to Gerald Finzi (1901–56) that 'for all his grim & rocklike exterior he is an almost pathetically sensitive human being – a man of sorrow & acquainted with grief' (HL to GF: 17 June 1932).

While he is now regarded as having led an uneventful life, and indeed some of the obituaries recorded this as having been the case, Ireland had a busy and varied career. In addition to the time spent composing, he was active as a performer, both as pianist and organist, as an Associated Board examiner and as a teacher. There were hectic periods when his diary was full, involving him in travel round the country. His busiest time was probably in the 1920s, at a point when his music was very popular, being performed by major artists such as Harriet Cohen (1895–1967), to whom he dedicated several pieces, including a transcription of J.S. Bach's 'Meine Seele erhebt der Herren', for her *Bach Book for Harriet Cohen* (1932). Other significant performers of his music included Beatrice Harrison (1892–1965), John Goss (1894–1953) and Roy Henderson (1899–2000). To take a slice of Ireland's life as a professional musician, in 1925, for example, he held an organist's post, he taught composition, undertook frequent tours for the Associated Board, worked as editor for the Clarendon Press Series for Oxford University Press, and had many public engagements as a performer of his own music as just a small sample of concerts shows.

6 January:	broadcast of his piano solos and accompanist to Ivor James (1882–1963) in the Cello Sonata
20 January:	piano solos and accompanist to Carl Fuchs (1865–1951) in the Cello Sonata, Leeds University
25 January:	accompanist to John Barbirolli (1899–1970) in the Cello Sonata, London
5 February:	piano solos, Leicester
12 March:	piano solos, Æolian Hall
27 March:	piano solos and pianist in the Phantasie Trio and the First Violin Sonata with Bessie Spence and John Dickson
30 March:	accompanist to Carl Fuchs in the Cello Sonata and pianist in the Phantasie Trio with Fuchs and William Primrose (1904–82), Manchester
31 March:	piano solos and pianist in the Phantasie Trio with Primrose and Fuchs
2 April:	piano solos, Wakefield
3 April:	piano solos and pianist in the Phantasie Trio with Primrose and Fuchs, Birmingham

Close friends, such as Thomas Dunhill (1877–1946), for whom Ireland had stood as best man, were truly loyal and supportive, and have left memories of his kindness and integrity. But Ireland also suffered from difficult personal relationships, and there are less salutary recollections of a grumpy, vulnerable man who was at one time an alcoholic. He taught composition and theory for many years, both privately and in his role as Professor of Composition at the

Royal College of Music. In the latter position he worked for one or two days a week, and had on average ten pupils. Of those he taught, E.J. Moeran (1894–1950) thought very highly of him, and described him as 'an exceptional counsellor', who gave 'unstintingly of his very best' (Moeran, 1931: 68). Conversely, the view of Benjamin Britten (1913–76) was that Ireland was unreliable and often drunk (in Mitchell and Reed, 1998: 211). Richard Arnell (*b.* 1917), recalled that:

> The lessons were given in a large, dark studio in the garden of his large, dark Chelsea house. In a sort of yellowish light from the skylight (there were no windows), not much could be seen but a huge piano, given him by some now vanished piano company. The keys were thick with dust and cigarette ash, and I am sure the instrument was never tuned. We would both sit at this monster, sometimes for two hours or more (the lesson was theoretically for an hour) while he stared absentmindedly at my music, making a few extremely telling comments, then digressing everywhere. He had a wonderful eye for a weakness and would spot it immediately.
>
> (Arnell, 1962: 39)

The same sorts of dichotomies and opposites can be found among comments from colleagues, family and friends. Ireland was a profoundly nostalgic man, given to reminiscing about an imagined, happier past, and the theme of remembrance runs deep in his output. He could be irritatingly evasive, but occasionally ardent and open. He eulogized spring and the English countryside, and in doing so betrayed an altogether happier and more effusive nature than has sometimes been suggested. In a radio broadcast Stephen Banfield proposed that the neglect of Ireland's music was possibly because he was 'rather unappetising as a person', but that this is to miss the 'gloriously free, intense, positive quality' of his music (Banfield, 1994). And Ireland himself wrote of the 'fire and inspiration' that he saw in his own music (EI: 2 Nov. 1945). From the expressive nature of the music it is clear that Ireland was a highly emotional person, and there is a dramatic contrast between his buoyant, uplifting music and that produced at moments of trauma. The composer wrote of himself and his family that 'we are liable every few years to some kind of "crisis", when everything in life seems impossible and unbearable, and one feels unable to face up to anything. I have had it several times ... ' (SI: 30 June 1948). From the music alone, it is evident when Ireland was suffering one of these crises. For example, the 1929 Ballade for piano was written at a time of great personal turbulence, with which the music is invested.

Although Ireland could be harping and petty, he could also betray a quirky sense of humour, and this again is manifest in the music in jaunty cameos and joyous ballads. Professional insecurity was one aspect of his nature, and he often questioned his lack of popularity. He was very particular about the manner in which people played his music, yet equally bemoaned the lack of performances.

Though Ireland was more directly involved with the British musical establishment than was his contemporary and friend, Arnold Bax (1883–1953), and though in a way better known, he did not find the same fame. A comparison between the two men accentuates the more private, secret nature of John Ireland. While Bax was knighted in 1937, appointed Master of the King's Music in 1942 and Knight Commander of the Royal Victorian Order in 1953, Ireland received no honours of any kind. Despite his national status, once his student days were over he did not really mix in artistic circles. While Bax consorted with renowned literary figures such as Laurence and Clemence Housman, James Stephens and Padraic Colum, Ireland was drawn to a writer, Arthur Machen (1863–1947), who himself is difficult to place: now little read, it is difficult to say whether his works are fantasy, horror or autobiography. Whereas Bax frequently travelled, to Germany, Austria, Russia and the Ukraine, Ireland was a very British figure who went abroad on only a handful of occasions, and then only to Europe. He met composers from other countries, most notably Ravel and Gershwin, but international figures such as these tended to touch fleetingly on his life (though less fleetingly on his music).

0.1 John Ireland by Edmond Kapp, 1932

Ireland's spiritual roots were in the 1890s and early 1900s. In a number of his pieces he harks back to the attendant images of these years, and in later life presented himself as the English gentleman. He read the Edwardians, and his music is a mixture of the progressive and static that characterized life in the first decade of the twentieth century. Just as it is impossible to label 'Edwardianism' by a single mood or symbol, so it is impossible to pin down Ireland by one 'type' alone. His music is rural, but there is also an urban side. It is full of pain and doubt, but also exudes total optimism. It is about reverie and speculation in the tradition of the Edwardian novel. Just as it is the little novels and bestsellers, minor productions that are so 'Edwardian', so it is often Ireland's miniatures that contain the essence of his nature. He was drawn to the fantasy and whimsy of the day, to the works of Ronald Firbank and Max Beerbohm, ghost stories and escapes into the past. And just as Edwardian England was full of polarities, so too is Ireland's music. Unlike Ralph Vaughan Williams (1872–1958), he never turned to English folk song for inspiration, and was much more interested in the music of Debussy and Ravel. But although his music subsumes many French influences, it is profoundly English, belonging to a particular age and sensibility, with its roots in English places.

Ireland did not write many lengthy works: there are no symphonies, no operas, and only a handful of pieces that last for more than fifteen minutes. Instead, his natural milieu was in smaller mediums, primarily piano, vocal and chamber music, and the *Sunday Times* obituary noted that he 'was at his best, however, on a smaller scale' (*Sunday Times*, 17 June 1962: 36). While some works, such as the orchestral overture *Satyricon*, have an immediate appeal, others are uncompromising in the demands they make of listener and performer, for example the piano piece 'Moon-glade', which yields a stark, compacted soundscape. While there are ballads in the best of ballad traditions, there are also songs that are denser, less immediately appealing than those of his contemporaries. The music demands concentrated listening and relistening. Some works were commissioned, most were not; and there is a fundamental difference between the two types.

Much of Ireland's output is closely inter-related, with a complex system of personal musical symbols, images and ideas infiltrating almost everything he wrote. As a result his music is difficult to categorize. The chamber pieces cannot be analysed in isolation from the piano music or the songs or the orchestral works, because they share so much common ground. The music is elusive because of fleeting motifs, glimpses of other works, half-recognized turns of phrase and recurring fingerprints. There are often extra-musical layers of meanings, with pieces closely linked to dates, places, people and literature, a feature that was noticed in early reviews of his music: 'One feels that Mr. Ireland does not consciously make up his mind to relate his art to life, but just that he cannot refrain from doing so' (*MMR*, Dec. 1918: 268). Because of these

personal associations and connections, a phenomenological criticism of
Ireland's music would have limitations. This is why, although the present study
is not a comprehensive biographical survey, the composer's life and music are
interwoven here. And while an awareness of the background informs the
music, the music itself serves as essential biographical material:

> The more or less meagre and ignoble facts tie the [composer's] balloon, his
> flotilla of balloons to the earth, and tracing the connections tells us something
> of the nature of artistic creation. The life of a [composer], which spins outside
> of itself a secondary life, offers an opportunity to study mind and body, or
> inside and outside, or dream and reality, together, as one.
>
> (Updike, 1999: A 10)

Unfortunately the surviving biographical material is sketchy, and there are big
gaps in our knowledge of Ireland's early life, though a picture of sorts can be
constructed from clues, both in the music and in letters. At various points in his
life, material was either destroyed or disappeared. Mystery surrounds most of
these 'spring-cleans'. It appears that Ireland himself periodically threw things
away, for example, like most people, when a big house move was imminent.
But it may also be the case that housekeepers took matters into their own
hands. Similarly, when Ireland's manuscripts were presented to the British
Library after his death, several contained systematic and thorough obliterations
of dedicatory words. It is unclear whether this was the work of Ireland himself,
or of another hand.

Ireland was a prolific letter-writer, and there is much surviving
correspondence, though very little from his youth or from the 1920s, the
decade in which he was producing his most intense, intimate music. However,
a surprising number of letters and other primary sources from the 1940s
onwards have survived. Some of the letters are to close friends, others to
musicians. They are one of the main ways in which it is possible to build a
picture of Ireland's personality, and are essential historical material. They
contain information on his composing methods, remarks on the political
situation, descriptions of places and throwaway lines that often give much
away. Just as there are polarities in the music, so it is evident from the letters
that Ireland was an enigmatic and contradictory figure.

To date there has been no book on the music of John Ireland, though
writings on Ireland not only as a composer, but also as a notable performer and
teacher, have appeared intermittently, from reviews of his earliest works to
longer articles on aspects of his compositional style. Two biographical works
have been produced. The first, published in 1969, was *John Ireland: Portrait of
a Friend* by John Longmire (1902–86). Longmire was a former composition
pupil and friend, and this work was an attempt not to write about the music, but
to convey something of the composer's personality and domestic and
professional life. In 1979 Muriel Searle's *John Ireland: The Man and His*

Music worked information on his output into a chronological biography, but included not a single musical illustration. Both these fundamentally hagiographical though evocative accounts have merits, but leave essential musical issues undiscussed and contain a number of factual inaccuracies. In 1985 Banfield devoted substantial parts of his *Sensibility and English Song* to discussion of Ireland's songs, this time with much greater insight into the meaning of the music. Since then there has been no further attempt to write about Ireland's output other than in short articles, though in 1993 Stewart Craggs' *John Ireland: A Catalogue, Discography, and Bibliography* appeared. Although this is a useful reference work, like the biographies it has shortcomings, and also like them, it is at the time of writing out of print.

In addition to these large-scale works there have been shorter articles and monographs on Ireland. The first significant pieces were written in 1919 by Edwin Evans (1871–1945), a critic and close friend of the composer. These remain among the most astute of any writings on Ireland's music. Noteworthy articles that followed this were in 1943 by Nigel Townshend and in 1946 by another friend and critic, Ralph Hill (1900–50). In 1954 there were two substantial pieces by Hugh Ottaway and the article for *Grove 5* by a former pupil, Peter Crossley-Holland (1916–). Frank Howes included a sizeable chapter on Ireland in his *English Musical Renaissance* (1966), but there was then a gap of several years before Colin Scott-Sutherland's *John Ireland* (1980). Composer Geoffrey Bush (1920–98) wrote on the composer in 1983 and 1993, Barbara Docherty in 1989 and pianist Alan Rowlands first in 1962, and at greater length in 1992 and 1993. The latter was another friend of Ireland. He first met him in *c.* 1956, when he went to play to him, and recalled that 'he greeted me with charm and talked animatedly for nearly two hours and I was soon to experience the pungency of his views and the dryness of his wit' (Rowlands, 1962: 71). One other perceptive writer on Ireland was Christopher Palmer, whose thoughts are preserved mainly as sleeve notes.

All of the writers above have commented in general terms on what they perceive to be the most striking characteristic features of Ireland's music, and all have cited two significant facets of his work. The first is Ireland's command of form; it is recognized that he was able to create and work within concise, organic structures. The second is that he had a great gift for melody; the term 'lyrical' is frequently applied. Geoffrey Bush, as Music Advisor to the John Ireland Trust until 1998, and both a pupil and friend of the composer, was perhaps the closest of these writers to the music. Nevertheless, he found the task of trying to capture the essence of the music in a few words an unrevealing exercise:

> A roll-call of stylistic features – beauty of line, subtlety of harmony, mastery of form, unfailing craftsmanship, sensitive response to poetry, a thorough grasp of the potential of instruments either singly or in combination – however

applicable it may be to Ireland's music does nothing to convey its inner character. A list of abstract qualities – strength of purpose, empathy with nature, quirky humour, profound feeling, and an even profounder reticence – is scarcely more helpful. The only way to understanding Ireland the composer is by direct contact with the music...

(in Craggs, 1993: xii)

Despite the disclaimer, Bush does begin to identify some of the hallmarks of Ireland's style.

One of the most powerful descriptions of Ireland's music came from a writer, Jocelyn Brooke (1908–66), commenting from the standpoint of a non-musician, with only a rudimentary knowledge of music techniques. Brooke, who found Ireland's music difficult and was not an immediate enthusiast, eventually became more than just an admirer, perceiving in the music a profound sense of place and of the past:

... with Ireland I was aware of [an] immediate impact: a sense, as it were, of *recognition*, as though, turning a corner in a strange countryside, I had suddenly caught sight of a familiar landmark. The simile is not accidental, for Ireland's music, at its most characteristic, evokes for me always the idea of a particular kind of *landscape*: a 'country of the mind', remote, mysterious yet essentially English. The scene I envisage, more often than not, is a prospect of bare chalk-downs interspersed with deep woodlands, vaguely apprehended in the bleak twilight of a winter's evening; there is a sense of far, illimitable distances, a hint, perhaps, of some *cor au fond des bois* echoing sadly beyond the lonely downland, on the crest of which the ancient earthworks stand silhouetted against a rainy sunset ...

(Brooke, 1958: 600)

Ireland himself professed a real liking for this interpretation by Brooke, and wrote to him after reading it, affirming that his music was an expression of a state of mind:

I wish I could write about your work as lucidly and understandingly as you have written about mine, most of which – the really significant thing – remains to the average hearer a mere sequence of notes and conveys none of that strange, secret 'territory of the mind' you and I so clearly share. It is a country unknown to them, hence neither you nor I can expect what is called popularity. But of course neither you nor I have aimed at that.

(JB: 8 Nov. 1958)

Descriptive writing in the manner of Brooke is one way of attempting to articulate something of Ireland's music, and will be revisited in Chapter 1. Another is to approach the music chronologically, and to devise compositional periods. The most decisive attempt to do this came from Crossley-Holland, who in *Grove 5* defined three natural periods. He saw the first of these as being 1903–20, a period in which an individual voice emerges from a traditional inheritance. The second was 1921–29, Ireland's most productive period, when much of his personal biography infiltrates the songs and the piano music. The years from 1930 were viewed as 'a period of clarification and larger works' (Crossley-Holland, 1954: 534). Others have also attempted to establish discrete stylistic divisions. Townshend saw 1920–30 as a time when Ireland was largely repeating himself and 1930 as a turning-point, with the Piano Concerto marking a move in a new direction and *Sarnia* (1940–41), and 'Le Catioroc' in particular, as the culmination of the search for something new. Ottaway discussed the piano pieces prior to *London Pieces* (1917–20) as being transitional works in which Ireland's true voice is not yet evident, with the Piano Sonata marking a reaching of maturity of thought, despite the limitations which he saw in this work. But a chronological route through Ireland's music is not necessarily the most useful methodology, given that there are motifs that recur over time and that there are very strong links between music of different periods. These connections also make it difficult to talk about the music by genre alone.

Another way of understanding Ireland's music is to approach it via literature. It might seem odd to come to a composer via a writer, but this is a very fruitful way into the heart of this music, a music whose spirit is often literary. Ireland would undoubtedly agree with this, having stated on a number of occasions that literature was as important to him as was music, and that no one who did not read Machen could truly understand his works. And Machen wrote to Ireland that the way into his own literary works was to read the autobiographical ones first, the notion being 'to interest the desired reader in the author, in the concrete; before you lead him to the author's all imagined world' (AM to JI: 17 Sept. 1941). The present book therefore starts not with the music, but with the composer himself, with his birth in 1879.

Chapter 1

Sonatas and fantasies: encountering Ireland

John Nicholson Ireland was born on 13 August 1879 in Bowdon, a prosperous Manchester suburb. He spent the large part of his childhood and adolescence in this area. His first home was a big Victorian detached house, 'Inglewood', St Margaret's Road. His father, Alexander Ireland (1809–94) (Plate 1), was born in Edinburgh, his family having moved from Orkney some generations earlier. He married Eliza Mary Blyth in 1839, but this partnership was cut short by his wife's death. He moved to Manchester in *c.* 1846 to become manager and publisher of the recently established *Manchester Examiner*, the rival paper to the *Manchester Guardian*. In 1865 Alexander Ireland married for a second time. His new wife, Anne (Annie) Elizabeth Nicholson (1839–93) (Plate 2), was of Cumbrian descent, and was herself an author and critic. Her father, Dr John Nicholson, was a scholar of oriental languages at Queen's College, Oxford; her brother Alleyne Nicholson a Professor in Aberdeen. The atmosphere in the Ireland–Nicholson household was therefore a literary one, and Alexander Ireland was acquainted with Thomas Carlyle, Ralph Waldo Emerson, Richard le Gallienne, Leigh Hunt and Walt Whitman. In addition to his role as a newspaper businessman, he published his own writings, including his recollections of Emerson and two works extolling the virtues of literature: *Cheap literature and the love of reading* (1882) and *The book-lover's enchiridion* (1883).

In 1866 Alexander and Annie were living in Alder Bank, Altrincham. Their first child, Lucy, was born in October that year, followed by another girl, Alice, in February 1868. The family then moved to Bowdon. Walter Alleyne (known always as Alleyne) was born in January 1871, and a third girl, Ethel, in January 1873. There was then a gap of a few years before the birth of John in 1879, when his father was seventy and his mother forty years old.

Ireland's mother Annie was the most influential figure in the early part of his life. Although she was in poor health, she lectured on literature, specializing in the poetry of Robert Browning. She published a number of works between 1885 and 1892, and is particularly remembered for her *Life Story of Jane Welsh Carlyle* (1891). Her last work, *Longer Flights*, published posthumously in 1898, includes a chapter entitled 'Train up a child', in which she sets out her parenting manifesto. Given that this was written in a period when obedience and duty were considered to be the most important aspects of a child's upbringing, her piece is remarkably forward-thinking. Although she says that a child should be taught to be 'straightforward, manly, brave, good and upright in his dealings, gentle, merciful, considerate' (Nicholson, 1898: 221), above all she stresses the futility of forcing a child in an inappropriate direction, saying that parents should observe 'patience and forbearance' (ibid.: 222). Perhaps Annie Ireland aimed to practise her suggested tolerance and support of an individual in her dealings with her son, John, but nevertheless it seems that Ireland had an unhappy childhood; comments in his letters refer to this.

The gap between the oldest and youngest child in this family was a big one, and did not make for good relationships between the siblings. Ireland described the fact that his brother Alleyne used to beat him 'mercilessly every night on my way to bed' (SI: 30 March 1948). Alleyne went to sea at the age of sixteen, and his writings were being printed outside Britain by 1897. His publications included political and travel works such as *Briton and Boer in South Africa* (1899). In 1907 he was employed by the University of Chicago, and became companion-secretary to Joseph Pulitzer from *c.* 1910. He wrote *Joseph Pulitzer: reminiscences of a secretary* (1914) and *The New Korea* (1926). After leaving Britain, there appears to have been little, if any, communication between Alleyne and John, and in 1948 the latter wrote that he had heard 'not one word for at least 30 years' (SI: 30 March 1948). Ireland's other recollections of his early family life testify to the cruelty of his upbringing. He recalled that he was 'shut in dark rooms with no food but bread and water, for 24 hours, for the slightest offence' (ibid.).

Of the three sisters, the youngest, Ethel, was the only one to maintain contact with John. She studied at the Royal Academy of Music (RAM), had some musical and literary works published, among them *Some new letters by Leigh Hunt and Stevenson* (1898), and married a linguist, Dr Anton Velleman, after which she moved to Switzerland. She was divorced during the First World War, and John was in touch with her at least until the Second World War, when she was living first in Venice, in 1939, and then in France, in Menton and Juan-les-Pins in 1940. She had two sons, the eldest of whom, Silvio (*b.* 1904), after an education at the King's College Choir School, Cambridge and at King William's School in the Isle of Man, did remain in contact with his uncle, visiting him in Chelsea in the 1920s. Silvio moved to San Francisco, where he took a new name, Henri Lenoir, and settled first as the owner of a café and eventually as a collector and dealer in fine art. Throughout Ireland's life there is affectionate and often lengthy correspondence between them. Silvio sent what were evidently very generous food parcels on a regular basis during and after the Second World War. Ethel's other son, Anthony (1906–89), worked for some time as a language teacher. He married and had three children, Nicholas (*b.* 1939), Caroline (*b.* 1941) and Adrian (*b.* 1945). He travelled widely, and found success as a playwright, with dramatic works including *Byron in Piccadilly* (1945).

While there were evidently problems within the Ireland–Nicholson household, John Ireland's formative years did foster a childhood interest in music. Ireland recalled that his first lessons were with his mother and that he was drawn to music from an early age:

> My sisters used to play the piano – Chopin and various things like that. And my mother, although she was not a professional musician, took a deep interest in music. I started playing the piano when I was seven or eight, but it wasn't until I came to London in 1893 that I began my serious studies. I can't remember precisely when I began composing, probably at an early age in my head, though I didn't put any of it down on paper until much later. I began writing music before I had any lessons in composition or any of the fundamentals.
>
> (in Schafer, 1963: 25)

In his very early years Ireland had a governess. His first experience of an educational institution, at the age of about eight or nine, was when he was sent to board at a local dame school (Plate 3). This was an unhappy experience, not least because he was made to stay there during the holidays, and because, according to Ireland, the three women who ran the school delighted to 'tyrannize' over him (SI: 30 March 1948). At about this time the *Manchester Examiner* suffered severe financial difficulties and eventually folded. The Ireland family then moved from Bowdon to Southport.

Ireland's next school was Dinglewood Preparatory School in Colwyn Bay, and he then spent two terms at Leeds Grammar School in the first part of 1893, during which time he lodged in the city. He studied music at both schools, learning piano, organ and violin, but he recalled that his early piano lessons were yet again uninspiring:

> I have the most unpleasant memories attached to my first piano teachers. They used to use a round, black and quite hefty ruler which would descend on my fingers the moment they got into trouble. But the difficulties didn't disappear as a result of the ruler treatment; they only became worse, and I became more and more terrified. At the age of ten I associated Beethoven with suffering and punishment.
>
> (in Schafer, 1963: 25)

The early musical training and the haphazard schooling was all rather unfortunate, and did not make for happy or useful early years. However, given that Ireland developed a profound knowledge and love of literature that continued for the rest of his life, it would seem that the family's associations with eminent writers made a much more lasting impression than did his formal education. Ireland himself testified to this. He remembered meeting le Gallienne and wrote that he had 'always been interested in literature as a consequence of my home life' (in Schafer, 1963: 26). He read widely and drew on many fine poems for inspiration. His output of some seventy songs uses poetry that is nearly always finely crafted: there are settings of Thomas Hardy, A.E. Housman, John Masefield, Arthur Symons and several Elizabethan sonneteers. Often he set newly published poems by contemporary writers, and there are also signs of eclectic and idiosyncratic literary tastes, such as his favouring of now little-known poets such as James Vila Blake. Ireland frequently prefaced his piano pieces with a passage from a poem, carefully chosen to reflect the meaning of the music. As an example, extracts from Victor Hugo's *Les Travailleurs de la Mer* and Charles Algernon Swinburne's 'Thalassius' are attached to the second and third movements of Ireland's piano suite *Sarnia* (1940–41). This work is a reflection of experiences during Ireland's stay on Guernsey between 1939 and 1940, and these two poets themselves lived on the island for short periods. And while there are inevitably some weak settings of poems, mainly from the early part of Ireland's career, there are many songs that show a real understanding of the poem's construction. For example, Housman's 'We'll to the woods no more' (1922) was based on a French *ronde*, hence its restricted rhymes and refrain. When Ireland set this in 1927 he mirrored the rhyme scheme in melodic repetitions.

On 28 September 1893, at the age of just fourteen, Ireland, on his own initiative, enrolled at the Royal College of Music (RCM). His sister Ethel was already at the RAM. She had registered in February 1891, and was studying piano, violin, elocution and modern languages and living in South Hampstead. Her younger brother moved in with her for a short time. Less than a week after he had started at the RCM their mother died, followed a year later by their father. Ireland and his sister were left in the charge of a guardian, and the next few years saw them moving frequently from lodgings to lodgings, Ireland taking work as an accompanist at smoking-concerts to supplement his income. It was the RCM that was to provide the first lengthy period of real stability in Ireland's life. His principal study was piano, with Frederick Cliffe (1857–1931), who had been Professor at the RCM since 1883. Second study encompassed organ and theoretical studies. Ireland's organ teacher was Sir Walter Parratt (1841–1924), who had also been at the Royal College for ten years, and who, from 1893, was Master of the Queen's Music. Ireland was awarded his Fellow of the Royal College of Organists (FRCO) at the age of fifteen. His harmony lessons were with James Higgs, who provided a grounding in the rudiments of music. By 1896 composition had been added to harmony, and a piano Associate of the Royal College of Music had been added to the FRCO.

During these first few years at the Royal College, Ireland also spent time getting to know the standard repertoire, and especially works by Beethoven, Brahms and Dvořák:

> I was able to attend many concerts, both chamber and orchestral. There were the Monday and Saturday 'Pops' at the old St. James's Hall where one constantly heard Chamber Music under such exponents as the Joachim Quartet, and so one became familiar with the classics, and the works of Brahms, who was still the greatest living composer. Also I attended the bi-weekly rehearsals of the RCM orchestra, which familiarized me with many works.

(JIT, 1)

One of the most interesting of Ireland's activities during his early years at the Royal College was his membership of the RCM Literary and Debating Society. This was established in 1896 and lasted for one year. The roll of membership included Evlyn Howard Jones (1877–1951), a pianist to whom Ireland dedicated some of his early works, and composers Gustav von Holst (1874–1934), Ralph Vaughan Williams, Fritz Hart (1874–1949), Dunhill, William Yeates Hurlstone (1876–1906) and Ireland. Meetings were held on Saturday afternoons, and were devoted to the reading and discussion of literary works, such as Carlyle's 'Essay on Dante'. Plays were read, with parts assigned to the music students, and there were also debates on musical issues. According to Dunhill, in 1896:

> The first meeting of the Christmas term brought forth two interesting papers by Vaughan-Williams and Von Holst respectively, upon 'Bayreuth' and 'Open-Air Music'. A debate on the motion by Vaughan-Williams 'That the Moderate Man is Contemptible' (which called forth many entertaining speeches on both sides) was held on the 15th of October, and other meetings included discussions on 'Pianoforte Music', 'The Socialism of William Morris', and 'The Philosophy of Schopenhauer'. There was also a reading of 'Cymbeline' and a debate upon the question 'Has Music reached its Zenith?'
>
> (Dunhill, 1908–09: 19)

Ireland was the instigator of one of the topics above, when he 'animadverted on Schopenhauer' (*MT*, Oct. 1958: 535). The meetings always concluded with a gathering for tea and buns at Wilkins' in Kensington High Street.

In addition to these activities, Ireland participated in concerts at the RCM, and began to write music, but it seems that he discredited and abandoned many of his very early compositions. There were a number of orchestral works that have not survived, including an overture, *Pelléas et Mélisande*, the *Prelude: Midsummer* and *The Princess Maleine*. From these first few years at the Royal College, little remains save for *In Those Days*, a piano work comprising two short pieces, 'Daydream' and 'Meridian', composed in 1895, and revised in 1941, though the later revision made few significant alterations to the original. 'Daydream' is a simple, diatonic work, with Brahmsian piano figuration. 'Meridian', also firmly diatonic, is an early example of Ireland's interest in the sea as inspiration. In 1896 there was a Communion Service in A flat major, and a *Pastoral* for piano, and in 1897 another piano piece, a Theme and Variations in E flat major, for which only the theme is extant.

Another work surviving from the early 1890s is an undated part-song for SATB chorus, 'The peaceful western wind'. The part-song was a genre that Ireland used throughout his life, and he produced a number of slight but always well-crafted pieces which punctuate moments of greater intensity in his output. Using a strophic text by Thomas Campion, in 'The peaceful western wind' Ireland establishes an archetype which he was to reuse with slight variations in his later part-songs. The three stanzas employ the same essential harmony, with only slight motivic variations. There is no sign that Ireland is depicting musically the meaning of the words, and the writing is essentially an exercise in simple four-part harmony (Example 1.1).

Example 1.1

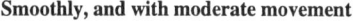

Smoothly, and with moderate movement

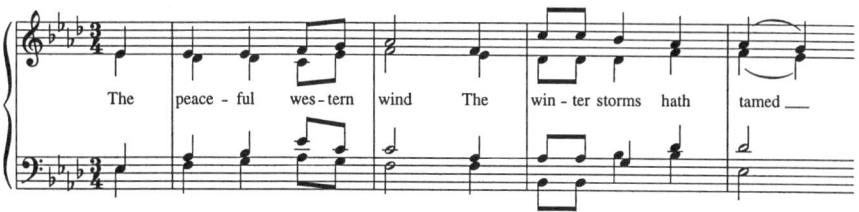

In March 1897 Ireland wrote his First String Quartet in D minor, and a few months later, in September, he completed his Second String Quartet in C minor. Neither work was published in his lifetime. The two quartets demonstrate that the young Ireland certainly had a good grasp of form and instrumentation, but though well crafted, these are student efforts, exploring the timbral and textural possibilities of the medium, and revealing the influences of Beethoven, Dvořák and Mendelssohn. Both quartets have a clear diatonic framework and follow a four-movement format, with a sonata-form first movement, a slow movement, a scherzo and a quick finale (in the case of the second quartet, a theme and variations). Both works, in particular the first quartet (Example 1.2, bars 25–9) have finales of an ebullient nature, a feature of all Ireland's chamber music.

Example 1.2

[Vivace]

In May 1897, between writing the first and second quartets, Ireland had become a scholar at the RCM and a composition pupil of Charles Villiers Stanford (1852–1924), whose own style of writing and demanding disciplined teaching methods had a considerable impact on Ireland, instilling rigorous craftsmanship in him.

Stanford also had a significant impact on the development of his pupil's personal harmonic language. Ireland wrote that it was Stanford who first 'expounded the modal scales' (*The Times*, 3 Aug. 1959: 10), and the introduction to and emphasis on the modal system of Palestrina certainly led Ireland to his own brand of modality. Between 1897 and March 1901 as Stanford's pupil, and during the first decade of the twentieth century, Ireland experimented with genres, structures and textures in an attempt to develop a personal voice. The major musical influences at this time remained Beethoven and Brahms, and even as late as 1911 Ireland was producing works such as 'Hope the Hornblower', relying heavily on the harmonic language of the first half of the nineteenth century. But there were also other important influences, including the music of Tchaikovsky.

While there are some piano works from the period to 1901, including *A Sea Idyll* in 1900, piano music does not feature prominently in Ireland's output at this stage, the main area of interest being chamber music. The two string quartets were followed in 1898 by a Sextet for clarinet, horn and string quartet, expanded from a single-movement 'Intermezzo' with the same scoring. In terms of its fomal concision it is an advance on the quartets, but there is yet little in the piece to indicate the direction in which Ireland was to move during the next two decades. In four movements, the Sextet is overtly Brahmsian in structure, harmony and texture, and even in melodic construction, as can be seen particularly in the opening of the 'Intermezzo' (Example 1.3).

Example 1.3

Allegretto con grazia

Given that Ireland had recently heard the renowned clarinettist, Richard Mühlfeld (1856–1907) performing Brahms' Clarinet Quintet in London, these derivative qualities are perhaps not surprising. The only shades of the later Ireland come in the finale, where there are glimpses of the floating melody lines which were eventually to mature into the fluid writing for clarinet in the 1943 Fantasy-Sonata. Ireland did not return to either the mixed chamber ensemble (save for a Trio for clarinet, cello and piano, rewritten as a Piano Trio) or to the string quartet. Referring to the quartets in correspondence many years later, he said:

> I wrote two, as a student – they were not so bad, either, but wouldn't do now. I have never had the temerity to complete another, though I have made one or two beginnings at different times. It is the purest form of music.

> (EL: 14 Sept. 1952)

Although this 'purest' music did not turn out to be Ireland's, the instruments of these early chamber works were all to be explored more fully. His writing for

French horn developed along very different lines, away from the sunny sounds of the Sextet to the bleaker timbres of the orchestral *Legend*. Clarinet, cello and violin all stimulated sonatas with piano.

Ireland's farewell to the RCM as a student was in 1901, marked by a performance of the 1899 orchestral Symphonic Prelude, 'Tritons'. After completing his studies Ireland was faced with the inevitable problem of earning a living, though he was by this time free of his guardians and had full access to the money inherited from his father. He was already working as a church organist and accompanist, and in addition took pupils in piano, organ and composition. After leaving the Royal College, Ireland continued with a self-imposed apprenticeship, experimenting with genres and different mediums. The diverse works of literature that he read exerted a profound influence from the outset, and vocal pieces in the form of part-songs, art songs and church music permeate the years 1900–10. The attraction of the small-scale, functional vocal work may have been for its sales value. Ireland continued to widen his knowledge of other music, and especially of contemporary French composers, whose influence on him was increasingly apparent in the first two decades of the twentieth century.

In 1904 Ireland completed an Orchestral Poem. This is an early example of the rhapsody-cum-fantasy one-movement structure that gradually developed into Ireland's favoured mode of expression. It has three sections: a modal Andante followed by an Andante molto moderato and an Allegro giusto that ends in A major. Although the sections are essentially three 'movements', the piece is monothematic. In the same year he arranged a Viola Concerto by Cecil Forsyth (1870–1941) for viola and piano. In 1905 he was awarded the Durham BMus, and in January 1906 produced a brilliant and virtuosic First Rhapsody for piano. Despite the merits of these early pieces, it is clear that Ireland did not regard them as serious, individual works of substance. Writing in 1936, he stated: 'I do not think any works of mine previous to the Phantasy [*sic*] Trio (1906 or 1907) are of any importance – I only regard them as studies, & as examples to myself of what not to do' (Cramer: 6 Sept. 1936). At the same time he wrote of his songs that he had 'over 70 in print, all of which I consider significant' (ibid.). As these 'significant' songs included some written before 1906, he was presumably saying that it was his early chamber and orchestral works that he did not value. The work he picked out as his first of real significance was the Phantasie in A minor for Piano Trio.

The choice of a one-movement 'Phantasie' was not Ireland's own, but was the brief for the entries for the 1907 Cobbett Chamber Music Competition. In 1905 Walter Wilson Cobbett (1847–1937), an amateur musician and businessman, in association with the Musicians' Company, established the first of a series of competitions in the field of British chamber music. His aim was to revive and modernize the early English 'Fancy'. Entrants were required to write a 'Phantasie' in one sectionalized movement. The first competition asked for a String Quartet, the second, in 1907, for a Piano Trio. The notion of a one-movement work with related sections evidently appealed to Ireland, as he returned to the 'fantasy' for chamber ensemble in 1943 (and he had already worked with coherent one-movement structures in the 1904 Poem and the 1906 First Rhapsody). The Phantasie won the second prize of £10, while Frank Bridge (1879–1941) took the first prize. Ireland's Phantasie was also successful in terms of the evident security of technique and the clarity of construction.

The piece, broadly speaking, is a sonata-form movement, with clearly defined exposition, development and recapitulation sections and differentiated first and second subjects in A minor and C major. It still owes something to Brahms, but Russian influences are clearly present, for example the recurring folk-derived swaggers, as at Letter E (bar 77), and it is also evident that Ireland had by this time heard and assimilated much French music. But even more striking than the audible influences is the fact that suddenly here is a truly individual work. The germs of motivic and textural aspects that are to develop as characteristics of Ireland's personal voice can be seen: soaring melodies, weighted appoggiaturas and moments of tremendous vigour. The opening piano-writing, against which the cello reveals the melody (Example 1.4), is an example of the fluid figuration, described by Ireland as 'a characteristic figure of accompaniment' (*JIT*, 2) that continues to feature in his later chamber works with strings.

Example 1.4

Also typical is the use of internal tempi variation: sudden animati give way to slower passages. Although this is a sonata-form movement, the 'development' section is actually a short slow movement contained within one new key, A flat major, whose main theme derives from the first subject. A recapitulation and coda follow, ending with great verve in A major. This type of brilliant, yea-saying conclusion (Example 1.5) had been seen to a lesser extent in the string quartets, and was to become a regular feature in Ireland's work.

Example 1.5

When he wrote this work, Ireland was clearly working to a predetermined sonata-form structure: his notes about the piece (*JIT*, 2) refer to it in purely analytical terms. He wrote of the opening that the principal subject is 'repeated with slight variations in detail', identified the bridge passage and discussed the genesis of the theme of the development section. The complete nature of the formal structure of the work, and the passionate nature of the string-writing, are all signs that by now Ireland was a much more assured composer, who knew where he was going. The Phantasie is the first of his works to show internal coherence, and the foundations for his later, tightly constructed monothematic movements, and in particular the 1943 Fantasy-Sonata, are laid here.

In the summer of 1908 Ireland began work on a sonata for violin and piano. It was not his first attempt at writing for a string instrument with piano; there were some abandoned early works for violin and piano, including a Sonata in C minor and a Sonata in one movement in G minor. He had also composed two short works for violin and piano, a Berceuse in 1902 and a Cavatina in 1904. These miniatures are charming salon works, relying on a simple, lyrical melodic line over a chordal piano part (Example 1.6).

Example 1.6

In 1909 Ireland completed his First Violin Sonata in D minor, and entered it for that year's Cobbett Chamber Music Competition. The sonata was a great success, winning the first prize of £40 from 134 entries. It was published in 1911, but not, however, performed until 1913, when Marjorie Hayward (1886–1953) – for whom Ireland had in the interim written another violin and piano piece, the Bagatelle (1911) – played it at the Æolian Hall, with the composer at the piano. It continued to be well received, and was reissued in 1915. One review commented on the amalgamation of influences and the emerging personal voice:

> The Allegro is full of the darkness and also of the tenderness of the North. It owes a little to Grieg, to MacDowell, and perhaps even to Brahms, but it is all the better for that. There is much more in it than the influence of these great masters. There are strong themes, novelly presented and well-developed, a constantly changing play of harmonic light, with clever technique for both instruments. The last movement is delightfully 'violinistic', whilst the slow movement shows the composer in a serenely religious vein of great ideality ...

(MMR, July 1915: 200)

Ireland was not entirely satisfied with the first version of the violin sonata and in 1917 he made some fairly substantial revisions to bowing and tempo markings, but also some structural cuts and alterations. He revised the piece again in 1944, at a time when he was rethinking a number of his early works.

Ireland's First Violin Sonata in D minor uses a three-movement model. It is a wonderfully fresh piece, a natural development of the new composer that was heard in the Phantasie. There are inevitably obvious influences on the music:

Brahms' chamber music textures, suggestions of Grieg and Sibelius in the major–minor juxtapositions and of Elgar in the rich harmonic climaxes. The impact of French music, not only of Fauré in the elegiac melodic writing, but also by this point of Debussy, is ever more pervasive. But although Ireland manipulates traditional structures, and works within a limited harmonic range, the piece is utterly his in its emotional changes of mood. His gift for writing melody is everywhere apparent, and his command of contrapuntal textures has changed entirely in the period following the early string quartets.

The first movement, Allegro leggiadro, is the strongest and most expansive of the three, and the most obvious extension of the form and content of the Phantasie. The opening (Example 1.7) with its lilting piano accompaniment and melody stealing out of the texture is very similar to the start of the earlier work.

Example 1.7

Ireland uses a sonata-form framework, with clearly defined first and second subjects. The first is forward-moving, in the tonic key; the second, at Letter B (bar 51), is more relaxed, in the relative major key. But now Ireland is not confined to the harmonic expectations of a sonata form movement, and there are wider excursions and more dramatic key moves than were seen in the Phantasie. Most striking is the recapitulation that starts in E minor at Letter E (bar 177), only in the coda at the Poco meno mosso (bar 315) returning to D minor.

The way in which Ireland develops his thematic material, particularly the second subject, is less through harmonic or motivic alteration than through nuances of accompaniment, articulation and emotional states, another technique that was to be developed as he established a personal voice. For example, the second subject appears at Letter D (bar 162) with the marking 'con tristezza', and is also presented 'sotto voce' (bar 299), then 'delicatamente' (bar 303). As in the earlier piano trio he develops his two main themes separately, but also in tandem. For example, the passage starting at bar 236 opens with four bars of the first subject, immediately followed by a version of the second. The movement has a rhythmic sense of ebb and flow that is typical of the composer's later impressionistic piano miniatures, and romantic juxtapositions of mood are an integral part of the music (Example 1.8, bars 75–80).

Example 1.8

Performance indications are particular and specific, and there are places where virtually every bar has some sort of marking. These markings serve two functions. On the one hand they help to articulate the structure of the movement; on the other they are there to exert a control over the performance situation, a practice that was to remain with Ireland throughout his life.

The second movement, the Romance, shows Ireland developing an individual approach to formal structures. The main melodic material of the movement is framed, at the start by rhapsodic piano flourishes; at the end by a three-bar chordal passage. There is one main melodic idea (Example 1.9), which is first presented on the violin, and which derives from the piano's introductory bars to the movement. This is an example of Ireland's lyrical writing at its simplest, accompanied by unadorned chords, and at this point with no hint of anguish in the appoggiaturas.

Example 1.9

This theme dominates, and is freely developed in a similar manner to the treatment of the second subject of the first movement: at Letter B (bar 44), for example, the tune is heard over a new shimmering accompaniment pattern, and at Letter E (bar 144) with more contrapuntal piano-writing. The introductory bars of the movement recur to separate presentations of the melodic material, first at bar 63, then at bar 138, and again at Letter F (bar 163) to announce the closing bars. There are also echoes of the first movement, for example the downward scale in bars 40–41, but these are occasional bars of reference, rather than a tight integration of material across movements. And there are new sections of music that are removed from the main material of the movement, such as the waltz-like affrettando at Letter D (bar 107) and, most strikingly, the piano chords at the Lento (bar 89) (Example 1.10). This sudden transition to a moment of solemnity, and a passage of parallel chords, is another new Ireland thumbprint.

Example 1.10

The third-movement Rondo shows Ireland tending towards a monothematic treatment, with the main rondo motifs closely interrelated. Here there are glances back at the melodic material of the Phantasie. Though at this stage it is difficult to identify any extra-musical associations, this sonata adheres to the formula that Ireland was to follow in most of his three-movement works, in that each of the movements has a different function. The middle movement, with its rich appoggiaturas, title 'Romance', and big climax, heralds Ireland's later slow movements, which are always 'about' love and people.

There was a gap of a few years after the completion of the First Violin Sonata and before Ireland's next significant work, and between 1908 and 1912 he produced only a handful of short pieces. These included an undated recitation for narrator and piano, 'Annabel Lee', and some church music. There were the unison and part-songs, 'The frog and the crab', 'In praise of May', 'A laughing song', 'Alpine song', 'At early dawn', 'In praise of Neptune', 'In summer woods', 'Slumber song', 'Spring', 'A cradle song' and 'Aubade'. And in 1912 there was a revisiting of Campion's words that Ireland had previously set as 'The peaceful western wind', this time in a work entitled 'See how the morning smiles', for two treble voices and piano accompaniment. Though he retained the A flat major tonality and the repeating verses, there were significant changes to the setting of the poem. During this period there was also a series of ballads written under the pseudonym Turlay Royce. Of these, 'Billee Bowline' and 'Hillo, my bonny', are hearty affairs. 'Love's window' has an archetypal Victorian sentimentality.

By 1913 it was clear that a much more assured and individual voice was emerging. In this year there were works for voice and piano, significantly the cycle *Marigold* and 'Sea fever'. Ireland also arranged some of his songs for voice and orchestra, including 'Here's to the ships!' and 'Youth's spring-tribute'. In retrospect these arrangements may be regarded as experiments towards writing an orchestral work, with the instrumentation of the latter song, which calls for celesta and harp, pre-empting that of *The Forgotten Rite*. There were also some piano works in 1913, notably *Decorations* and *Preludes*, and a Trio for clarinet, cello and piano, performed in 1915. What is evident from the works of 1913 is Ireland's passion for French music. Later in life he wrote of Maurice Ravel's harmonic idiom: 'one gets a flavour for it, like oysters or some strangely flavoured dish. Melodically, Ravel's tunes are nearly all cast in some one or other of the Greek 'modes' – as indeed are many of my own' (ARLG: 5 Aug. 1943). And from this point on there is an increasing use of modal tunes in Ireland's own output.

In 1915, soon after writing a short anthem intended for use by troops serving in the war and a Rhapsody for piano, Ireland began work on his Second Violin Sonata in A minor. He completed this in January 1917, having in the meantime set three of Eric Thirkell Cooper's *Soliloquies of a subaltern somewhere in*

France. For the Second Sonata he clearly drew on his earlier experiences of writing for the combination of violin and piano, although this work is nevertheless very different from the first sonata, and in many ways can be seen as a landmark in Ireland's composing career. *The Times* reported that

> ... as the result of a music prize competition arranged by the committee of a fund for assisting musicians in wartime, Mr Albert Sammons, Mr William Murdoch and Mr Percy Pitt, who acted as judges, have awarded the prize of 40 guineas for a violin and pianoforte sonata to the composition sent in by Mr John Ireland.
>
> (*The Times*, 7 Feb. 1917: 2)

The first performance was given on 6 March 1917 by violinist Albert Sammons (1886–1957), to whom it is dedicated, and pianist William Murdoch (1888–1942). The work was an immediate success with the general public, primarily because it was perceived as being war-inspired and was both expressive and inspirational at a time of need. The performance of Sammons and Murdoch contributed to the emotions evoked by the piece: both men were on leave from service with the Grenadier Guards, and performed in khaki uniform. Sammons was recruited to the Grenadier Guards in May 1916. He served mainly as a bandsman at home, but also went to France as part of an expeditionary force in May 1917. He was something of a national symbol, as a photograph of him playing the violin atop a tank in Trafalgar Square implies (Figure 1.1, p. 36).

Frank Bridge, Ireland's exact contemporary and fellow Stanford pupil, was so impressed by the work that he wrote to the composer:

> Until I send you a line or two I shall not be able to get your new work out of my head. Not that I shall ever lose the impression – that's impossible – but while the recollection is so vivid I feel I must write and tell you how overjoyed I am with the Sonata ... Its power is tremendous. I have the greatest faith in its future ... It is not only for the comparatively small circle of people who are interested in British music, but for the whole world, regardless of nationality ... It is possible that you may not think this is your *best* work, but personally I am convinced it is not only a landmark in your own history but also in that of contemporary music ... I feel proud that any one of us has produced such a work ...
>
> (in Hill, 1946: 105)

The work demonstrates a major advancement in the sophistication of its construction. Like the First Violin Sonata, it does use traditional structural models, but these are now worked with great flexibility. Ireland manipulates and develops melodic cells within each movement, and also across all three movements of the work. But despite the strong melodic links, each movement retains a distinct character. This work shows clear stylistic developments on its predecessor in that there is evidence of a much more individual harmonic language, combining richly layered chords with modal tendencies.

The first movement, the Allegro, uses modified sonata form. The exposition presents a sequence of closely related melodic cells which grow out of the melody of the first four bars (Example 1.11).

Example 1.11

The rhythmic impetus of this opening theme drives the movement, but there are many moments of repose, and as in the First Violin Sonata, the contrasts between 'vivo' sections and passages of relaxation are sudden and frequent. The second idea (bar 18) is in a different vein from that of the opening. Here the violin's more lyrical melody is accompanied by 'leggiadro' offbeats. From bar 46 these offbeats are developed more fully as a second subject, before an expansive and tonally secure third melodic idea, now in F major (bar 56). At Letter F (bar 88) a short section marked 'rubato' leads to a reiteration of the material of the opening theme in preparation for the development. As in the Phantasie Trio, the 'development' is essentially a short, lyrical 'movement', in which a transformed version of the opening melody is placed first over an intoning pedal (Example 1.12, bars 101–6).

Example 1.12

A new motif is then introduced (see Example 1.17a on p. 29) that separates presentations of the transformed first subject. At the Tranquillo (bar 131) this is now marked *una corda*. A short three-bar accelerando in the piano part leads the way to the recapitulation. This is basically a modified repeat of the exposition, with the former F major theme now in A major. The coda that starts at Letter L (bar 231) is in two sections. The first part combines the first subject with an expansive violin melody (part of which is shown in Example 1.20a, p. 30), and the last ten bars are a return to the driving rhythms that opened the movement.

The second movement, Poco lento quasi adagio, uses ternary form, but also has a framing introduction and conclusion. The opening twelve bars divide into two six-bar phrases, where bars 7–12 are a repeat of 1–6, but with a number of melodic and harmonic alterations. The interplay between the violin and the piano's right-hand melody (Example 1.13) is crucial to the evolution of the rest of this movement.

Example 1.13

After this interweaving introduction the first main theme is heard at Letter A (Example 1.14, bar 15), the violin's melody played out over the piano's right-hand chords and left-hand walking quavers.

Example 1.14

In bar 29 this melody is combined with the melodic pattern of bars 1–2, after which the passage from bar 35 emphasizes the E flat tonality. The central section of the piece has a change of time signature to $\frac{12}{8}$, and a change of key to G flat major (bar 40). This section is dominated by a new melodic idea (Example 1.15), and also a reappearance of the subsidiary theme heard in the development section of the first movement.

Example 1.15

At Letter D (bar 45) this is repeated, this time in G major, and then at Letter E (bar 52) in inversion in A major. At the end of this section, starting at bar 67, a solo violin line, based on a conflation of the two melodies of Example 1.13, leads to a recapitulation of the main theme (Example 1.14) and a repeat and elongation of the E flat major passage of bar 35.

The finale moves back from E flat major to A minor. It opens with a short section marked In tempo moderato, which has the forward momentum and dotted rhythms of the first movement. The Con brio that follows is an assertive conclusion to the work in A major, its main theme (Example 1.16) entirely buoyant.

Example 1.16

While there are interruptions to this *joie de vivre*, such as the brief excursion to B flat minor in bar 62, and the return to the material of the In tempo moderato at bar 155, these are swiftly banished. In bar 228 there is an 'alla burla' version of the theme of the Con brio, now in E flat major, and at Letter L (bar 324) a light, offbeat section that leads to a brilliant close. The overall key scheme of the sonata, which opens in the tonic minor and ends in the tonic major, with the central movement built on the key of the diminished fifth, becomes a recurring trait in Ireland's works from this point on.

Each of the movements is tightly constructed, in the sense that the melodic material within a movement is interrelated. At the same time there are motivic links between the three movements, and these are so strong as to place this work as a benchmark in the development of Ireland's creation and treatment of structure. For example, the new passing motif of Movement I (Example 1.17a) is much more fully developed in Movement II (Example 1.17b), and one of the cells of I (Example 1.18a) is transformed into the main substance of Movement III (Example 1.18b).

Example 1.17a

Example 1.17b

Example 1.18a

Example 1.18b

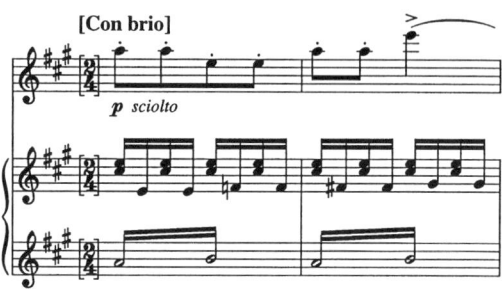

Similarly, the inversion of the third idea of II (Example 1.19a) reappears in III (Example 1.19b).

Example 1.19a

Example 1.19b

There are some phrases common to all three movements. Examples 1.20a, b and c show the versions of one of these metamorphosing melodic lines, as it appears in the first, second and third movements.

Example 1.20a

Example 1.20b

Example 1.20c

Ireland found it lamentable that the tightness of construction of this work was not always perceived by the listener. After reading Eric Blom's adverse criticism of the structure of this piece he wrote that the 'appreciation of my 2nd Violin Sonata is certainly very welcome, even if he does say the structure is "loose", which is utter nonsense, and only means he does not know the work well enough to appreciate the extreme subtlety and skill employed in the construction, and the way the various parts are related to the whole' (EC: 18 March 1941).

If the above formalistic analysis reveals something of the 'subtlety and skill employed in the construction' and 'the way the various parts are related to the whole', it does not reveal the essence of the piece. Although most writers on this and other works by Ireland have perceived coherence of structure as being an essential part of the composer's writing tools, which indeed it is, a purely neutral analysis fails to get to the heart of the music, and in fact has limitations for any works written after the Phantasie Trio, the last piece of which Ireland spoke in purely abstract musical terms. It tells us that Ireland could write a good sonata, but it is not only in terms of its structure that the Second Violin Sonata is such an important work at this stage in his career. What the above approach does not do is engage with all the images, ideas and connections that are so powerful and vivid in Ireland's music, and with which this work brims. Indeed, 'few works are more fascinating store-houses of those recurrent "self-quotations" or "private symbols"' (*Birmingham Daily Post*, 30 Oct. 1961: 6) which are an integral part of his compositional technique.

All the authors included in the Introduction deployed a descriptive language in their approaches to writing about Ireland's music. The various attempts to evoke the essence of his work in words have discerned contrasting sensibilities within his output. Because of this, there are certain phrases that have recurred in descriptions of his music. The common ground shared by these writers, and the fact that historically Ireland's output has been spoken of in terms of its expressive qualities, point the way to an interpretative method of looking at the music.

Another factor that supports a hermeneutical approach to Ireland's music is that nearly every work bears a descriptive title: only the handful of works with generic titles such as Sonata, Sonatina and Rhapsody do not. Ireland himself left various clues that his titles were intended to carry some weight. There are many letters in which he talked of the specific connections between certain pieces and a place or a person. He also wrote in more general terms that his titles 'give some idea of the emotions involved' (in Schafer, 1963: 33), and that personal experiences often instigated a composition. For example, of *Legend*, he wrote that it was inspired by the Sussex Downs: 'Things like that would often start up certain thoughts and images, and these would be reflected in my music' (ibid.: 34). The fact that a piece does not have a graphic title does not mean that it is not inherently programmatic. The 1915 Rhapsody for piano, for example, is both a freely evolving web of musical motifs and a composite intermingling of Ireland's images and ideas.

Virtually every piece by Ireland is, in Barthes' words, 'in communication with at least one other structure' (Barthes, 1977: 16), namely a literary text of some sort. This may be the title, a caption or the words of a song, or all three. The totality of the meaning of the music is thus carried by two different structures, one musical, one linguistic. Some of Ireland's titles are specific in their placing of the work: 'Amberley Wild Brooks' (1921) assigns an exact location to the piece. In addition, Ireland frequently appends a literary quotation to his piano miniatures. Where he does this, the words seem to be there in order to quicken the image, to load it with 'a culture, a moral, an imagination' (ibid.: 26). The title and added quotation are 'kindred suggestions' (Evans, 1919b: 395), and attempt to make explicit the musically implicit. They can also project secondary images onto the main idea. For example, the short piano piece, 'The boy bishop' (1941) has two literary descriptors in addition to the title, one an explanation of the title, the other an ambiguous biblical epigraph.

On the whole it would seem that the title was fomulated *after* the completion of the composition, even if the idea was already there. The fact that Ireland often changed the title of a work several times before its publication, weighing up the best descriptor, in most cases did not alter the fundamental meaning of the piece: 'Chelsea Reach' (1917) was originally 'The River: an Impression', for example. The work was 'about' a river, the final title pinning down its exact location. Conversely, Ireland's decision to call the middle movement of *Sarnia* (1940–41) 'In a May morning' rather than 'Boyslove' was a way of capturing the essence of the piece in a manner that was suggestive rather than explicit.

Recognizable 'codes of feelings', which are not necessarily revealed though a neutral analytical method, are discernible across the whole spectrum of Ireland's works. One useful way of approaching these codes of feelings is by drawing on methodologies of literary theory, specifically hermeneutics, reception theory, semiotics and narratology, and various writings have been used as starting-points for the present study. A stage further on from this, and a stage closer to the music, is topic theory: Robert Hatten's decision to integrate perspectives from semiotics, music theory and music history into his study, *Musical Meaning in Beethoven* (1994) was a fruitful one, and offered a useful model for an analogous study of Ireland's music. A number of topical fields can be distinguished across the spectrum of Ireland's works. His world, his plot, his setting and his characters can be recognized in his music through the sign system he deploys.

One useful book consulted on the route to a greater understanding of Ireland's music was Nikolaus Pevsner's *The Englishness of English Art* (1956), in which Pevsner looked at the national characteristics of the art of England, dividing his work into categories by subject matter. His aim was to extract the Englishness from English works of art, both in terms of the spirit of a particular age and in terms of an identifiable national character. In doing so he cited certain traits which transcend time, such as the penchant for understatement and a distrust of rhetoric. This work is remarkably relevant to a discussion of Ireland's musical style, and Ireland sits comfortably as Pevsner's reticent Englishman finding large-scale genres and the 'Grand Manner' unattractive, while taking naturally to the British talent for 'exquisite water-colours and miniatures, things on a small scale' (Pevsner, 1956: 80).

Through a combination of historical writings by and on Ireland and a variety of theoretical methodologies, it has been possible to establish a taxonomy of topics in Ireland's output. In order to do this it was necessary to decide which one of a work's various aspects is most 'pertinent for a coherent interpretation of it, and which ones remain marginal and unable to support a coherent reading' (Eco, 1992: 146). I have guarded against over-interpretation, and the establishing of the topic system with regard to Ireland has been through a consideration of internal evidence in the music in conjunction with its biographical and literary backgrounds. There have been earlier attempts to class Ireland's works under 'topics', but these have never been fully formulated. For example, John Longmire, in an obituary on the composer talked of the range of moods evident in his music, which included 'lyricism', 'mysticism', 'irony' and 'strength' (*MO*, 85/1018, July 1962: 599).

Ireland's works can be divided into six main topical fields by spirit, which form three opposing pairs: Anglo-Catholicism and Paganism; Country and City; Love and War. Many of his works are clearly situated within one of these topical fields, while others are more ambiguous, hovering between worlds. In other pieces topics mingle, with no single area foregrounded. Each of these topics has 'its special tone, its special combination of elements' (E. Wilson, 1993: 21). Ireland differentiates between topics primarily by structural and harmonic means, but also through timbre and motif. While there are melodic motifs that carry one particular meaning, many of his little motifs are not allied to any particular topic, though they *are* redolent of more general meaning. For example, there are many instances of 'yearning' phrases involving weighted melodic appoggiaturas. There are exuberant upward flourishes, usually employed at the close of a work or movement. A meandering, fluid solo melodic line often appears at a pivotal moment in a piece. And there are persistent 'fingerprints' across his output, such as the frequently used $^5^3^5$ and $^5^3^4^5$ patterns.

There are also large-scale structures that recur across Ireland's output, particularly ternary forms and monothematic creations. And there is often, though not always, a correlation between structural and expressive types. There are aspects of Ireland that cross topics, such as his strong response to place. It is therefore possible to place Ireland's works within these topical fields, but without adhering to a rigid set of criteria. He himself spoke of certain works as having common meaning: in 1921, for example, he wrote of a 'connection between this work [*Mai-Dun*] & the finale of my piano sonata ... Perhaps also it has some relation to "The Forgotten Rite" ' (EE: 7 Dec. 1921).

The pairs of topics are important both for their biographical aspects and for their musical characteristics. The English Church, for example, was something that was central to Ireland for its spiritual and historical associations, and there is a corpus of works for church performance. Conversely he had a pagan side, and many writers have referred to his 'dark, latent exoticism' (Townshend, 1943: 65), the 'influences of pagan antiquity' (Hill, 1946: 102) and his sense of 'the immanence of the supernatural' (Bush, 1993: xi). Aspects of his works have often been described as pantheistic and demoniac.

Ireland's response to nature has been recognized as fundamental to his musical style. Hill commented on the fact that Ireland was 'susceptible' to 'natural scenes' (Hill, 1946: 100) and Banfield wrote about his 'vivid images of nature' (Banfield, 1985: 165). But he was also a man of the city, with its popular and vulgar aspects, its many faces. There is a 'sanguine' John Ireland (Ottaway, 1954: 262), and one with a 'vagabondish' humour (Crossley-Holland, 1954: 538). His is the London of Hogarth, and his London portraits have the detail of Hogarth the observer and recorder of life.

The subject of Ireland and 'Love' has its own polarities. There is an effusive, longing side; his music is described as 'ardent' (Hill, 1946: 103) and as 'yearning' (Crossley-Holland, 1954: 535). But it is also 'static and repressive' (Townshend, 1954: 73) and he was a man who was 'bottled up' (Howes, 1966: 225). Pevsner writing of the detachment of Reynolds might equally apply to Ireland, who has his own secrets, and whose musical pictures similarly keep 'long silences. Or, to put it differently, the English portrait conceals more than it reveals, and what it reveals it reveals with studied understatement' (Pevsner, 1956: 79). Ireland's obituary in *The Times* noted this, saying of his music that 'understatement is its essence' and that works such as *The Land of Lost Content* 'communicate far more than they declare' (*The Times*, 13 June 1962: 12). There is also a more robust side to Ireland, and the word 'rugged', first applied to him by Evans in 1919, has assumed an air of authority in subsequent writings, though only Evans went on to link the 'ruggedness' of Ireland with war specifically, adding the terms 'heroic' and 'martial'. Child, in 1920, extended this to 'tough and manly' (*MT*, Aug. 1920: 556).

These descriptions are an introduction to the topics that will be explored in musical terms in the chapters that follow. The fact that different topics appear across Ireland's output reflects his conscious connection of musical style with meaning. As well as the pieces that fit comfortably into a single topic, there are also large-scale works within which topics appear and disappear in the form of motifs and harmonies linked in a syntagmatic personal narrative.

So how might an interpretive way of looking at Ireland's music help to reveal more of the essence of the Second Violin Sonata? Up to 1917 Ireland's works tend mainly to have either no particular topic (the Sextet and the Phantasie) or a single, clearly identifiable topic (*The Forgotten Rite* and 'An island hymn'). In the Second Violin Sonata Ireland brings together a number of different, and even opposing, topics, and introduces motifs that reappear in some of his later works.

The piece was a product of emotions provoked by the First World War, as Ireland confirmed in 1948, in the aftermath of the Second World War: 'It is a more exciting and full-blooded work than the D minor. Written in 1916–1917, it now becomes applicable to the stormy times we are living in again' (EC: 5 March 1948). And in 1950 he again wrote of its connection with its age: 'It would seem that this sonata appeared at just the right, the psychological moment, and that it expressed in music something which everybody was feeling' (*JIT*, 1). From these comments alone it would seem logical to consider this work as belonging to a 'war' topic, and many writers have done this in vague terms, regarding the sonata as moving from tension and questioning through pathos to optimism. However, against this background Ireland allows other topical areas to emerge, sometimes fleetingly, but also at times in quite extended sections. There are also glances back at the piano Rhapsody and forward to 'Chelsea Reach'.

At this stage in the present study it is not appropriate to explore the work in detail, given that the six main topics and their defining musical characteristics have yet to be discussed. An interim step is to use the descriptive phrases set out by Evans. Thus the first movement is not only a tightly wrought A minor Allegro, but also defines the drama of the piece with its 'rugged vigour' (Evans, 1919c: 458). The second movement is both a contrasting E flat major slow movement, and 'concerned with lyrical solace' (ibid.). The third movement is a relaxation of tension, in which 'even the humour of the last section gathers a flavour of the heroic from the context' (ibid.).

The Second Violin Sonata is a key work in Ireland's output both in terms of its constructional qualities and in its presentation of the themes and ideas that were now to be developed as an integral part of his personal style. It was also a landmark in terms of its performance and reception. Ireland's association with Sammons was a beneficial one, as Ireland himself acknowledged:

My personal association with Albert Sammons began during the first war, when he had already achieved a considerable, even unique, reputation as the finest English exponent of his instrument. Naturally his playing was known to me, and I particularly remember superb performances given by him of the solo part in the concertos of Elgar and Delius. His qualities as a violinist were personal, and entirely different from those of any British or foreign performer of his time. He had a steadiness of sustained, singing tone, under perfect control, which I have never heard except in the playing of Ysaÿe. His bowing and left-hand technique reached such a degree of co-ordination and perfection that one was unconscious of them as such. When he played a work, whether chamber-music or in conjunction with the orchestra, one was conscious only of the music, to which he gave sensitive and completely satisfying expression. As a personality, like all great artists he was essentially modest, humble and ever open to learn.

I first came to know him soon after my 2nd. Sonata for violin and piano was completed. It was decided that he and William Murdoch should give this work its first public performance, which took place in the Æolian Hall in March, 1917, before an audience in which many leading musicians were present. At that time Sammons and Murdoch were privates in the Grenadier Guards, and were of course in their khaki uniforms: both of them young and boyish-looking, radiating youth and energy.

For me it was an electrifying occasion. Little of my music had been publicly heard, and I felt that my fate as a composer was to be decided at that particular moment in time, as proved to be the case. On that I need not enlarge. It was probably the first and only occasion when a British composer was lifted from relative obscurity in a single night by a work cast in a chamber-music medium.

[Sammons] always impressed me as a true artist, selfless and of deep integrity, a man whose mind, personality and consummate art commended one's unqualified respect and admiration. And it is in this light that he will ever be remembered by all who heard him and knew him; while his great qualities as an artist and teacher will, one feels sure, be passed on through a younger and rising generation.

(*JIT*, 3)

The day after the first performance the work was taken on by a publisher, and the ensuing reviews of this 'electrifying' occasion were unanimous in their praise, the *Musical Times* round-up of the February and March events of 1917 describing it as a 'brilliant specimen of his powers' (*MT*, April 1917: 168). The intention is to return to this 'brilliant' sonata in Chapter 8, to get to its heart after exploring the six main subject areas in Ireland's output. The first and longest-lived lure was the Anglo-Catholic Church.

1.1 Albert Sammons, Trafalgar Square, *c.* 1916–18

Chapter 2

Anglo-Catholicism

John Ireland's deep-rooted and long-lasting relationship with the Anglican Church had a complex and profound impact on his life. Ireland was a practising Anglican for most of his life, and read the Bible on a regular basis. His faith was genuine, but as he grew older, increasingly tinged with doubt and cynicism. There are two particularly valuable sources of information on Ireland and the Church. One is the collection of letters he wrote to Father Kenneth Thompson (1904–91) between 1936 and 1961, in which he frequently refers to religion and related issues. Thompson's own feeling was that despite some problems, Ireland was a Christian whose religious beliefs were solid:

> Amid many doubts & fears (especially at the end of his life ... naturally then perhaps ... concerning survival & the future life) John was a sincere & faithful Anglican Christian – soon (I think) after his arrival in London he, accidentally as it were, wandered into a very high Anglo Catholic Church (I believe it was St Mary Magdalen's Paddington) & was henceforth attracted to AngloCatholicism.
>
> (KT to CSS: 20 Sept. 1976)

Despite his underlying faith, throughout his life Ireland revealed misgivings about religion, most often at times of stress, such as in July 1936, when a close friend, Percy Bentham (1884–1936) died of blood poisoning. For Ireland, a traumatic incident was often the catalyst for an outpouring, and a questioning of the reason for religion. On this occasion Ireland was effusive, hating the crematorium funeral service for its perfunctory nature, and talking of the problems attached to the Christian faith:

> At my time of life, seeing the impermanence and transitoriness of all things, one could wish to attach one's mind to something permanent, such as Catholicism, & the idea of a God who changeth not. I have often discussed this with Bentham. But, on the other hand, I cannot see why, if there is a God who knows individually the life of all His creations ... that a man of blameless life, of the purest of pure hearts, of the very finest & most stable character, can be struck down, & wasted, in this way, – causing the very bitterest grief to all his relatives & friends.
>
> (EI: 17 June 1936)

As Ireland grew older, his expressions of dissatisfaction with the Church of England became more frequent. For example, in 1944 he wrote to Arthur Robert Lee Gardner (dates unknown), a friend and former cleric:

> I am much interested in what you say about the Christian faith. If, as you say, you are definitely convinced of the existence of a Holy Spiritual Influence on

this earth – and that the Christian faith is a fact – then you have got a good deal further than I have. I <u>used</u> to think so – but now I feel very uncertain about it. I am much more certain that there is an <u>Evil</u> Spiritual Influence on this earth – which is very much in evidence, & even seems to have convinced the former sceptic, Joad. If I could really feel convinced of the other proposition, I think I sh^{ld} feel the only logical thing to do w^{ld} be to become a Roman Catholic – which faith combines Christianity with Magic. Indeed, I wish I could! At present, I am unable to experience that personal contact with Jesus Christ which seems to be the essence of Christianity, as a practising religion.

(ARLG: 23 July 1944)

Ireland's hints that Roman Catholicism might be more appropriate for him than the Church of England are primarily directed at the former's greater emphasis on rites and traditions:

The deepest religious emotion I have ever felt has been at the Ceremonies on the Thursday & Friday before Easter – and what <u>we</u> cannot have – the Ceremonies on the Saturday before Easter as practised by the Roman Church – something absolutely age-long & everlasting – the re-kindling of Fire – <u>Lumen Christi</u>.

(KT: 16 July 1936)

Ireland frequently bemoaned the lack of ritual in the churches he attended, and it would seem that for him one of the main attractions of the Church was its ceremony. It is from his letters to Thompson that we get an idea of the other appeals of the Church, such as its austerity and distance, and also a spirit of place of particular church buildings. Ireland's religion was not only about a private and public relationship with a Christian God, and most of the churches with which he was associated had something special about them in terms of their location, architecture, or historical connections. The Anglican Church was also the backdrop for a community of priests and acolytes; and the proximity of youths and clerics, with whom Ireland seemed to empathize, was another lure. It was a fantasy world as well as a real one.

The second interesting source of information on Ireland's life within the Church is a collection of parish magazines relating to his association with St Luke's, Chelsea. These contain a surprising amount of material on the repertoire and activities of the choir he conducted. But while the Anglo-Catholic church had a vital influence on his life, it had a less immediately striking impact on his music. With the exception of a few works, Ireland's church music is not the most significant area of his output, and discussion of this repertory has been largely omitted from previous surveys of his music. Much of this music – in the shape of utilitarian services, organ music and hymns – is functional and impersonal, rooted in a style inherited from the Victorians, with little trace of an individual voice. But there are also androgynous modal tunes, hymns to love and beauty, ambiguous works that are neither wholly sacred nor wholly profane, such as 'The sacred flame', 'The holy boy' and 'The boy bishop', which have erotic and personal extra-musical associations. And it is also the case that aspects of his 'church' style permeate his secular chamber and orchestral works.

Most of Ireland's church music was designed with a specific choir and situation in mind. The bulk of it dates from the early part of his career, during his time as organist at St Luke's, but there is also a renewed interest after 1940. This was a year in which Ireland both found and lost a personal heaven on Guernsey, where he was living at the time, and a man who expressed such affection for his stay on the island, and his association with the island's churches, was likely to leave evidence of this affection in the form of works inspired by his time there. As a result there are a number of church pieces that date from during and immediately after 1940.

Ireland's corpus of works for the Church sits rather curiously within his output, and there are several reasons for this. He was working as part of a religious institution which had long-established musical foundations and an expectation that its composers would work within certain constraints. Because of this, Ireland's church pieces owe much to the models of Stanford and his predecessors. Ireland's church music offers little to tax the performers, so it would also seem that he never had access to a truly satisfactory choir, though it may also be that he was mindful of the lucrative market for music for amateurs.

Even at the time of publication, Ireland's church music was regarded as lightweight, functional music. The organ Capriccio was reviewed in 1912 as 'charming', of 'lighter form' and 'within the powers of those possessing even moderate technical skill' (*MT*, June 1912: 384). His church music was always perceived as 'easy', and nearly all the early reviews use this word to describe this area of his output. At the same time it was generally well received: his word-setting was declared 'graceful', and the works were 'heartily commended' (*MT*, June 1914: 388).

Ireland's output of music for the Church, while not extensive, encompasses choral works and a number of pieces for organ. The choral pieces divide into four categories: services and canticle settings, hymn tunes, carols and anthems. The services belong to a distinct musical world in which the harmonic language has little in common with Ireland's 'secular' style. It is a mixture of the modal and diatonic language of his predecessors, with basic root position chords and restricted, simple melodic lines. The word-setting is syllabic and there are many unisons. The movements of the service settings are linked by phrase repetitions, head motifs used in the manner of Stanford, and the whole seems to be an essay in functionality. The style of the services and canticles, which are evidently written with a run-of-the-mill choir in mind, changes little from the early examples to the later works.

The hymn tunes mainly revolve around Ireland's associations with Geoffrey Shaw (1879–1943), co-editor of the *English Hymnal*, and with Sir Sydney Nicholson (1875–1947) of *Hymns Ancient and Modern*. The hymns come from three distinct periods in Ireland's life. There is one very early tune from 1906, a cluster from 1918–25, and then one in 1947. Like the services, for the most part they have a functional, practical purpose, and as such are straightforward and syllabic. There is a tendency toward alternating duple and triple meters, and Ireland's favoured subject matter is the Resurrection.

In addition to the hymns there are four carols for soprano, alto, tenor and bass (SATB). The carols do not have a single recurring theme, but they do use mainly traditional texts. History and the birth of Christ are connected musically by way of modal tunes and deliberate musical archaisms. Triple metres predominate, and all the carols have strong, lilting melodies. They feature unisons and share melodic material.

Ireland's three anthems for choir form the most interesting part of his church music. Though each is scored for different forces, they have a single striking concordance, in that all three draw on texts relating to Christ's Passion. All are imbued with a sense of drama and have erotic undertones. They also have structural correlatives, in that they are sectionalized according to the meaning of the text, yet derive all their melodic material from the opening bars of the work. It is in these pieces that Ireland chooses not to maintain a dissociation of sensibility, mixing topics much more freely than in his services, which belong very clearly to an enclosed world.

2.1 The choir stalls, Holy Trinity, Sloane Street

Composing music for the Church was not the only professional association that Ireland had with the Anglo-Catholic world. He began his musical career as an organist, and worked in this capacity for much of his life, and it is therefore rather surprising that his output for this instrument is so small. There are just ten published works for organ, and all bar one of these date from before 1911. Ireland was somewhat unusual in having been both a professional organist and a professional pianist, and the cross-currents are evident in the music, which mixes functional processional, song accompaniment and light music elements.

Ireland entered the Royal College as a first study organist. There he studied with Sir Walter Parratt, the organist of St George's, Windsor. At the same time he spent his formative composition lessons scrutinizing and emulating the polyphony of Palestrina. His early musical training was therefore primarily aimed at a career in church music. His first known post was a temporary one, as deputy for Vaughan Williams at St Barnabas, South Lambeth for six months.

The next post was more significant. In *c.* 1897 Ireland became the deputy organist at Holy Trinity, Sloane Street, Chelsea. This was an appealing vacancy owing to the facts that the highly esteemed Sir Walter Alcock (1861–1947) was the principal organist and that the church possessed a fine four-manual organ by J.W. Walker and Sons, built in 1891 to the specifications of the church's previous, equally esteemed, organist, Edwin Lemare (1865–1934). Some years later Ireland wrote that in the mid-1890s, 'Holy Trinity Sloane Street was a fashionable Church, and had the reputation of the best musical service in London' (*JIT*, 4). In many ways this post suited Ireland well: the services were appealingly ritual-laden, and the ecstatic, full-blown nature of the decorative interior would have contributed to the overall experience. When Ireland took up the post at Holy Trinity it was a relatively new church, consecrated in 1890, the last work of the architect John Dando Sedding, a leading member of the Arts and Crafts movement, much affected by the heady nature of the Anglo-Catholicism of the 1880s. The church was filled with carving, statuary, ornamental metalwork and stained glass, including a magnificent window designed by Edward Burne-Jones and William Morris. But it was the choir stalls (Figure 2.1) that demonstrated the most striking mingling of sensuous beauty with religious formality and tradition. Made from dark oak with bronze panels, they are crowned with reliefs of important figures in the history of the English church. One of these represents John Keble, a figure to whom Ireland returned at the end of his life.

Holy Trinity had a daily evensong at 6 o'clock with the choir of boys only, followed by a choir practice. The full choir sang at the Sunday services. Ireland played for evensong two or three times a week, and for all the Sunday services in the summer months, and had to attend the choir rehearsals, which were conducted by Alcock. Ireland recalled that:

It must be noted that there was no choir school, all the boys being selected from the Holy Trinity Church School, but in those days they were mostly the sons of servants of the gentry who at that time lived in the neighbourhood ... Moreover, every year the Church provided them with a seaside holiday of a fortnight, some of the Church officials and clergy being in charge, which laid the foundations for a fine esprit-de-corps which led to the happiest co-operation in the choir work of the Church, and the kindliest relations between all concerned. I myself was always invited to join these pleasant vacations, and they were delightful times I shall never forget.

(JIT, 4)

It was while at Holy Trinity that Ireland first began to write for the Church, and there are three associated works. The first was a Communion Service in A flat, one of his earliest surviving pieces, performed presumably shortly after he had joined Holy Trinity, as the score indicated that it was for use at the church. This setting is for boys and organ only, seemingly intended for the weekday services, and while simple, diatonic and unsophisticated, as might be expected from such an early piece, it has moments of drama. Ireland's setting of the Credo is an overt expression of the transition from burial to resurrection. The words 'And was crucified also for us' are set to an intoning B♮. At 'And the third day He rose again' the voices divide into two parts for the pictorial ascendance into heaven and the return to A flat major. This crudely passionate response was to be developed as a part of his church style. This service also contains an early example of a sweet, 'saintly' aspect of Ireland's church music in the Sanctus, a triple time 'song' with the simplest of melodies floating over moving parallel triads.

The dramatic approach was continued in Ireland's biggest work for Holy Trinity, Vexilla Regis (1898), a setting of a translation of words by Bishop Venantius Fortunatas. This Hymn for Passion Sunday was Ireland's first contribution to the anthem repertory. He was only nineteen when he wrote the piece, and despite its very early date and the inexperience of the composer, Vexilla Regis is an exciting work showing signs of Ireland's potential. It was performed at the church, but then, like so many of the early pieces, withdrawn by the composer, and not published until after his death. It is the first of his extended musical approaches to the Passion, and it presents Christ's sacrifice as something momentous, with fitting music of exaltation and solemnity. It is primarily Ireland's choice of instrumental forces that creates the feeling of ritual. In this work he chose to write for soli SATB, chorus SATB, organ and a brass quintet consisting of two trumpets and three trombones. In octaves the brass contribute to and enhance the laudatory nature of the opening, but are omitted in the central soli section where the words focus on Christ's suffering.

Although it is sectionalized in a manner that pre-empts the much later work for chorus and orchestra, These Things Shall Be, the entire piece emanates from the opening melodic idea. From this, Ireland derives two smaller motifs: a rising perfect fourth usually followed by a falling tone or semitone and a rhythmic pattern involving stepwise movement. These two motifs form the basis of all sections of the work, subjected to unison appearances, imitative entries, transposition, inversion and rhythmic transformations. At this stage in Ireland's life, the Passion stands for glory and achievement, captured in harmonies and textures emerging from Ireland's musical heritage, though even at this early stage, some of the melodic climaxes hint at an ecstasy in the suffering.

There are two distinct types of music in *Vexilla Regis*, and these two types are the essence of Ireland's church style. The first is the grand response, exemplified in the extended instrumental introduction and the C major affirmations, as at bar 96 (Example 2.1). This is the prophetic, the eternal, the absolute confidence in the greater glory of God. In passages of this type, which have an emphasis on chordal writing, major tonalities and rising vocal fanfares, Ireland is drawing on a musical tradition that encompasses his English predecessors and stretches back to Handel.

Example 2.1

The other aspect of Ireland's church topic is the sweet transcendence that was seen in the Communion Service in A flat. Here, a new section of music, starting at bar 128, moves to E major to muse amid the glory. This 'sweet' churchiness relies for its effect on lyrical tunes, in which phrases end with apppoggiaturas. The accompaniment in these instances is chordal, simple and often has an abundance of dominant sevenths (Example 2.2).

Example 2.2

In this work Ireland was also experimenting with contrapuntal writing, especially in the closing Amen, in a way that was never again seen in his music. The grandiose choral work for the Church was abandoned by Ireland after *Vexilla Regis*, probably for practical reasons. As a Hymn for Passiontide, and requiring large forces, its performance outlets were limited. Ireland's only other work associated with Holy Trinity was of a very different nature, a short, charming 'Vesper hymn'.

Unfortunately for Ireland and for Holy Trinity, Sir Walter Alcock was much in demand and along with the Rector, Canon Fyton, soon left for St Margaret's, Westminster, taking some of the best choristers with him. On account of his age and inexperience, Ireland, despite the fact that he often conducted the full service himself, was not elevated to the post of principal organist. Instead, the organ post at Holy Trinity's sister church, St Jude's, Turk's Row, Chelsea, was assigned to him at some point between 1897 and 1900. Later in his life he harked back to the days at Holy Trinity, when he had 'a marvellous choir of 40 splendid boys' (KT: 17 July 1939), and acknowledged his debt to Alcock, whom he thought was a fine musician.

Ireland's period at St Jude's was a brief one. It was the custom to take the choristers at this church on an annual holiday, as it had been at Holy Trinity, and during this time Ireland went with them on seaside trips to Deal, Herne Bay and Worthing. This custom, albeit on a much more modest basis, was also practised at Ireland's next, and musically much more significant, post as organist and choirmaster at St Luke's, Sydney Street, Chelsea.

Ireland took up his new appointment at St Luke's in July 1904, as successor to Everard Hulton. The rector at this time (from 1902 until 1930) was the Reverend Henry Edward James Bevan (see Plate 5) who, like Ireland, had moved there from Holy Trinity, where he had been the rector from 1895 to 1902. Bevan had taken over from Gerald Blunt, who had been rector since 1860, and presumably the appointment of Ireland was at Bevan's request. Ireland's duties involved playing the organ, but also training the choir. Later in 1904 it was reported that:

> it [was] to the training of the boys that Mr. Ireland ha[d] especially directed his attention, since he felt that there was here great need for improvement. At the close of the summer holidays he announced that he should require regular attendance at the week-day services and practices, and also that he would hold a practice every day of the week. The result, even during the past month, has been a very great improvement in the quality of the singing.

(St Luke's, 11/1904: 231)

St Luke's (Figure 2.2), built in the Gothic style by James Savage and consecrated in 1824, is a magnificent building in terms of its grandeur and excellent acoustics, its tall tower the most striking feature.

By the time Ireland came to the church, it had already acquired a strong sense of tradition and history, having associations with Dickens, who was married there in 1836, Charles Kingsley, whose father was rector from 1832 until 1860 and Thomas Carlyle. Its organists, too, had included renowned

2.2 Engraving of St Luke's, Chelsea, 1827

musicians, the first, in 1824, Sir John Goss (1800–80), later organist at St Paul's Cathedral. Despite all these positive aspects, and the fact that St Luke's had a proper, paid, surpliced choir, this church was never entirely to Ireland's taste. He disliked the style of the services, which were insufficiently ritualistic for him, and the church possessed an inferior organ, built by the firm of Nichols in 1824.

The period at St Luke's generated the bulk of Ireland's church music. More importantly it introduced him to figures who were to play important roles in his career outside the Church. These included the curate Paul Walde (dates unknown), who became a lifelong friend, and with whom Ireland stayed at Little Sampford Rectory in the 1940s, and also the cleric A.R. Lee Gardner, who was a friend of Ireland from c. 1908 to at least 1954, and who later gave up Holy Orders to become a crime writer. A number of the boys also played significant roles in Ireland's life, three in particular. These were Charles Markes (1900–85), Bobby Glassby (c. 1900–34) and Arthur George Miller (1905–86), all of whom will be discussed in Chapter 6. Of these figures, Gardner, Markes and Glassby can be seen in Plate 5.

Nearly all of Ireland's organ music dates from his time at St Luke's. Some of it appears to have been intended for use as voluntaries, but there are other works that seem to belong more to the world of the civic organist. Ireland himself gave a short organ recital at the church every Sunday evening after the service, but there is no record of what he actually played at these events. His own organ pieces are a mixture of lyrical elegy and exuberant fanfare, and it is clear that he was also drawing on light music repertories.

Before coming to St Luke's, Ireland had in 1902 written an Elegiac Romance, an extended recital piece, the longest and by far the most densely textured and chromatic of his organ pieces. It is difficult to discern influences specific to organ repertoire: neither Parry nor Stanford had published anything much for organ before this date, and it would seem that the piece is more generally rooted in a nineteenth-century chromaticism, overtly romantic. The piece is an elegy on a single theme, used as the basis of an expansive exploration of tonality and texture. The writing is often pianistic, and owes something to the orchestral transcriptions for organ that were popular at this time. Although this is a very early and undeveloped work, which relies on simple harmonic sequences, it, like *Vexilla Regis*, promises something that in the church music remained unfulfilled. Ireland never again attempted grandeur in his organ music, and the four pieces that followed this, in 1904, were in complete contrast. These were the Intrada, the Villanella, the Menuetto-Impromptu and the *Marcia popolare*, whose style signalled a move away from thick textures towards a more dance-based approach.

The Intrada is a very straightforward, hymn-like movement in F major. The most interesting of the 1904 pieces is the Villanella, which is surely a piece of light music. Ireland may have been influenced by Fauré's use of the term 'villanella' for some of his song titles, and indeed by the 'villanelle' of Chabrier and Dukas. This piece has the light, witty characteristics expected of a villanella, with its simple, singable melody and chromatic cadences (Example 2.3).

Example 2.3

The Menuetto-Impromptu is a delicately chromatic dance (Example 2.4), in the manner of Alexandre Guilmant (1837–1911), and there are similarly light, sometimes camp, touches to the Villanella. When, in 1941, these two were arranged for orchestra by Leslie Bridgwater, they were published appropriately as 'salon' pieces. Ireland himself reworked the Intrada, Villanella and Menuetto-Impromptu in 1944 and republished them as a *Miniature Suite*.

Example 2.4

For a few years Ireland wrote nothing for the organ, but then, in 1911, three new works appeared. The Capriccio was a continuation of the light music vein, with its whimsical opening and subtle chromatic touches. The other two works, *Sursum Corda* and *Alla Marcia*, were published as a pair and were dedicated to Ireland's former organ teacher, Sir Walter Parratt. They were reviewed as serving well 'as voluntaries before and after service' (*MT*, Jan. 1912: 32), and that is essentially what they are. Both are tonal and only rarely depart from a four-square phrase structure. *Alla Marcia* is a simple affirmation of faith, its celebratory fanfares and secure, unwavering pedal part resounding in praise. To effect this Ireland deploys inherited traditions such as triadic, trumpet-derived passages and extensive repetition of the main two-bar motif. In the section from bar 20 to 40, a new idea interrupts, but despite driving the music away from the tonic key, it never succeeds in dominating and is swiftly swept away in a procession towards a confident close in G major.

Ireland wrote nothing else for the organ during his time at St Luke's. Given that he spent until 1926 there – that is, another fifteen years – this is surprising, and one can only assume that he did not particularly like writing for the instrument. His corpus of organ music is thus a curious one: a single essay in nineteenth-century harmonies and textures, a collection of salon pieces and a handful of functional works for practical use. It was not here that Ireland was to find his natural medium for musical expression.

Ireland's involvement with St Luke's was quite extensive, particularly during his early years in the post, and his name appears at regular intervals in the parish magazines that survive (these go up to and include 1923). During this time there were few changes of personnel. Bevan was Rector for the duration of Ireland's employment, and another long-serving preacher was Hugh Otter-Barry, who left in 1915. Beck was the organ-blower, Capel C. Peacey another cleric, and Charles Hindes the vestry clerk until 1926. All of these figures can be seen in Plate 5. The impression from reading the registers of service and minute books is that music was a fundamental but not terribly significant aspect of the church. As early as 1905 there were reports in the parish magazine that the organ was not in good shape:

> The vagaries of an English winter are always trying to those who are reluctantly compelled to acknowledge that they have passed the prime of life, and we were sorry to hear our old friend the organ evidently suffering from the effects of the alternating frost thaw and fog which prevailed during the Christmas season. There can hardly be any necessity to assure the congregation that Mr. Ireland was in no way responsible for the alarming and disconcerting groans which marred the services on Christmas evening and New Year's Day. It was simply a case of bronchial catarrh, from which the organ has made a speedy and satisfactory recovery without any further relapse.
>
> (*St Luke's*, 2/1905: 39)

In the same year the magazine carried reports of a need for new music, and for fund-raising for this purpose, with Ireland as the enthusiastic musician involved in this process. And in April 1905 it was noted that the choir would have new surplices.

In the early part of his time at St Luke's, Ireland was very involved with the social life of the church, and reports of dinners and outings often mention him as being present. The music performed in the services in the first decade of the century was limited in date and repertoire, and largely confined to Ireland's predecessors. The list of music for 1905 shows that Stanford in B flat was a regular feature, along with services by Alcock, Charles Harford Lloyd (1849–1919), Henry Thomas Smart (1813–79), John Stainer (1840–1901), Arthur Sullivan (1842–1900) and Thomas Attwood Walmisley (1814–56). Ireland wrote two works for the church in this year. These were the hymn tune 'Eastergate' (the title of which, like many of Ireland's hymn tunes, has personal meaning, in this case a reference to an early visit to a place of the same name in West Sussex) and a Magnificat and Nunc Dimittis in A major. During this time, Ireland's connections with Holy Trinity and with Alcock were maintained, primarily through Bevan's continued friendship with his former organist. Alcock regularly attended dinners and services, and the report of March 1906 read:

The officials and adult members of the Choir were most hospitably entertained at dinner at the Rectory on February 2nd. The Rector, of course, presided, and the company was rather larger than usual, including all the gentlemen of the Choir with one exception, Messrs. Ireland, Peach and Penrose, the Rev. L. McN. Shelford, and two very welcome guests, the Rev. W.M. Le Patourel, Precentor of Holy Trinity, Sloane Street, and Dr. Alcock, Organist of the Chapels Royal and formerly of Holy Trinity. After dinner, in which full justice was done to the ample fare provided by Mrs. Bevan, the evening was given up to informal speeches, and later on to still more informal glees.

The Rector's health was proposed by Mr. Murley, solo tenor, in an admirable speech, and, in replying, the Rector called attention to two features which he was glad to say he had always noticed in connection with St. Luke's Choir. The one was the general *esprit de corps* and keen interest displayed in the work; the other was the absence of the too professional spirit, which so often mars a Choir where all the members are paid. He congratulated the Choir on these two characteristics, and hoped that they might always remain their pride and ideal. After speeches from Mr. Shelford and Mr. Ireland, the toast of "the Visitors" was proposed, and Mr. Le Patourel and Dr. Alcock were called upon to respond. Both spoke in glowing terms of the happy six years when they had worked together under the Rector at Holy Trinity, and then went on to remind us that they had each on different occasions been present at St. Luke's on a practice night, when they had been immensely struck with the results of Mr. Ireland's training. Dr. Alcock especially said that he felt he might congratulate himself on a most distinguished pupil. A very enjoyable evening closed with a vote of thanks to the Rector and Mrs. Bevan for their kind hospitality.

(*St Luke's*, 3/1906: 64)

The traditional choir outings that had been a feature of life at both St Jude's and Holy Trinity were also a feature of St Luke's, though here they were confined to day trips. In 1906, for example, the choir had an excursion to Littlehampton, which involved a long and arduous train journey, with changes at Arundel and Ford. There, the members of the party bathed, had lunch, went for a drive and then bathed again before a three-hour journey home, with Ireland and Bevan presiding over the 'more sedate carriage' (*St Luke's*, 9/1906: 190). There were other choir gatherings, including outings to Kew Gardens, rounders matches and suchlike.

In 1907 Ireland dedicated his Te Deum in F to Bevan, a work again rooted in nineteenth-century harmonic language. The vocal textures are unambitious, using mainly unisons and chords, and little counterpoint. In a manner derived from *Vexilla Regis*, there are expressive moments of drama and sentimentality.

At this time Ireland was evidently held in high esteem at St Luke's. Reports in the parish magazines often mentioned performances of his music outside the church. By 1909 a new curate was referred to in the magazines: the Reverend C.P. Walde (Paul Walde), whose name was added to the lists of those involved in extra-curricular church activities. The 1909 choir outing to see *Dick Whittington* at the Drury Lane Theatre was led by Walde, Ireland and another figure: Archer. This was J. Stuart Archer, the new assistant organist. Another new name of 1909 was W.F. Albon, a choirboy who went on to become Ireland's assistant at St Luke's in the 1920s.

The period from about 1909 to 1912 was the heyday of Ireland's time at the church. Music at this time included more Stanford in B flat, and a continued enthusiasm for Smart, Stainer and Walmisley. The parish magazine list of music for February 1911 is very typical:

SUNDAY, February 5th (*5th Sunday after Epiphany*)
MATINS AND HOLY COMMUNION – Te Deum, *Ireland*; Benedictus, 35;
Holy Communion, *Garrett*; Hymn during Communion, 559; Pater noster,
Lemare No.2.
Hymns, 320, 242, 528.
AFTERNOON SERVICE – Hymns, 217, 228, 341.
EVENSONG – Service, *Lloyd*.
Hymns, 531, 38, 82.
Anthem, "He, watching over Israel," *Mendelssohn*.

SUNDAY, February 12th (*Septuagesima*)
MATINS AND LITANY – Te Deum, Benedicite, *Stainer*; Benedictus,
Stanford in B flat.
Hymns, 301, 535, 295.
AFTERNOON SERVICE – Hymns, 340, 339, 240.
EVENSONG– Service, *Walmisley* in D.
Hymns, 83, 514, 161, 168.
Anthem, "The Heavens are telling" *Haydn* (Creation).

SUNDAY, February 19th (*Sexagesima*)
MATINS AND HOLY COMMUNION – Te Deum, *Stanford* in C;
Benedictus, 114; Kyrie, *Stanford* in G.
Hymns, 172, 277, 316.
AFTERNOON SERVICE – Hymns, 536, 512, 336.
EVENSONG – Service, *Stanford* in C.
Hymns, 373, 176, 184, 588.

SUNDAY, February 26th (*Quinquagesima*)
MATINS AND LITANY – Te Deum, *Stanford* in C; Benedictus, 146.
Hymns, 536, 210, 555.
AFTERNOON SERVICE – Hymns, 210, 334, 260.
EVENSONG – Service, *Stanford* in C.
Hymns, 273, 520, 192 (T.370).
Anthem, "O love the Lord" *Sullivan.*

(St Luke's, 2/1911: 30–31)

In 1912 Ireland wrote a second church anthem, the 'meditation' for Passiontide, *Greater Love Hath No Man.* For this, Ireland chose to draw on an existing compilation of appropriate passages from the Old and New Testaments. This came from a booklet of Bible readings, *Daily Light on the Daily Path*, given to him by his mother. Ireland read these regularly, and the text for 'Greater Love' was that of 3 October, as was confirmed by Thompson. The sentiments of the words are reflected in four musical sections, as indicated in the layout below:

(i) Many waters cannot quench Love, neither can the floods drown it. Love is strong as death. (Song of Solomon viii:7 and viii:6) Greater Love hath no man than this, that a man lay down his life for his friends. (John xv:13)

(ii) Who His own Self bare our sins in His own Body on the tree, that we, being dead to sins, should live unto righteousness. (1 Peter ii:24)

(iii) *(That we, being dead to sins, should live unto righteousness.)* Ye are wash'd, ye are sanctified, ye are justified, in the Name of the Lord Jesus (1 Corinthians vi:11); Ye are a chosen generation, a royal priesthood, a holy nation, That ye should shew forth the praises of Him Who hath call'd you out of darkness into His marvellous light. (1 Peter ii:9)

(iv) I beseech you, brethren, by the mercies of God, that ye present your bodies, a living sacrifice, holy, acceptable unto God, which is your reasonable service. (Romans, xii:1)

The words belong together by way of their shared meaning each passage considering aspects of Christ's Passion and more generally, the notion of 'sacrifice'. Ireland matches these sentiments with four distinct types of music, but provides unity of meaning through motivic, and to a lesser extent, tonal, unity. Thus each of the main sections of music derives from the opening melodic line, as shown in Example 2.5, where (ii) is an inversion of the opening of (i), (iii) an elaboration of (i) and (iv) a development of (iii).

Example 2.5

In terms of the distinct characters of the four sections, the first is passionate, fervent and heartfelt, a celebration of love and sacrifice, in which Ireland's 'sweet transcendent' and 'affirmative' church types are combined. The opening music is tonal, with Elgarian harmonies underpinning the lyrical melody. At the repeat of the words 'Many waters cannot quench Love', the harmonic alteration from an E major (bar 5, beat 3) to an E minor chord (bar 13, beat 3) highlights the poignancy of the words and melody. The line 'Love is strong as death' provokes assertive, stirring choral unisons, a new fanfare idea derived again from (i) (Example 2.6).

Example 2.6

The climax at the words 'Greater Love hath no man' (Example 2.7) is all the more powerful after the previous unisons.

Example 2.7

The second, 'transcendent', section uses two solo voices to ponder on Christ's actions and the third moves on to look at the outcome of the resurrection for mankind. This is the 'affirmative' type, with the words 'Ye are wash'd' sung to the same music as the word 'Fulfill'd' that was seen in Example 2.1. This section is resolutely tonal, primarily a succession of root position chords and unisons with the fanfare motif prominent. The final words are rather an afterthought, with more evidence of modal thinking than anything that has gone before

The other work of this year, 1912, was a Benedictus in F, to be added to the Te Deum. It was also at about this time that Ireland was beginning to develop his friendship with the young chorister Charlie Markes, using him as an assistant from time to time. Markes evidently devoted much of his time to life at the church, as is clear from surviving documents.

In 1913 Ireland dedicated another work to Bevan, the Office of the Holy Communion in C. This setting, reviewed as 'well within the powers of the average parish church choir' (*MT*, June 1914: 388) is typical of Ireland's services, with its simple melodic lines and harmonic movement. Again, root position triads dominate, and the word-setting is almost exclusively syllabic, as seen in the Gloria (Example 2.8). The whole is held together by a recurring scale motif.

Example 2.8

The Jubilate Deo in F that followed in 1914 deploys an unashamed diatonicism, and it is evident that Ireland was by this time using an entirely separate, functional style for his church services and canticles. The Jubilate Deo and the Communion Service are very distant from Ireland's secular works of this period, which include the song-cycle *Marigold* and *The Forgotten Rite*. The Jubilate Deo, reviewed as 'tuneful' and 'straightforward' (*MT*, April 1914: 246) rarely strays from the tonic key, and in the opening few bars sticks resolutely to root position chords. The vocal writing is almost exclusively homophonic, with only occasional passages where Ireland thins the texture. The 1915 Magnificat and Nunc Dimittis were a continuation of the same, and these works, along with the Jubilate Deo and the Benedictus all used the same Gloria, derived from motifs from the Te Deum.

By 1915 the impact of the First World War was being felt and the choir was in decline, with numbers diminishing as members enlisted to serve at the Front. Services at St Luke's in this and the next few years also reflected the impact of the war, with an abundance of anthems focusing on the subject of peace, and war litanies being said every fortnight. By this time the Ireland services and canticles were an integral part of the repertoire of St Luke's. It is evident from the parish magazines that the war greatly changed the life of the church, and there were no longer the lavish dinners with beautifully decorated tables or the community outings. The Rector declared financial problems, and the magazines increasingly referred to war activities. Nevertheless, Ireland continued to compose throughout these straitened times, and in 1917, the parish magazine reported the success of Ireland's Second Violin Sonata and advertised tickets for sale for the performance of the Second Piano Trio in June of that year.

Once the war was over Ireland produced only a handful of religious works, including a Benedicite in F and some hymn tunes: 'Irene', the chorale-like 'Mighty Father', 'Fraternity', 'Love unknown' and 'Chelsea'. By far the best of these is 'Love unknown', composed in 1919, and first included in *The Public School Hymn Book* in 1920. The words, by Samuel Crossman, were suggested to Ireland by Shaw, their subject once again Christ's Passion. The compelling feature of this tune (Example 2.9) is the way in which Ireland creates a sense of ebb and flow with his mixing of ³⁄₈ and ³⁄₂ bars, and his flexible word-setting. The shift of emphasis in the words is matched by a folk-influenced tonal device, a move to a new key centre based on the flattened leading note D♭ of the original tonic E flat major, a key Ireland tended to associate with serenity and religious faith.

Example 2.9

My song is love unknown,
my saviour's love for me;
love to the loveless shown
that they might lovely be:
but who am I, that for my sake
my Lord should take frail flesh and die?

The music sung at St Luke's after this point continued much as before, and the repertoire of 1920 and 1921 was very similar to that of ten years earlier, save only that there was more Ireland. The choir outings had resumed, and in the meantime W.F. Albon had become the assistant organist. In 1923 his place was taken by Leslie Woodgate, a pupil of Archer and a student at the RCM. This is the last year in which there is extant information on the St Luke's choir and its activities as recorded in the parish magazines.

In 1925 Ireland produced the hymn tune 'Chelsea', yet another setting of words about the Resurrection, linked thematically to his earlier piano work, 'Chelsea Reach'. He was still very involved with the church, and in this year submitted estimates for the building of a new organ. But on 29 October 1926 the minutes of St Luke's Parochial Church Council recorded that 'Mr John Ireland had been compelled by the stress of his many other engagements, to resign the post of Organist and Choirmaster at St Luke's after having occupied it for the past 23 years'. The new organist was Guy Eldridge, but the new organ was not installed until 1932.

The year after leaving St Luke's, Ireland wrote the first of his four carols for SATB, the modal, graceful 'New prince, new pomp'. This was his last piece of music for church use for some time. Upon his departure from St Luke's in 1926, Ireland ceased to work as a professional organist and did not do so again until 1940. It would also seem that he discontinued his allegiance to St Luke's, as by about 1932 he had become a regular worshipper at St Cuthbert's, Kensington. The ritual of this church, 'with its beauty & mystic symbolism', 'greatly moved him' (KT to CSS: 20 Sept. 1976), and Ireland, along with his friend Percy Bentham, became quite involved with the church. The Priest-in-Charge at this time was Kenneth Thompson (see Plate 20). This was a meeting of minds, and Thompson was to become a close friend of the composer. His position as a cleric and his obvious empathy with Ireland's music and sexuality were powerful attractions, and from 1936 to 1962 the two met regularly and corresponded frequently. Fourteen years after Ireland's death, Thompson wrote to Scott-Sutherland that the composer 'regarded me as his Chaplain, so to speak – and one to whom he could talk intimately about his personal affairs' (KT to CSS: 20 Sept. 1976).

In 1936 Thompson left St Cuthbert's and moved to Sussex to be chaplain at Lancing College, and the following year added to this post that of lecturer and librarian at Chichester Theological College. His friend's move to a county that held a strong appeal for Ireland evidently prompted the composer to think similarly, as in 1937 he mentioned that he was considering a post at Chichester Cathedral, a passing thought which came to nothing. In any case, Ireland was at this time spending most of his time living in Deal in Kent, attending St Andrew's, Deal, but finding it 'a very half & half church as regards ritual' (KT: 14 July 1938).

In 1939 Ireland left England for Guernsey, ostensibly to consider settling on the island, and in 1940 he renewed his formal links with the Church as Director of Music at St Stephen's, St Peter Port (Figure 2.3). He wrote to Paul Walde:

> You may be amused to hear that I have been induced by supplications, threats and cajolery, to become, more or less informally, Director of Music at the only ritualistic Church on the Island. For a long time I have felt I would like to play the organ again and to handle a choir, not too strenuously – and I was influenced by the fact that at this Church (St Stephen's), there is a splendid up-to-date 3-manual Walker organ, with all-electric action, which no local organist has ever been able to tackle, except with disastrous results – also, as you know, Popery has always had a strong appeal for me, and in the morning, services are all thoroughly Popish, with the Mass in most of its glory. The music is simple, being mostly plainsong (the only *real* Church music) ...
>
> (PW: 12 June 1940)

The rector at this time was the Reverend Thomas Hartley Jackson, who was there from 1927 until 1946. Important choristers included Martin Le Page, Peter Lihou and Andrew White, and once again these youths were to have an impact on Ireland's output. The post proved to be a fulfilling one, as the church was far more concerned with ritual than St Luke's had ever been, and this appealed to Ireland, as he wrote soon after taking up the post:

> Ritually they do the Mass rather well, with everything, including incense and the Gospel procession; the music is rather a jumble, but one could not alter that, I fear. The choir is not bad, for a place like this – there are about 8 boys & 2 or 3 girls & some men. They sing in tune & with a fair quality. They sit up in the west gallery where the organ is, but the organ console is in the chancel.
>
> (KT: 1 March 1940)

A few months later he was still expressing his delight in the ceremony of the church, describing the Mass as:

> ... performed in a highly efficient manner from the stage-managing point of view. The servers and acolytes are drilled to every movement and every inch. It is a change from the hypocrisy and banality of St Luke's, Chelsea – also from the frantic and 'Heath-Robinsonish' organ I had there to play on.
>
> (PW: 12 June 1940)

Surviving members of the choir have given somewhat different accounts, remembering not so much the ritualistic elements of the service as Ireland's manner, which they recall as rather distant, intolerant and demanding of exceptionally high standards at the two rehearsals and two services each week. The choristers were not trained musicians and so all the music was learnt by ear, including Ireland's own Communion Service in C. Ireland had other, less important, connections with another of Guernsey's churches, St Saviour's, where he performed as organist on occasion, and he became friendly with its rector, Reverend Edward F. Wood.

One of the main attractions of Guernsey was the cross-fertilization between the churches and their ancient past, the sacred buildings on Guernsey appealing to Ireland as much for their pagan foundations as for their Christianity. St Saviour's has a menhir to mark the entrance to the church, as does Ste Marie, Catel, and the main attraction of St Martin's church was the 4000–year-old Neolithic stone menhir, 'La Gran-mère du Chimquière', outside its gates. In his letters from Guernsey, Ireland alluded to this juxtaposition of the sacred and the secular on the island, mentioning the contrast between the many beautiful churches and the pagan relics.

In addition to the secular works from this period, there exist manuscript workings for a mass specific to the rituals of St Stephen's, the Missa *Sancti Stephani*. This is very much in line with other services by Ireland, with extreme harmonic and melodic simplicity, though this work is more clearly modal than earlier services. Ireland omitted the Credo on the grounds that St Stephen's always substituted a local Credo into a mass setting in order that the

2.3 St Stephen's Church, Guernsey

congregation could participate at this point. He wrote to Thompson in September that he had 'practically finished a simple mass – quite simple, though in 4-part harmony ... I will dedicate it to you, if you like' (KT: 10 Sept. 1941). It is the only one of his works dedicated to Kenneth Thompson, who by this time had become a Navy chaplain, and it remained unperformed until 1994, when the choir of St Stephen's sang it as part of that year's D-Day commemorations.

On his enforced return to England after the German invasion of Guernsey in 1940, Ireland once again turned his hand to church services. In 1941 he produced a Morning and an Evening Service in C and the Ninefold Kyrie, intended for use with the 1913 Communion Service. Also in 1941 Ireland made an effective choral arrangement of 'The holy boy', and wrote 'A New Year carol', the opening of which shared melodic germs with the earlier 'New prince, new pomp'.

The Second World War saw Ireland maintaining connections with the Church of England. In 1940 and 1941 he lodged first in Radlett and then Banbury, attending services in Oxford and Christ Church, Banbury, where a friend, Walter Trinder, was organist. In 1942 he was living in Little Sampford Rectory, Saffron Walden, with his friend Paul Walde. Dreams and regrets seem to be the main theme of these wartime years, and Ireland wrote of his fantasies for the future, which included Thompson taking up a post as a country cleric, with Ireland as his organist:

> ... when the war is over, you must take a country living, or ... in a small town, where we can work up a large choir & I will be your organist & choirmaster. I really mean this. I will live with you in the Rectory or Vicarage.
>
> (KT: 25 Nov. 1943)

At this time Ireland was also reading theological matter, including H.G. Wells' *Indictment of the Roman Church*.

In 1944 Sydney Nicholson commissioned a new work from Ireland, to be performed in Durham Cathedral as part of a Royal Schools of Church Music summer holiday course. This was *Ex ore innocentium*, for which Ireland again chose to use the topic of Christ's sacrifice, this time approached from the viewpoint of the child, using words by Bishop W.W. How:

I　　It is a thing most wonderful,
　　　Almost too wonderful to be,
　　　That God's own Son should come to heav'n
　　　And die to save a child like me.

II　　And yet I know that it is true:
　　　He chose a poor and humble lot,
　　　And wept, and toiled, and mourned, and died,
　　　For love of those who loved him not.

III   I sometimes think about the Cross,
      And shut my eyes, and try to see
      The cruel nails and crown of thorns,
      And Jesus crucified for me.

IV   But even could I see him die,
      I should but see a little part
      Of that great love, which like a fire,
      Is always burning in his heart.

V   And yet I want to love thee, Lord;
      O light the flame within my heart,
      And I will love thee more and more,
      Until I see thee as thou art.

It is a personal blend of genres used by Ireland: a mixture of solo song, unison song and anthem. By this time the themes of Christ's Passion – sacrifice, suffering and love – had become closely entwined with the innocence of the angelic choirboy. By 1944 Ireland had a much greater self-knowledge and awareness of his attraction to the beauty and purity of the choirboy (as will be discussed in Chapter 6), and his references to the first performance made play of the appearance of the boys, who looked 'perfectly ravishing, in light blue cassocks and ruffs' (KT: 6 Sept. 1944).

Ex ore innocentium ('From the mouths of innocents') falls into five sections determined by Bishop How's verses, all related motivically, in a manner akin to, but more simple than, that of *Greater Love Hath No Man*. Considering the advanced harmonic language deployed by Ireland in the works that immediately preceded and followed it, this work, with its root position chords, stands out as being again in a distinctive 'church' vein, and here it is the transcendent type that is foremost. Verses I and V are in E flat major, their profession of wonder matched in a melody of an innocent artless quality, supported by rich appoggiaturas (Example 2.10).

Example 2.10

These outer sections are the assurance against which the central verses muse and reflect. Every one of the five verses contains a swooning, emotional climax, a high point both in terms of pitch and expressive qualities. The most striking of these outpourings of Passion comes in the third verse, where the music swiftly moves from gentle contemplation to dramatic conclusion (Example 2.11).

Example 2.11

As a whole the work is highly effective, potent in its juxtaposed simplicity and eroticism. By all accounts the choirboys for whom it was written found it very congenial, and according to Nicholson they 'really loved it & showed it by their singing: it was most expressive & everyone present felt it to be a really lovely work. You have <u>absolutely</u> hit the nail on the head' (SN to JI: 19

Aug. 1944). After the performance the boys signed a declaration of their appreciation of the piece.

Once the war had come to an end, Ireland made several attempts to resume one of his positions as organist. He wanted to return to Guernsey, but was told that his former post was not free. There is also correspondence from 1945, in which he says that 'The Rector of St Luke's, Chelsea has written to me to say his organist (who has been in the R.A.F.) is not returning ... I have been to see the Rector, and it is clear he would very much like me to be concerned' (JL: 4 Dec. 1945). Despite the fact that during the war years Ireland had expressed his regrets at having given up the post, this possibility of returning never came to fruition. Ireland did, however, continue to write church music on a very occasional basis. A 1947 commission from Nicholson was the hymn tune 'Sampford', its title a reference to the rectory where Ireland had stayed during the war. Once again he set a Passiontide text, returning to the oscillating $\frac{3}{8}$ and $\frac{6}{8}$ of 'Love unknown'. During the 1940s and 1950s, Ireland became less and less involved with the Church of England, and expressed his doubts about his own belief at increasingly regular intervals. Again, he alluded to the attractions of the ritual of the Roman Catholic church:

> I, too, have long felt how unsatisfactory the C of E is. Yet I find, for myself, that the alternative – the R. C. – has something definitely "foreign" about it which goes greatly against the grain. There is also much that is tawdry and displeasing in certain external details, and I personally am not constituted to accept the extreme & emotional veneration of the B. V. M. which seems such an important part of Roman practice – and so inescapable.
>
> Perhaps I am not really a Catholic at all, but only attracted by what Catholicism has in common with pre-Christian paganism – i.e. the general idea of sacramentalism, wh. is so closely allied to magic. You yourself use the words "the super-natural", wh. cover a great deal more than Christian or Catholic doctrine.
>
> (LS: 16 March 1946)

Thompson, too, suffered crises of faith, and in 1947 converted to Roman Catholicism and left for Rome to train for the priesthood. Ireland was ultimately unconvinced, and wrote that he himself was unlikely 'to fall for it, as I am too complete a Pagan – and you too, I think, are too conscious that God's good gifts are there to be enjoyed, to acquiesce in and lend yourself to all this negativeness and asceticism' (KT: 30 Dec. 1947). A few weeks later Ireland reiterated these sentiments: 'You have too much of the artist in you to conform to the leaden outlook of Romanism towards earthly beauty ... This theory of repression does not seem to conform to the immense creativeness of the Deity – or to be in harmony with it' (KT: 4 Feb. 1948).

By 1949 Thompson had returned to the Anglican Church, although his correspondence with Ireland continued to debate the pros and cons of Roman Catholicism. In 1950 Ireland spent five weeks in Ashington, West Sussex, after which visit he wrote that the 'Sussex churches are singularly disappointing in that they simply stink of Protestantism (instead of incense!)' (KT: 25 June 1950). The correspondence indicates that in 1951 Thompson was once again suffering personal doubt. In 1952 Ireland was reading and discussing with Thompson Joad's *Recovery of Belief*.

In the last few years of his life Ireland rediscovered his interest in writing for the Church, and there is a sequence of works and revisions, including 'Island praise' in 1955, which is a reworking of 'An island hymn', and another carol in 1956, 'Adam lay ybounden', whose melodic shape and harmonies resonate with references to 'The holy boy'. The last two works that Ireland wrote were associated with the Church, a return to his musical roots. Both of these were in 1958, the first a remarkable setting of Psalm 23, the second the valedictory organ work, *Meditation on John Keble's Rogationtide Hymn*. Both of these will be discussed in Chapter 9. Curiously, just a few months after writing his last two works, Ireland stated that he could no longer be regarded as either Catholic or Anglo-Catholic (KT: 4 Sept. 1958). Kenneth Thompson summed up the oppositions and connections between the composer's attraction to Christianity and to Paganism when he wrote in 1976:

> The corpus of his Church music is extensive ... It is in this, of course, that he chiefly expresses that side of his nature ... In his instrumental music – though religion & faith must underlie everything he wrote, as part of the man – it is his love & worship of the Devil in creation that is predominant, & this is his Pagan mysticism, if you like ... there was a tension (I think) between John's love of Nature & his sense of the mystery behind it, his Paganism – & his Christian faith. Paganism with its immersion in the transitory has a sense of being finally doomed & unsatisfying especially in relation to the homosexuality often allied to it ... Christianity ... stands for the permanent in & behind nature.
>
> (KT to CSS: 20 Sept. 1976)

It is true that Ireland's works that have Pagan links and motivations have the 'immersion in the transitory' set down by Thompson. Ultimately Ireland's belief in the Christian faith was stronger than his attraction to Paganist philosophies, and this perhaps accounts for the qualities of transcendence and affirmation in the church music.

Chapter 3

Paganism

'A Pagan I was born, & a Pagan I shall ever remain' (KT: 16 July 1936). Although this statement, prompted by the death of a close friend, might appear to be in conflict with Ireland's lifelong association with the Anglican Church, his Christianity has affinities with his paganism. Ireland's fascination with the ritualistic aspects of religious ceremony was matched by a preoccupation with pagan rites. It was an attraction of similarities, but also of oppositions. While the allure of church ritual was its controlled structure and detachment, the appeal of pagan ceremony lay in its unbridled liberation and loss of control. There are a significant number of 'pagan' works in Ireland's output. Some take as their subject matter a specific rite or a named pagan place, or both. There are other pieces which, though unarticulated by title, carry pagan meaning, or which are pantheistic, celebrating the ecstatic side of nature. These are among the best and most individual of his works, and have generally been received as such. William Mann, in 1969, wrote of Ireland that 'he really makes contact when he turns to introspection – to magic and mystery and psychic contact through ancient monuments with our ancestors in the remote past' (Mann, 1969: 9).

Although London was his permanent home for most of his life, Ireland was drawn to country sites of historic significance, specifically those places in which the presence of the past could be keenly felt, where there might be 'a sense of something vaguely sinister, which would do harm if it could … of something muffled up and recalcitrant; of something which rises upon its elbow when no one is present and looks down the converging paths' (Forster, 1972: 355). These were usually burial sites and other spots of previous intensive activity such as chalk-pits and flint-mines, places which had 'morphic resonances' (as discussed in Sheldrake, 1993 and 1994), and which for Ireland precipitated experiences that were encapsulated in his compositions. Identification with a place and its pagan past seems to have been a real driving force behind Ireland's music.

The South Downs and the Channel Islands exerted a particular fascination on account of their long barrows, tumuli and dolmens, and Ireland was a frequent visitor from early in his life, and later a resident: on Guernsey in 1939 and 1940, and ultimately in West Sussex. These places were important for their prehistoric sites and relics, but also for the whole experience that they gave to the composer: beauty, serenity and wilderness brought together in a landscape with personal overtones which he could interpret in his music.

Ireland shared this sensitivity to the past with other contemporary musicians, but above all with writers, and there are numerous examples of novelists and poets working in the late nineteenth and twentieth centuries who have attempted to engage with the continuity of history and an ancient, pagan past. Ireland's surviving library contains a preponderance of poetry and prose in which the writers share some of the composer's preoccupations with landscape, its history and its atmosphere. It seems that he sought out literature which alludes to memory, ritual and place. Ireland read the novels of Richard Jefferies, Machen, Sylvia Townsend Warner, Forrest Reid and E.M. Forster. He liked the shadowy references to past civilizations in the poetry of Thomas Hardy and Walter de la Mare, and the Sussex connections of John Masefield and Hilaire Belloc.

Of these writers, Ireland was particularly drawn to the work of Machen. Machen was born in the Welsh village of Caerleon-in-Usk, claimed as the seat of King Arthur, and the site of a Roman amphitheatre. In 1880 he moved to London. After a few years working as a translator, he began writing his own novels and semi-autobiographical works. The middle years of his life were spent as a travelling actor with Sir Frank Benson's Shakespeare Repertory Company, and from 1914 he worked as a journalist. Machen was a member of the Hermetic Order of the Golden Dawn (under the names *Frater Avallaunius* and *Filius Aquarti*), along with writers W.B. Yeats, Aleister Crowley, Algernon Blackwood and Bram Stoker. Although, like Ireland, Machen was a practising High Church Anglican, for many years he researched into fairy lore, shamanism and the occult, and wrote works of fiction and articles on these subjects, including 'Paganism' for Lord Alfred Douglas in 1908. Now little known, he was at one time admired by Oscar Wilde, Masefield, Siegfried Sassoon and Sir John Betjeman.

Machen's fascination with Britanno-Roman life and its reverberations on the landscape served as a stimulus for Ireland, helping him to tune in to the spirit of place, the *genius loci*. Ireland first became acquainted with the writer's work in 1906, when he bought a copy of *The House of Souls* of that year, and wrote retrospectively in 1957 that he had been 'a worshipper of Machen ever since' (AR: 28 Sept. 1957). The two men knew one another from 1933 onwards, and occasionally met and corresponded. Ireland read all of Machen's work, and found the novel, *The Hill of Dreams* (1907), deeply compelling. In many ways this work is an exemplification of what it was that attracted Ireland to Machen's world. Its main protagonist, Lucian Taylor, is drawn repeatedly to the 'outland and occult territory' (in Palmer, 1988: 174) of an ancient Roman fort. His youthful interest in the place culminates in his eventual withdrawal from reality into a dream existence in which he sees only people of the past. His deterioration towards death is accelerated by his use of laudanum to assist him in his hallucinations. Like Charles Baudelaire before him and Aldous

Huxley after him (though unlike both, not a user of drugs himself), Machen believed that taking substances such as mescalin and lysergic acid could lead to a revitalized consciousness, and he promoted the delights of tobacco-smoking and alcohol in a number of his works.

There were many reasons why *The Hill of Dreams* would have appealed to Ireland. A mixture of fantasy, horror story and mysticism, its language is derived from that of the Symbolists. The central character, Lucian, is a lonely figure, who spends much of his time on solitary walks or in contemplation. Elements of nature play a strong part in Machen's writing, transforming places into different places, an idea that came to be important to Ireland in his own later works. In *The Hill of Dreams*, while sunlight 'transfigure[s] the meadows and change[s] all form of the earth' (ibid.: 179), sunset invests 'the old Roman fort ... with fire' (ibid.: 176). Machen's delicate descriptions of places and of sensations produce a positively physical, sensual effect:

> The hot air seemed to beat upon him in palpable waves, and the nettle sting tingled and itched intolerably; and he was alone upon the fairy hill, within the great mounds, within the ring of oaks, deep in the heart of the matted thicket. Slowly and timidly he began to untie his boots, fumbling with the laces, and glancing all the while on every side at the ugly misshapen trees that hedged the lawn. Not a branch was straight, not one was free, but all were interlaced and grew about one another; and just above ground, where the cankered stems joined the protuberant roots, there were forms that imitated the human shape, and faces and twining limbs that amazed him. Green mosses were hair, and tresses were stark in grey lichen; a twisted root swelled into a limb; in the hollows of the rotted bark he saw the masks of men. His eyes were fixed and fascinated by the simulacra of wood, and could not see his hands, and so at last, and suddenly, it seemed, he lay in the sunlight, beautiful with his olive skin, dark haired, dark eyes, the gleaming bodily vision of a strayed faun.
>
> (in Palmer, 1988: 181–2)

One of Machen's relatives, the poet Sylvia Townsend Warner, was another important influence, and Ireland read much of her work. Like Machen, she was acquainted with the composer, met him on occasions in the 1920s, and he was at one point considering writing an opera based on her story, *Mr Fortune's Maggot* (Harman, 1989: 78). Townsend Warner began her career as a musicologist, before turning writer in 1925 with the publication of her first book of verse, *The Espalier*. Some of the poems in this collection, including 'The Green Valley', show her attempting in words to tap in to what Ireland was trying to convey through music. In this poem memories are triggered of a distant, elusive and yet palpable past, 'grassy slopes, and the cart-track winding, so' (Townsend Warner, 1985: 33).

Townsend Warner and Machen both deal with 'ecstasy', physical and mental, in their writings. While Townsend Warner's was a bodily state, Machen's ecstasy was a solitary condition, often wine-induced, and disconnected from place. The more hedonistic, nature-induced ecstasy which pervades some of Rupert

Brooke's poems also appealed to Ireland, as did, much later in his life, the alternately rapturous and detached writings of Jocelyn Brooke, with whom he formed a close friendship in his last years, and whose books resonate with direct references to Ireland's music.

While Ireland had a lifelong partiality for writers whose concerns were pantheistic, historic or pagan, there were particular periods when this interest surfaced strongly. 1913 was an important year for him, as was 1933. The 1920s saw the production of a number of pagan works, and the topic re-emerged in 1940. In every case Ireland was either living in or visiting a place of particular historic significance with resonances of the past.

In 1913 Ireland produced *The Forgotten Rite* and completed a collection of three piano pieces grouped together as *Decorations*. The first of these, 'The island spell', was an evocation of a Jersey idyll, begun in 1911 and finished on Ireland's return to Jersey in the following year. In sketches for this piece the slow reverie ended in a blaze of brilliance. Ireland decided to detach the original ending and use it as a separate piece, the third of the *Decorations*, with the title 'The scarlet ceremonies'. This title derives from a short story, 'The White People', contained within Machen's novel, *The House of Souls*. Ireland said of this story that it had 'astounding qualities', at which he 'never cease[d] to marvel'. Intriguingly he wrote that 'Machen told me something about "The White People" which, I think, is not known to anyone except myself' (AR: 28 Sept. 1957). The central part of the story is the diary of a young girl, who spends her time escaping into her own private fairyland. Her nurse has introduced her to some of the forbidden, magic traditions of a witch-cult, one of whose rites is practising the 'scarlet ceremonies'. The ending of the story is ambiguous, and has instigated diverse interpretations. The most popular, as suggested by writer H.P. Lovecraft, is that the young girl is discovered dead after an encounter with Pan in the desolate landscape she frequents (Lovecraft, 1945: 91–2). Pan the goat-god was a recurring symbol in Machen's writing, and a significant influence on Ireland's music. He owned a statue of Pan, and this stood on his piano for many years, as can be seen in Plates 4 and 18.

Born in Arcadia, the offspring of Hermes and Dryope, Pan was both divine and human, a somewhat mysterious, many faceted creature – a fusion of opposites. He was a musician, the creator of the panpipes from the nymph Syrinx. He was a benevolent pastoral figure, the shepherd responsible for Arcadia's herds, a 'sort of fugitive, hidden among leaves' (Lawrence, 1936: 22). Yet he was also a lustful beast associated with ecstatic bacchanalian rites. Pan could inspire impulsive actions, cause panic and bring death to those who looked upon him.

Ireland's interest in Pan, which is manifest in two significant works, can be seen as part of a widespread rekindling of interest in paganism, with Pan as figurehead, which took place in artistic circles from the mid-1880s to about 1940, articulated primarily, but not exclusively, in literary works. The list of poets and novelists who focused on one or many of the characteristics of Pan is extensive, particularly in England, but also in France, the USA and Ireland. Pan appeared in short lyrical poems as well as grandiose epics, evoked variously by W.E. Henley (*London Voluntaries*), Francis Bourdillon (*A Lost God*) and de la Mare ('They Told Me' and 'Sorcery'). In the 1870s and 1880s Swinburne wrote several poems which deal with Pan's activities, including 'Pan and Thalassius', as did both Robert Browning and Elizabeth Barrett Browning a few years earlier, the former's depiction of the lascivious Pan in 'Pan and Luna' a different beast from the latter's laughing, piping Pan in 'A Musical Instrument'. Pan featured in short stories by Forster and Huxley, and was a shadowy figure lurking in the background of much of the writing of D.H. Lawrence. Pan appealed to composers too, among them Debussy, Charles Koechlin (1867–1950) and Albert Roussel (1869–1937) in France, Sibelius and Nielsen in Scandinavia, and in England to Ireland, Granville Bantock (1868–1946), Bax and Arthur Bliss (1891–1975). Pan's relatives include fauns, bassarids, satyrs and ægipans, but it is difficult to differentiate between them, and the word 'faun' is often used to mean Pan himself.

The reasons for the interest in Pan are complex. With the erosion of rural areas in the latter part of the nineteenth century, artists sought solace in an imagined, escapist era when man's relationship with nature was instinctive and harmonious. For some, Pan was regarded as a benevolent, enlightening figure. His spirit was pervasive to such an extent that he was frequently portrayed not as a mythical personage, but as being alive, walking freely among us, appearing 'in homely guise of hedger-and-ditcher or weather-beaten shepherd from the downs' (Grahame, 1898: 69). Ireland was sympathetic to the problem of vanishing rural environments, and in the latter part of his life expressed his thoughts that 'The Great God Pan has departed from this planet, driven hence by the mastery of the material & the machine over mankind' (KT: 29 May 1952).

It was perhaps inevitable that a movement away from traditional, Victorian English religious values towards a type of paganism which eventually became highly fashionable in European circles, should be the outcome of this focus on the importance of nature. And inevitable that Pan should then be adopted as a symbol of the decadence of the late 1890s and early 1900s. With his repellent countenance and physical similarities to the devil figure, Pan had always had a sinister side to his nature. He is often depicted as a bringer of death – in 'The Music on the Hill' by Saki and 'The Man Who Went Too Far' by E.F. Benson – or as a provoker of violence and depravity. The illustrations of Pan by Aubrey Beardsley for *The Yellow Book* were associated with perversion, and Pan's occult and more unpleasant associations culminated in his adoption by Aleister Crowley as a Satan figure, a phallic anti-Christ symbol to be worshipped. Forster, in his *Aspects of the Novel* (1927), cited the Pan school, among them Robert Hichens, Benson, Nathaniel Hawthorne and Reid, as having satanic associations. This horrific side of Pan did seem compelling to Ireland, much as sites of antiquity, and especially those associated with black magic rituals, exerted a fascination. From time to time he expressed an attraction to, but also a fear of, black magic, and wrote to Thompson in 1946 that 'as you know, I am far from repelled by an admixture of the occult and magic, of a genuine kind' (KT: 23 Jan. 1946).

Pan as a sexual symbol was not exclusive to satanists. As a lustful god, impulsive and yet unfulfilled, he was used by many writers to represent both uncontrollable and repressed desires. In a number of novels and short stories, Pan appears as a symbol of sexual liberation, a conferrer of enlightenment, or as an antagonist – the dark side of the landscape. E.M. Forster's interest in Pan was directly related to his own religious and sexual uncertainties, and the goat-god makes brief appearances in *The Longest Journey* (1907) and *A Room With a View* (1908). One of Forster's early short stories, 'The Story of a Panic' (1902), was the fruit of a moment of inspiration during a visit to the Vallone Fontana Caroso above Ravello. In this story, an awkward teenager is visited by Pan whilst staying in Italy, resulting in an immediate and total spiritual liberation. For D.H. Lawrence, Pan was also a catalyst, a dark figure and instigator of inner turmoil. Pan was the powerful, dangerous key to self-awareness. In this sense Pan would have appealed to Ireland, given his own self-questioning and his identification with Pan as an isolated figure who fails to achieve a fulfilling relationship with a woman. Lawrence was also a favourite with Ireland, and he read many of his works, including *The White Peacock* and *Aaron's Rod*.

For composers, a literary text often provided the impetus for their Pan pieces, with Stéphane Mallarmé, Paul Verlaine and Swinburne being the most frequently used poets. Both Bax and Bantock drew on Swinburne's *Atalanta in Calydon*, and both had a period of focused attention on the corybantic carousings of Pan and his relatives. Ireland preferred the more sinister Pan of Machen. For Ireland, Pan was a symbol of the *genius loci*, a reclusive, lonely, yet Dionysian creature, hideous to women, and a figure common to pagan and Roman Britain, to the Victorians and to Ireland's own generation, linking different times and places. His first significant Pan-inspired piece was his orchestral tone-poem, *The Forgotten Rite*, written in 1913 at a time of great interest in the goat-god: Ravel's orgiastic *Daphnis et Chloë* was performed by the Ballets Russes in 1912, Bax's programmatic and exuberantly bacchanalian symphony *Spring Fire*, based on Swinburne's *Atalanta in Calydon*, was written in 1913 (as was his short story 'Ancient Dominions', a tale of pagan ritual), and Debussy's *Syrinx* appeared in the same year. Bantock's massive choral ballet, *The Great God Pan*, was finished in 1915. When the *Ballets Russes* visited London in 1913, Ireland heard Stravinsky's *Sacre du Printemps*. This experience had a tremendous impact on him. Writing late in his life of performances which he felt had been significant moments in his career as a musician, he singled this out, describing the work as having 'the power of calling up something from the subconscious mind – some racial memories, perhaps, of things long hidden, and belonging to a remote and forgotten past' (*JIT*, 5). Grainger, writing to Ireland in 1956, described Ireland's music in similar vein: 'your thrilling music, which chills my marrow with its deep echoes of the shadowy past' (PG to JI: 9 April 1956).

'The scarlet ceremonies' and *The Forgotten Rite*, both completed in 1913, were thus part of a wider movement of ritualistic and Pan-inspired works. The piano work contains two distinct musical responses to the notion of pagan rites. The first is brilliant, virtuosic, 'demonic', and this was to be developed in a number of the works that followed between 1913 and 1943. The second is the 'incantatory' use of winding melody, as in bar 47. In this piece, the theme of the central incantation is derived from that of the outer revelries.

While 'The scarlet ceremonies' has literary associations, *The Forgotten Rite* had specific connections with place. Ireland's regular visits to the Channel Islands, begun at some point before 1908, continued each year from 1908 until 1914, and he spent a large part of every summer (six to eight weeks or so) in Jersey. There is evidence that Jersey, with its many pagan sites, partly inspired *The Forgotten Rite*. Ireland wrote in a letter to conductor Kenneth Wright:

> It's a work I felt much about. I wrote it after being alone for 6 weeks in Jersey, and one felt so intensely, painfully, in fact, the indescribable beauty of the light, the sea, and the distant other islands. At that time, one felt that the very thinnest of material veils separated one from the actual Reality behind all this smiling beauty ...
>
> (KW: 10 Sept. 1928)

Two of the stunning prehistoric sites on the island were being excavated while Ireland was on the island, the dolmen Les Monts Grantez in 1912 and the dolmen La Pouquelaye de Faldouet in 1910. The most impressive of all Jersey's prehistoric sites is one which would have held particular appeal for Ireland: La Hougue Bie is a pagan site sanctified by the erection of two Christian chapels on its summit. These sites were associated with forgotten rituals, some sacrificial, some concerned with fairy magic and some with witchcraft.

The Forgotten Rite is essentially an evocation of Pan, although Ireland referred to the piece more imprecisely as a 'religious ceremony' (KT: 23 Jan. 1946). Ireland's *Forgotten Rite* is probably closer to Mallarmé's hazy, swooning eroticism than to any other type of Pan visitation, and the size and makeup of the orchestra is clearly influenced by Debussy's orchestra for *Prélude à l'Après-midi d'un faune*. This Pan is a genial visitor, leaving no aftertaint. Here Pan = country = sex. The work is about sensation and enchantment, the static opening chords and the sensuous nature of the orchestral writing establishing a dream world akin to Debussy's earlier faun-inhabited afternoon.

The structure for all of Ireland's pagan works is a type of musical narrative with peculiarly personal extramusical references. The structure most often includes an explicit setting and an event, usually a single incident, and sometimes a plot and characters, though there is little in the way of specific characterization. He favours ternary structures, at the start of which a mood is set up, followed by a central section in which conflict or confrontation occurs, after which there is a return to the original, now altered scene. This had already been seen in 'The scarlet ceremonies'. The structure of *The Forgotten Rite* is also a basic ABA format, where the outer sections establish and then revisit a situation.

While there are other of Ireland's works which use a ternary structure, what immediately locates this landscape as a pagan one is the opening chord sequence, hovering on a second inversion chord (Example 3.1). A two-bar distant timpani roll sets the scene, and the feeling of suspense is enhanced by the string upbow that is then used to introduce the ⁶₄ chord in bar 3. The unresolved, and thus mysterious, ungrounded, sound of the second inversion chord is a feature which permeates a number of the pagan works, and this particular motif (Example 3.1) was one to which Ireland periodically returned.

Example 3.1

Another prevalent harmonic characteristic of Ireland's pagan works is the use of major/minor juxtapositions. Sometimes these are dramatic, large-scale key contrasts, but there are also more subtle examples, which seem to be not entirely pagan, but more generally associated with 'religious' feeling, and also feature in the Anglo-Catholic works. A typical instance of subtle harmonic alterations of this nature comes in bars 7–10, where the F minor chord of bar 5 is transformed into an F flat major chord in bar 9 (Example 3.2).

Example 3.2

The backdrop for this particular Pan vision is thus a chord sequence that in its hymn-like part movement has links with the feeling of ceremony of Ireland's church music: he described it as 'slow in movement & mystical in feeling' (HS: 6 Aug. 1928). What follows is a symbolic flute call, an archetypal panpipe melody, with its limited note range. This is to be pivotal in the work (Example 3.3).

Example 3.3

For many composers, Pan's most important role was that of pastoral musician, and the number of works entitled or alluding to Syrinx testifies to this. Supple, hovering melody, often a monody, was the starting-point for many composers portraying Pan in music (as eerie piping often heralds Pan's appearance in novels and in poems). There is a preponderance of works for unaccompanied flute, but unconfined, floating melodies and roulades are also a pervasive feature of piano works and orchestral music. Pan's pipes have many powers. His melody may be plaintive, 'piercing sweet' (Browning, 1990: 204), or may act as a reviver or catalyst. The sound of the panpipes can induce inebriation, terror or euphoria. These distinct powers are represented in the various Pan pieces. Koechlin's solo flute pieces, *Les chants de Nectaire* (1944), present Pan both as pastoral goatherd (explored through fluid, unmetered, arching melodic lines) and as frenzied dancer. Within the bounds of a larger work, where Pan's pipes are part of a bigger world, usually associated with a woodland scene, the pipes, not always played by the flute, often herald an event. Nielsen's orchestral 'nature-scene', *Pan og Syrinx* (1917–18), after the opening flute call, uses a chromatic cor anglais line to darken the soundscape and to propel the scene from peaceful woods to wild bacchanale. In *The Forgotten Rite* the flute's short, six-note motif (Example 3.3) is a call to attention, invoking the mysterious emergence of Pan.

What follows in bar 17 is a transformation of the opening chords, and a brief but ecstatic climax after which the panpipe motif is transferred to the trumpet in bar 23 for the revelation of the gigantic reality of Pan's presence. The impact of the emergence is marked physically by an intake of breath – a slight break before the music and the scene move on. From bar 26 there is a hushed, 'reverent' version of the opening chords. The function of the first section of the work is therefore to set a scene of reverie, to introduce the Pan motif and thus Pan himself, and to oscillate between moments of ecstasy and of calm. The central section, the Poco più lento, from bar 36, is a pastoral F major idyll, in which the panpipe call is developed, no longer a signal, but fundamental to the whole. Taken up first by the oboe, it is now a more expansive melody (Example 3.4).

Example 3.4

The motif permeates this section, the music continuing to oscillate between effusive climax and restrained contemplation. To effect the departure of Pan, Ireland returns to the original flute motif, this time played by the piccolo (bar 60). Just as the brighter trumpet timbre and the use of the full orchestra signified the manifestation of Pan, his disappearance is marked by a final, other-worldly presentation of the motif by the celesta over sustained string chords, the opening D♭ chord now in root position.

The Forgotten Rite is the first major statement of Ireland's fascination with Pan. 'Le Catioroc', the opening piece of his piano suite, *Sarnia*, completed on his return to London from Guernsey in 1940, is an unequivocal representation of a very different manifestation of Pan. In a letter to Edwin Evans, Ireland wrote of the connection between these works, saying that the suggestion 'that ['Le Catioroc'] is in some sense related to *The Forgotten Rite* is true, though the latter is concerned with a less sinister or "whiter" side of these things' (EE: 28 Sept. 1957).

The Channel Islands had attracted Ireland as a place to live for some time, and his decision to move to Guernsey in 1939 was partly because of its opposing Christian and pagan cultures (his first letter to Kenneth Thompson from the island mentions good churches and pagan relics in the same sentence). For most of his time on the island he lived in Fort Saumarez, on the west coast, very close to two significant pagan sites. Le Creux ès Faies, a burial chamber in the immediate vicinity of Fort Saumarez, was associated with the fairy tradition in Guernsey. Near by was Le Catioroc, a headland on the west coast, on which a neolithic burial chamber, Le Trépied dolmen (Plate 16), is situated. This was reputed to be the scene of witches' sabbaths in the sixteenth and seventeenth centuries, and the last surviving site of pagan rituals on the island.

Ireland's 'Le Catioroc' is closely related to one of Machen's early novels, *The Great God Pan* (1894), and bears a quotation from *De Situ Orbis*, a geographical work written in about AD 50 by cosmographer Pomponius Mela. The passage quoted was originally a description of a bacchic orgy on Mount Atlas:

Silet per diem universus, nec sine horrore secretus est; lucet nocturnis ignibus, chorus ægipanum undique personatur: audiuntur et cantus tibiarum et tinnitus cymbalorum per oram maritimam.

[All day long, heavy silence broods, and a certain hidden terror lurks there. But at nightfall gleams the light of fires; the chorus of ægipans resounds on every side: the shrilling of flutes and the clash of cymbals re-echo by the waste shores of the sea.]

Ireland and Machen corresponded on the subject of Mela, and on Guernsey as a pagan place. Machen stated that he had always understood 'that though Guernsey is, officially annexed to the Bishopric of Winchester; it is, in fact, rather in the Archdiocese of the Demon' (AM to JI: 18 March 1941). Ireland came to the Mela quotation via Machen's *Great God Pan*, in which the words appear as an accompaniment to

> ... the frightful Walpurgis-night of evil, strange monstrous evil, that the dead artist had set forth in hard black and white. The figures of fauns and Satyrs and ægipans danced before his eyes, the darkness of the thicket, the dance on the mountain-top, the scenes by lonely shores, in green vineyards, by rocks and desert places, passed before him: a world before which the human soul seemed to shrink back and shudder.

(Machen, 1993: 61)

The first edition of *The Great God Pan* was illustrated with a Beardsley drawing of a faun (Figure 3.1). The book was influential in both England and France, where it was translated by Paul-Jean Toulet and read by Maeterlinck and Debussy. The work tells of a doctor who performs an operation on a young woman, during which she sees Pan. The intention is for the vision of Pan to reveal realms beyond common experience. The reality is that the vision leaves her an idiot, but she gives birth to a child, Helen Vaughan, who grows up to bring death and destruction to friends and acquaintances. The Mela citation comes from a point in the story where the drawings of one of Helen Vaughan's victims are being examined. Although Ireland attached the quotation after completing the piece, he had read the Machen story some years previously, and these words became associated with the atmosphere of the burial chamber and its surroundings at Le Catioroc. This is borne out both by the original title for the movement – 'Ægipans' Headland' – and by the piece itself, which in its musical language articulates the quotation in structure and in spirit.

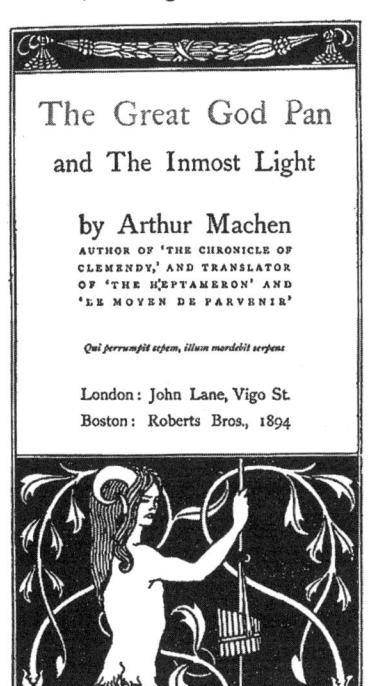

The Great God Pan

and The Inmost Light

by Arthur Machen

AUTHOR OF 'THE CHRONICLE OF
CLEMENDY,' AND TRANSLATOR
OF 'THE HEPTAMERON' AND
'LE MOYEN DE PARVENIR'

Qui perrumpit sepem, illum mordebit serpens

London: John Lane, Vigo St.
Boston: Roberts Bros., 1894

3.1 Beardsley, frontispiece to *The Great God Pan*, 1894

Mela's words describe the two different faces of a single place: what is latent by daylight is a real terror by night, a site of pagan revelries. Ireland's piece correlates to this. It is a single place with two different atmospheres contained within another ABA structure. In effect it is the musical equivalent of Todorov's 'ideal' narrative, which 'begins with a stable situation which is disturbed by some power or force. There results a state of disequilibrium; by the action of a force directed in the opposite direction, the equilibrium is re-established; the second equilibrium is similar to the first, but the two are never identical' (Todorov, 1977: iii). There are parallels with Forster's 'Story of a Panic', in which the visitation of Pan(ic) effects a character transformation; and also with Kenneth Grahame's chapter, 'The Piper at the Gates of Dawn', in *The Wind in the Willows*, where Pan's presence transforms the landscape.

'Le Catioroc' opens with a stable situation, a presentation of the main melodic motif, rooted in a desolate minor tonality (Example 3.5), underpinned by a tonic pedal for the first sixteen bars.

Example 3.5

The equilibrium is disturbed first rhythmically (bar 33) and then tonally (bar 39), to create a state of disequilibrium by bar 45 (Example 3.6).

Example 3.6

The same tonal force used to initiate the state of disequilibrium recurs to re-establish equilibrium. As in *The Forgotten Rite*, the landscape is a pagan one, and a Panic wilderness specifically, not because of second inversion chords, but on account of other melodic, harmonic and rhythmic nuances. Here Ireland makes use of pagan, 'uncivilized' harmonies. The outer sections of 'Le Catioroc' emphasize open, bare fifths, benign pastoral turned primitive by way of the minor tonality and the added dissonant appoggiaturas, chromatic inner lines and false relations.

That the movement derives from a single melodic idea is typical of much of Ireland's music. But the fact that the melodic line, essentially fluid and pulsating, which, in the outer sections of the piece, evolves through a series of roulades and sighing, drooping, enticing phrases such as that in bars 12–14 (Example 3.7), makes this a pipe melody, once again heralding a pagan event. It is not insignificant that the piece is dedicated to a Guernsey flautist, and friend of Ireland, Alfred Sebire.

Example 3.7

[Quasi lento]

These are not pipes of pagan mirth, however, but play a darker, 'strange, unending melody ... phrase after phrase' (Benson, 1992b: 113). They have the traits of Keats' 'undescribed sounds, that come a swooning over hollow grounds' (Keats, 1978: 116). The panpipe melody both establishes and disturbs the state of equilibrium. The increasing complexity of the ornamented A minor phrases gives way to a series of graded roulades (Example 3.8: bars 34, 36, 43, 44).

Example 3.8

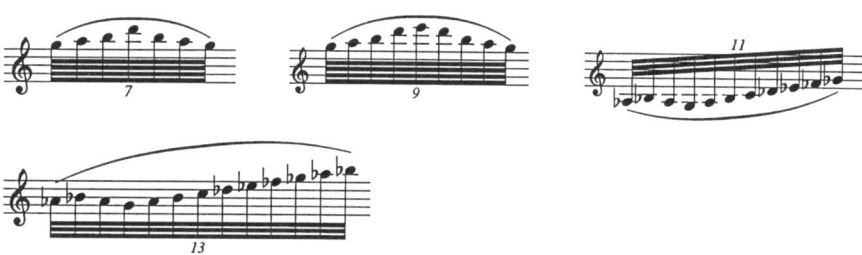

The last of these roulades leads to the oscillating B♭⁷/f⁷ chords in bar 45 (Example 3.6) and the ensuing central bacchanalian music. In this section Ireland's ægipans are fleet of foot, almost Gallic in the use of dotted rhythms. The relationship between this and the opening 'brooding' music is a close one, with the melodic outline of the new dotted rhythm of bar 48 derived from bars 3 and 4 (Example 3.9).

Example 3.9

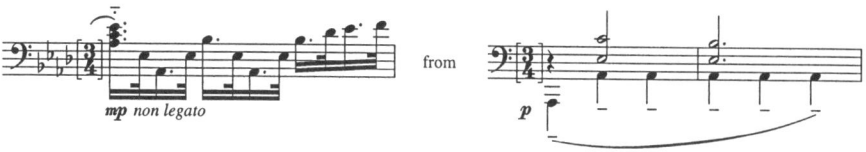

What starts as a rather refined A flat major gradually moves to a state of increased euphoria, with strings of dominant ninth chords and wild triplet rhythms (Example 3.10; bar 67). There is a decided bawdiness in the central section of the piece – Pan was derided by Huxley as an oafish goatfoot in his short story 'Cynthia', and Ireland's revels have a definite air of the carnivalesque, brought about primarily through the disjointed, leaping rhythmic patterns featured here.

Example 3.10

The dominant ninths become more frenzied in frequency and in dynamic markings, and lead towards a climactic version of the oscillating Bb^7/f^7 chords in bar 81. The ægipans' dance then dissolves into descending chromatic scales towards the re-establishment of the original equilibrium.

Listening to 'Le Catioroc' with Ireland in 1945, Thompson described it as opening with 'rather sinister Panique music – the part of the Isle of Guernsey indicated is full of legend & belief in witchcraft. The middle portion of the piece is a sort of wild Bacchic & Satyr Dance' (KT's insertion into KT: 25 Nov. 1945). Ireland had already made specific connections between Pan and 'Le Catioroc' in a letter to Clifford Curzon, who gave the first performance, stating that 'there can be no doubt that Pan was worshipped there … the essence underlying Pan, the Satyrs, the Fauns, is a world of hidden, forbidden beauty connected with Nature … now entirely overlaid by science and civilization' (CC: n.d.).

'Le Catioroc', along with 'In a May morning' and 'Song of the springtides', is part of a suite of movements, *Sarnia*, which is 'about' Guernsey (Sarnia being the Roman name for the island). Ireland made connections between *Sarnia* and *The Forgotten Rite*. He wrote of the latter as 'a highly concentrated expression of one idea' and described *Sarnia* as 'an extended work comprising several contrasted ideas and much diversity of material' (KT: 23 Jan. 1946). *Sarnia* might also be regarded as a later, explicit version of the implicit sentiments of the Piano Sonata; an unnamed pagan place named. While the first movement of the Piano Sonata (which will be discussed in Chapter 8) mixes topics, moving from darkness through vernacular jocularity to attainment, 'Le Catioroc' has its own vernacular elements in the dance of the ægipans, but ends in darkness. The central movement of the Piano Sonata is concerned with sexuality and landscape, but sexuality veiled. The central movement of *Sarnia*, 'In a May morning', is about a specific person, the young boy Michael Rayson, in a specific setting. This is made clear by the dedication, references in letters and the Victor Hugo poem attached to the movement. The third movements of both pieces are pantheistic works, rhapsodic outpourings. Both quote from previous movements, and both feature pagan signals, the Piano Sonata referring back to the opening of *The Forgotten Rite*.

The last movement of *Sarnia*, 'Song of the springtides', is concerned with the heady side of nature, rather than being about the sea specifically. Its original title was to be the less poetic 'The Daffodil Fields', but eventually Ireland decided on 'Song of the springtides', a title he abstracted from Swinburne as being 'rather appropriate to the music' (KT: 4 May 1941). Swinburne was a poet whose main concerns were with the wild, sensuous side of nature, and his works had appealed to Ireland from an early stage in his career. Much of Swinburne's work expresses an ecstasy induced by communing with nature, and 'Song of the springtides' is imbued with this sense of ecstasy. It shares structural and harmonic features with the finale of the Piano Sonata, using similar tonality shifts.

Ireland's evocation of ancient places was not confined to sites of Pan worship, but extended to other places of historic interest. Just as stays in the Channel Islands inspired several works, so too trips to West Sussex provided an important source of inspiration. Ireland visited Sussex frequently for many years and maintained a pied-à-terre in the heart of the county in the 1920s and 1930s, and again from 1950. It is significant that he chose to spend the last nine years of his life living opposite Chanctonbury Ring (an Iron Age enclosure turned Roman temple) on the South Downs. Like Le Catioroc, it became the site of a witches' coven, and many legends and local lore are connected with the place. The attraction of such places for Ireland was particularly important in the 1920s, during which years he regularly visited Sussex and also pagan sites in Dorset. This was the period when he knew Sylvia Townsend Warner. There are two references to him in her diaries of 1928. The first describes dining with him, then returning to Gunter Grove and watching him turn into a 'demented stranger' (Harman, 1995: 15) as he recounted his miserable personal relationships. The second entry records Townsend Warner's reactions to a number of Ireland's works after their next and last meeting.

> In the evening to the BBC John Ireland evening. Trio – 1919 [*sic*], too noble for my taste, songs by Hardy, Dekker (very good, an excited talking vocal curve, almost like hens) and the love and friendship set. Then the Sonatina, with a Sabbath last movement based on Lolly. This I really liked. It has an excitement of the wild brain, instead of the usual wild body orgy. Then two songs from A.E. Houseman [*sic*] with a piano epilogue and a cello sonata that I should enjoy on a second hearing, but they were playing against time, and it didn't emerge. A very beautiful serious child named Perkins [*sic*], who reminded me of Bea ten years ago, turned over, tense with anxiety to turn over right. Her hands were ice-cold with nervous exhaustion when I talked to her afterwards. She, I, Ireland and Edward Clark went on to a late dinner. There was a wireless in the restaurant, and we listened to a very

good Blues. I thought how close the analogy is between Jazz and plainsong: both so anonymous, so curiously restricted and conventionalized, so perfectly adapted to their metiers, both flowing with a kind of devout anonymity. Talked of Holst, and how the beginning of Egdon Heath is like Holst improvising with his thumb. Ireland drew a horse with smoke and a water-butt, a fire engine, three aeroplanes and God regardant on the table-cloth with creative seriousness. I liked him this time, perhaps he was only drunk that evening.

(ibid.: 16)

Townsend Warner's mention of the Sonatina refers to the fact that the last movement is based on her novel, *Lolly Willowes* (1926). Lolly Willowes is a spinster who decides that a sedate life with her relatives in London is not all that she would want. She moves to the village of Great Mop, where she makes a pact with the devil and discovers that she is a witch. It is not difficult to see why Ireland was attracted to this novel, with its echoes of the same sorts of sentiments as those expressed by Machen:

> Her mind was groping after something that eluded her experience, a something that was shadowy and menacing, and yet in some way congenial; a something that lurked in waste places, that was hinted at by the sound of water gurgling through deep channels and by the voices of birds of ill-omen. Loneliness, dreariness, aptness for arousing a sense of fear, a kind of ungodly hallowedness – these were the things that called her thoughts away from the comfortable fireside.
>
> In this mood she would sometimes go off to explore among the City churches, or to lose herself in the riverside quarters east of the Pool. She liked to think of the London of Defoe's *Journal*, and to fancy herself back in the seventeenth century, when, so it seemed to her, there were still darknesses in men's minds.

(Townsend Warner, 1993: 76–7)

At Great Mop, Lolly is invited to a witches' sabbath, where 'they whirled faster and faster, fused together like two suns that whirl and blaze in a single destruction' (ibid.: 192). She dislikes this public display, and later finds her own, more solitary, way of communing with Satan. Although Ireland liked Townsend Warner's works, he was not convinced by them to the same extent that he was by those of Machen, and he wrote to Jocelyn Brooke that 'Sylvia Townsend Warner has something in "Lolly Willowes" – something akin to that strange territory I so clumsily spoke of. But she tinges nearly all with an underlying irony which is sometimes stimulating but often destructive' (JB: 21 Aug. 1957).

Ireland's Sonatina (1926–27) picks up this sense of irony. The 'Lolly Willowes' finale is an expression of the pagan sabbath in the novel, and another example of the 'demonic', orgiastic response. Here the harmonic language is stringent, the melodic phrases short. The whole movement is derived from brittle, clipped rhythms and ostinati figures. In the central section Ireland writes a sequence of cross-rhythms (Example 3.11) which lead inexorably towards an ecstatic, climactic section before returning to the original motifs.

Example 3.11

Ireland's language in this work has similarities with the style of some of the songs of Peter Warlock (also known as Philip Heseltine, 1894–1930) of this period. Ireland was acquainted with Warlock from about 1918, and in the late 1920s spent some time in his company, along with E.J. Moeran, John Goss and Augustus John. A woodcut in the anthology *Merry-Go-Down: A Gallery of Gorgeous Drunkards through the Ages* (1929) depicts from left to right Moeran, Ireland, Alec Rowley (1892–1958) and Warlock drunk, dressed in Elizabethan costume (Figure 3.2). It must have been a somewhat curious relationship, given Ireland's innate cautiousness and conservatism, and probably only came about because of Ireland's friendship with his former pupil Moeran.

3.2 Woodcut from *Merry-Go-Down*, 1929

Ireland's obsession with the south of England was manifest not only in his decision to settle in Sussex in 1953, but also in a number of his compositions which have close links with that county, and also with Dorset. Three of these were inspired by specific historic sites: *Mai-Dun* (Maiden Castle in Dorset), the Cello Sonata (The Devil's Jumps in West Sussex; the work will be discussed in Chapter 8) and *Legend* (Harrow Hill in West Sussex). The first of these works was the orchestral 'symphonic rhapsody', *Mai-Dun*, completed in 1921. During the 1920s Ireland visited Dorset several times, and there are surviving photographs of Maiden Castle, the earthworks near Dorchester, from a holiday in 1923 (Plate 10). The piece was thus linked to a real place visited personally by Ireland. But like many of his works it also has literary connections. *Mai-Dun* is the name that Thomas Hardy gave to Maiden Castle. The Hardy connection is significant. Hardy's own explorations of the grotesque aspect of a close kinship between man and the landscape, the landscape both as a place of refuge and as a place of terror, were well known to Ireland, and he set a number of Hardy's poems in the 1920s. Hardy's 1885 description of Maiden Castle in the short story, 'A tryst at an ancient earthwork' evokes its splendour and drama:

> At one's every step forward it rises higher against the south sky, with an obtrusive personality that compels the senses to regard it and consider. The eyes may bend in another direction, but never without the consciousness of its heavy, high-shouldered presence at its point of vantage. Across the intervening levels the gale races in a straight line from the fort, as if breathed out of it hitherward. With the shifting of the clouds the faces of the steeps vary in colour and in shade, broad lights appearing where mist and vagueness had prevailed, dissolving in their turn into melancholy gray, which spreads over and eclipses the luminous bluffs. In this so-thought immutable spectacle all is change.
>
> (Hardy, 1997: 134)

A letter from Ireland to Adrian Boult (1889–1983) confirms that the portrayal of an ancient hill fort was the intention behind his orchestral work.

> I do not know if MAI-DUN is being transmitted on the Home programmes ; if it is, I shall listen with the deepest interest. As the music was inspired by what is the most remarkable prehistoric fortification in this country, if not in Europe, and the thought of the strife and determination it represents still, perhaps the music will have an added significance in these days when England really is a beleaguered fortress ... And may the triumphant closing section be prophetic, in its microcosmic way!
>
> (AB: 22 May 1941)

The work is an evocation of the Briton community at Maiden Castle, and its invasion by the Romans under Vespasian in AD 43. To effect this, Ireland presents the listener with a sequence of contrasting musical episodes, which represent action and counter-action. Ireland's description of the work as a 'rhapsody' is apt, as there is no clear narrative, and the action is not chronological. He wrote of this piece to Jocelyn Brooke that it begins 'in medias res, so to speak' (JB: 22 Dec. 1957), plunging the listener straight into battle, without any preliminary scene-setting. There are two main types of music in this piece. One represents battle – the 'action' in the work, achieved through a sense of propulsion via driving, forward-moving rhythms and a full orchestral sound featuring sound effects such as *col legno* and focusing on the brass. Repetitive bass patterns and a recurring motif (Example 3.12) establish this as music of conflict, just as they do in Ireland's war pieces.

Example 3.12

Example 3.13

In the second type of music, the 'counter-action', the emphasis is melodic rather than rhythmic (Example 3.13; bar 104). The mood is tranquil, at times soaring, and individual woodwind and brass instruments emerge from the orchestral texture.

These two types of music alternate, representing the fort at war and the fort at peace, and also appear in combination (as at the L'istesso tempo, bar 191, where the lower strings pursue their music of war beneath the melody of the upper strings and flute). The effect is not of an evolving plot, but is rather an impression of an incident, past and present mixing in Ireland's imagination. His approach in his other, later, orchestral work influenced by a historic site was very different. Where *Mai-Dun* is a musical interpretation of a massive focal point on the landscape with a well-known past and a history in paintings and literature, *Legend* turned away from the public eye to a more private, personal place, a landscape impossible to see without being within it; an experience known only to the participant.

In *Legend* (1933), for piano and orchestra, Ireland adopted a clear narrative, told from the point of view of autodiegetic narrator. He alluded to the structure as such, writing that 'the form is dictated by the emotional sequence of ideas, & grows from the material' (HR: 24 Oct. 1933). The 'emotional ideas' were, according to Ireland, the result of a strange occurrence whilst he was walking in a remote spot on the Sussex Downs, close to Chanctonbury Ring, Harrow Hill (Figure 3.3). Harrow Hill is an inaccessible spot, the site of neolithic flint mines, an Iron Age enclosure and a medieval lepers' colony. For a fleeting moment Ireland saw a group of children dancing, dressed in archaic white clothing. This incident was akin to a similar one described by Machen in his short story, 'The Happy Children', and Ireland's experience was later recounted by Jocelyn Brooke:

> The composer was staying, as he often did, in West Sussex, and one day took a picnic lunch to a remote spot on the downs which had for him a peculiar and inexpressible attraction. Soon after he had sat down and unpacked his sandwiches, he was suddenly aware that a number of children had invaded the open space in front of the bank on which he was sitting. His first feeling was one of annoyance at being thus unexpectedly disturbed in so lonely a place. A moment later he realized that the children were in fact no ordinary children: they played and danced together on the downland turf, but in complete silence; and they were dressed in white garments of a curious and archaic pattern. Ireland watched them for some time: that they were 'real' enough he had, at first, no doubt whatsoever. Then reason reasserted itself: could they be real – these silent, dancing children in their strange white raiment? The composer glanced away for an instant, then looked up again: the 'children' had vanished.

(Brooke, 1964: 7)

Later, Ireland wrote a full account of the experience to Machen, hoping, no doubt, that the writer who had so often described similar occurrences, would proffer some explanation of the mysterious children on the Downs. But Machen

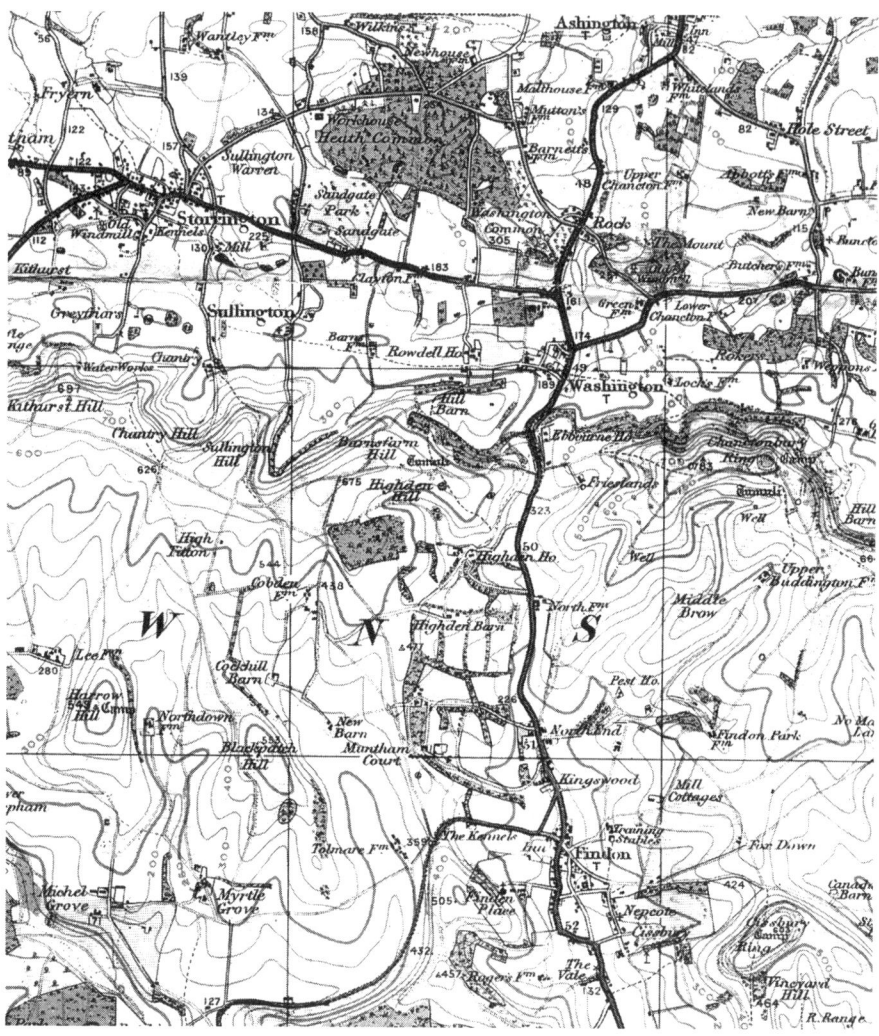

3.3 Map of the area of West Sussex showing to the north the village of Ashington; below this Ireland's house, Rock Mill (marked Old Windmill); below this, Chanctonbury Ring; and to the south west, Harrow Hill, 1931

was not to be drawn: his reply came on a postcard, offhand and laconic: 'Oh, so you've seen them too, have you?' (ibid.). Although Ireland maintained that the experience was real, it may have been that he was projecting his knowledge of Machen's stories about uncanny appearances on to a familiar landscape: 1933 was the year in which he first met Machen, and *Legend* was dedicated to the writer.

As had happened in Jersey some twenty years earlier, Ireland happened to be in an area of historical interest at a time when it was undergoing archaeological exploration. The barrows known as the 'Devil's Humps' at Kingley Vale, a few miles to the west, were excavated in April of 1933, and a catalogue of the Sussex barrows was published in 1934. Ireland spent much of 1933 living in a cottage in Ashington, writing that he was 'keeping out of town as much as I can, so as to be able to concentrate better, moreover, to be near the material which is the basis of this music' (HR: 24 Oct. 1933). *Legend* is 'uncanny' in the Freudian sense, in that it is a representation of something which is uncertain, concealed, with the distinction between imagination and reality blurred. It corresponds to Freud's definition of the 'uncanny' as 'that class of the frightening which leads back to what is known of old and long familiar' (in Dickson, 1988: 340).

One of the early ideas for a title for the work was *Queen Fridias*, a title which seems likely to have been culled from one of the books in Ireland's library, Allcroft's *Downland Pathways* (1924). There are two chapters in Allcroft's book that refer to the relevant parts of the county. 'Harrow Hill' bears the following description:

> The footsteps of other men you may find at every turn, but of the men of other days. Their roads and tracks immesh all the lower slopes of the hill, starred here and again with the usual *memento mori* in the form of a barrow.
>
> (Allcroft, 1924: 184)

From Harrow Hill an old lepers' path (the path that was purportedly the source of inspiration for *Legend*) leads to an area of land known as 'Friday's Church', containing two Bronze Age barrows and an ancient spring, as described in the chapter 'Burpham':

> No name is better known to the *indigenœ* than is 'Friday's Church', yet there is nothing to be seen that the wildest imagination could interpret as pertaining to a chuch – nothing at all, indeed, save the remnants of a cluster of small barrows long since spread by the plough … if you consult an older generation … you may be told that 'Queen Fridias was buried here'.
>
> (ibid.: 222)

The origins of the programme behind the piece are therefore complex: an amalgam of real and read experiences. In the work Ireland makes great play of timbral symbolism and the potency of suggestion through colour. He uses music to unlock a world: a specific sound acts as a gateway from one world to another.

The instrument he uses to do this is the French horn, the horn traditionally a gestural instrument. As such it has both a literary and a practical history, and its magical powers have pervaded many works of fiction. Jack's horn, in *Jack and the Beanstalk*, brings down the giant's castle, and the realm of Asgard was guarded by the magic horn of Heimdall. In Ariosto's *Orlando Furioso*, Astolpho possessed a horn which was capable of putting to flight brave knights and savage beasts. The horn is often a symbol of transportation between realms. In C.S. Lewis' *Prince Caspian* the horn is used to call people from one world to another. In its summoning of the High Kings of Narnia the horn is 'loud as thunder but far longer, cool and sweet as music over water, but strong enough to shake the woods' (Lewis, 1974: 89) And for Machen, in *The Hill of Dreams*, it is the note of the Roman trumpet, calling and recalling, that fills

> all the hollow valley with its command, reverberat[ing] in the dark places in the far forest, and resonant in the old graveyards without the walls. In his imagination he saw the earthen gates of the tombs broken open, and the serried legion swarming to the eagles. Century by century they passed up ...
> By hundreds and thousands the ghostly battle surged about the standard, behind the quaking mist, ready to march against the mouldering walls they had built so many years before.

> (in Palmer, 1988: 199)

Legend opens with a solo intoning French horn, using repetitive, resonant, oscillating seconds, fifths and sixths (Example 3.14). The horn call is not only a summons in the literary sense, but it is also a literal horn call – a *ranz des vaches*, with its reiterated short phrases. It derives from earlier examples, most obviously Rossini's *Guillaume Tell*.

Example 3.14

This sets the scene for a dark, brooding evocation, with appropriate instrumental colours: Ireland selects subterranean clarinets, primeval bassoon and distant timpani rumblings. In the opening section the orchestral texture is sparse, often just a soloist or a pair of instruments. On to this primitive landscape Ireland projects a piano soloist as protagonist: the person entering into the experience. The opening horn motif is compressed and taken up by the pianist (bar 28), at which point another 'signal' instrument, the gong, confirms the crossing between worlds. The horn motif is then developed by the cor anglais. The piano protagonist is given a solo passage to mark the entrance into the sombre, ancient scene, the lepers' path. Here Ireland chooses to use a deliberately archaic harmonic language. The prevailing atmosphere is created by the predominant use of a minor mode, and the melodic line is an elaboration of the 'Dies irae', supported by the antiquated parallel intervals first heard in the clarinet parts, now tolling against the plainsong melody (Example 3.15).

Example 3.15

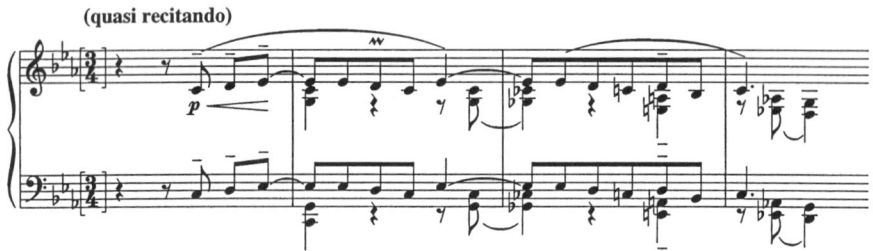

This melodic motif builds up to a new, dramatically different central section, introducing the dancing children figures into the landscape (Example 3.16).

Example 3.16

To do this Ireland deploys a more delicate, ethereal soundworld, with a new melodic idea in the bassoons and horns, accompanied by discreet touches of percussion (triangle and tambourine). The legato phrases of the piano solo give way to a much lighter articulation, over which interjections of the opening *ranz des vaches* are heard. The pianist takes up the new idea, the narrator joining his vision, and there is an ensuing movement towards a climax. The horn theme gradually takes over as the children depart and the narrator is led away from his vision. The final section of the work features the original horn invocation, this time also pervading the string section. *Legend* thus takes the protagonist along the ancient lepers' path to Harrow Hill and back again, with the concluding music subtly changed, the protagonist altered by the experience.

Ireland's musical representations of pagan experiences are not restricted to physical encounters. He was also interested in sensations, pagan in substance, of a nature that is harder to define, and in customs and traditions. A recurring influence on his music was John Brand's *Observations on Popular Antiquities*. This book records English ceremonies and customs, both Christian and pagan, which were originally collected by an earlier writer, Bourne, and added to and commented on by Brand. Ireland's piano piece *Month's Mind* was written in 1933, the same year as *Legend*, and was prefaced by a quotation from Brand:

... days which our ancestors called their 'Month's Mind', as being the days whereon their souls (after death) were had in special remembrance – hence the expression of 'having a Month's Mind', to imply a longing desire.

The quotation refers to an ancient historic custom whereby it was possible to arrange for a 'Month's Mind', often a grand service and feast, to be said once a month after death. These 'Mynde Days' were days when the soul was held in special remembrance. Brand's explanation of the phrase as meaning 'longing desire' derives from the eighteenth-century usage of the term, and implies a sort of premonition of one's own remembrance after death. For Jocelyn Brooke, *Month's Mind* exerted a particular fascination, to the extent that he wrote a poem with the same title. The reason for his fascination with the piece was that, for him, it had 'that peculiar quality of impersonal, almost mystical nostalgia which is to be found in all the most characteristic works of this composer' (Brooke, 1990: 100). Brooke saw the work as being 'a country of the mind' (ibid.), a concentrated quintessence of the sensibilities to be found in Ireland's music:

> The dominant image evoked is of a wooded and remote countryside, silent and frost-bound in the early twilight of a winter's evening. It is the dead season, yet there is a subtle, half-realized feeling of spring in the air: a stirring of bird-life in the woods, the catkins lengthening upon the hazels, the first celandine, perhaps, gleaming precociously in the sheltered hedgerow. After a day of rain and unbroken cloud, the western sky is suddenly clear, a broad rift of brightness palely green over the humped outline of the woods: the days are 'drawing out', and the land itself seems to extend with the lengthening days, one is suddenly aware of far, illimitable distances. The dimension of Time, also, is extended in this country of the mind, Uricon or Camelot lie beyond those farther woods; and on the beech-crowned hill, where the cromlech rises stark against the rainy sunset, the ancient and bloody rites are celebrated anew, and the beacon fires are lit for Beltane or Samhain.
>
> (ibid.: 100–101)

Brooke was a frequent visitor to Ireland's house in the latter part of the composer's life, and even toyed with the idea of writing a biography of the composer. As was mentioned in the Introduction, Ireland's opinion of Brooke's descriptions of his music was that they showed real understanding. The main characteristics that Brooke identifies in the music are nostalgia, an austerity and bleakness and a sense of a connection with the past, the effect of 'longing desire', or 'yearning', which is created mainly by Ireland's use of falling phrases (particularly the characteristic patterns used in bars 3–4, bars 8–9 and bars 42–3).

Month's Mind is a concentrated example of Ireland's pagan style. It contains all the kernels of Ireland's music in this vein, and tonally and motivically has strong links with Ireland's other pagan works. The structure is again a ternary one and, as in 'Le Catioroc', a harmonically disruptive climax at the end of the central section leads to recapitulation and re-equilibrium. The unresolved second inversion chord permeates the piece, the opening three chords and the oscillation around a single, central note (Example 3.17) having their roots in the opening of *The Forgotten Rite*.

Example 3.17

This is the same sort of pivotal writing used in 'Song of the springtides', which deploys similar tonal–modal–tonal routes and analogous left-hand quaver movement (Example 3.18).

Example 3.18

The pivoting around a key note is a feature of *Month's Mind*, and this centrality is not restricted to melodic patterns; the chords in bars 11–13 are basically variations on a single note and its potential harmonizations, as are the right-hand chords in bar 14. The effect of this is a musical ebb and flow. Occasionally there are moments of stasis, where the same chord is repeated (the section from bar 21 to 28). The parallel chords (at bar 57 the same penitential perfect fourths that were used in *Legend*) and false relations that recur throughout *Month's Mind* are a hallmark of Ireland's 'pagan' harmonic language.

Ireland's paganism is thus concerned both with pagan ritual and with pagan place. In Simon Schama's description of Arcadia in his *Landscape and Memory*, he talked of its two faces: 'shaggy and smooth; dark and light; a place of bucolic leisure and a place of primitive panic' (Schama, 1995: 517). He wrote of the golden, pastoral, tamed side of nature as opposed to the untamed labyrinth and wilderness. In Ireland's landscapes we see the same oppositions. His pagan sites are the shaggy, dark places of primitive panic, but there are also places which are smoother, lighter and altogether more bucolic, quiet without being menacing.

Chapter 4

Country

While Ireland's pagan places were the downlands of southern England and the ancient monuments of the Channel Islands, these territories had another, different aspect, without the expanse, the wilderness and the momentous events. Where the pagan, 'upland' locations all involved a climb up hidden paths to hills, promontories and barrows, the same regions also had a 'lowland', and much more contained, benign side. There was a Sussex that, like Rupert Brooke's Grantchester, might be 'flower-lulled in sleepy grass' (Brooke, 1970: 68), inviting Edward Thomas' 'sublime vacancy / of sky and meadow and forest and of my own heart' (Thomas, 1975: 131). And there was a pre-war Jersey of heady summers days and seaside holidays. Ireland's country was a place of romantic idyll, a personal Arcadia. The pieces that belong to this topic are almost exclusively piano music and songs. They are all small pieces, elegiac and melodious: water-colours in music of time and landscape.

Just as Ireland's pagan settings had more genial counterparts, the poets to whom he turned because of their pagan interests also had more radiant aspects, and could evoke rosy country visions. While Ireland was drawn to the poetry of Thomas Hardy because of the poet's preoccupations with landscape and history, he also set Hardy's blithe ballads and sunnier transcriptions of nature. All of Ireland's Hardy-inspired works were written in the 1920s, the first being *Mai-Dun*. Then, in 1925, at a time when he had been visiting Dorset, Ireland wrote four songs to words by Hardy. These are in a very different vein, and encapsulate a number of the features of the composer's country topic. The first was 'Great things', a joyous ballad in four stanzas in C major. This is Ireland utterly convincing in a rollicking, vernacular mode, far removed from the sinister visage of the countryside. Here he is not pursuing a solitary climb to some dark burial site, but sitting in a rural inn imbibing. The style of this song is akin to Warlock's musical celebrations of a rustic life involving alcohol, dancing and love. There is a tremendous rhythmic momentum: accents and offbeats prevail, and as a result passages where the words describe movement, such as 'Spinning down to Weymouth town' (bars 9–10) and 'The dance it is a great thing' (bars 28–9) have a real sense of sparkle in the corresponding musical propulsion.

The sequence of settings entitled *Three Songs*, also of 1925, is a collection of Ireland's different types of response to the friendlier aspects of nature. The first, 'Summer schemes', is a simple, lyrical eulogy, two souls together against an idyllic backdrop. The ballad-like nature of the piano's introductory bars, with its left-hand quaver accompaniment and right-hand melody, sets the scene for the opening words, 'When friendly summer calls again'. But as the sound of bird-song starts to 'flood the plain', there comes a brief episode of what in Ireland's music might be termed 'nature-ecstasy'. This happens in bars 17–18, where there is a moment of stasis, with oscillating, shimmering right-hand chords. This technique was used by Ireland at a much earlier date, and will be discussed more fully at the end of this chapter, with regard to the song 'Earth's call'. In 'Summer schemes' the ecstasy seems to be reserved for nature itself. The second of the set, 'Her song', is a nostalgic ballad in three stanzas, with a modal melody and a simple chordal piano part. 'Weathers', the third song, is a straightforward pastoral response, even marked 'Allegretto pastorale'. It is in compound time, C major and has a lilting accompaniment. What characterizes all of these songs, and sets them apart from the pagan music, is that there is no cataclysmic event. Each response is enclosed and uncomplicated.

Ireland's nature pictures are part of a long tradition of music and landscape. His country scenes belong to the image of rural England that became synonymous with the notion of 'Englishness', but there are also obvious ways in which he drew on French responses to place and sensation. However, there are no depictions of foreign landscapes, and in every case Ireland turned for inspiration to Britain's climate, water and inland meadows. Unlike many of his contemporaries, including Finzi, Holst, Herbert Howells (1892–1983), Ivor Gurney (1890–1937), Hubert Parry (1848–1918) and Vaughan Williams, Ireland did not experience the lure of the West of England, and he never attempted to depict the Severn counties in music. His preferred landscapes, and holiday destinations for much of his life, were the counties of Dorset, West Sussex and Wiltshire, and the coastlines of Kent and Norfolk.

In 1922, for example, he holidayed in Norfolk. A set of photographs of the vacation (*JIT*, 6) contains evidence of his favoured country pursuits. He was not alone, but travelled with his former chorister Arthur Miller (who will be discussed in Chapter 6). It seems that Moeran was also involved at some point, as there is a photograph in which he appears. Ireland and Miller were in the county for about four weeks, and visited Stalham, Bacton (the home of Moeran) and the Broads. Time was spent taking boat trips (see Plate 8) and picnicking (see Plate 9). It was very much a rural idyll. The same locations held their appeal and were visited and revisited. Nearly ten years later, in 1931, Ireland spent a week in Norfolk and three weeks in Herne Bay, Kent, and this was in addition to regular visits to Sussex. The Channel Islands were another favourite holiday location. As was discussed in Chapter 3, Ireland was a regular visitor to Jersey before the First World War, and he also knew Guernsey, Sark and Alderney.

Every one of the significant nature pieces, which really only discounts the part-songs, is in some sense autobiographical. The places with which they are associated were well known to Ireland, hence the predominance of southern landscapes. Like the pagan settings, the locations are real ones, but now without the intrusion of historic figures. Nevertheless, they also have imagined, or remembered, solitary aspects. Ireland's country is a musical synthesis of sounds, sights and sensations, which in addition often has literary overtones, and he was drawn to particular landscapes for their literary connections. In his nature pictures Ireland attempts to capture the essence of a particular, usually identified, place, or to evoke a season. But they are also musical representations of personal experiences against a rural backdrop, involving the 'poetic conceit of feelings inspired by Nature' (Hatten, 1994: 92). For example, the piano piece, *Equinox*, written in the autumn of 1922, in its constant, rapid figuration, is a depiction of wind upon the South Downs, but also an entwining of an aspect of nature with a turbulent personal emotion.

There is not a single 'countryside' John Ireland, and there are different ways in which his country is manifest in his music. In one respect this topic is easy to recognize, simply because of the established common currency of musical symbols on which Ireland draws. But there are also works that straddle this and the love topic, in that they are expressions of ecstasy in an idyllic landscape, using motifs personal to the composer. And although there are different manifestations of the country in his music, they have in common a feeling of quiescence, in which time and action stand still in reverie, trance or relaxation. Ireland was very receptive to season, particularly April and May, and wrote a number of rippling piano pieces that rely on florid figuration as a means of encapsulating lyrical idyll. There is also a body of nature impressions in which the senses rule. These are closely allied to the subtle images and evocations of the Symbolist poets and influenced by the techniques of Debussy and Ravel. Ireland wrote a number of waterscapes which focus on Britain's rivers and seas, the characteristic features of which are derived from traditions of representing water in music. There is the composer as Edwardian traveller, whose own rather limited Wanderlust is expressed through songs and piano music. There are straightforward ballads, and there is an Ireland who draws together these different aspects of seasons, places and people in evocations of West Sussex and in suites of 'green' pieces. By far the easiest of the country aspects to define is Ireland's 'pastoral', simply because it has clear characteristics that appear in all its manifestations, the earliest of which was in 1896.

In 1999 a previously unknown work by Ireland was discovered at the Royal College of Music. This was a short piano piece, completed on 20 August 1896 while the composer was staying in Pontwgan, in the countryside of north Wales. It is simply entitled *Pastoral*. Though this is an early student work, written before Ireland began his studies with Stanford, facets of the piece show that he was attempting to symbolize the pastoral in music. It contains germs of the composer's pastoral style that were to be refined over the next twenty years.

In his book, *Musical Meaning in Beethoven* (Hatten, 1994), Robert Hatten, drawing on the earlier theoretical writings of Leonard Meyer and Leonard Ratner, set out his understanding of what constituted the 'pastoral' in music. From roots of 'rustic simplicity' (ibid.: 80) he traced the evolution of the pastoral to a different state of 'sublimity, suggesting spiritual grace, serenity, or transcendence' (ibid.: 80). Whilst his observations are primarily directed towards music of the first half of the nineteenth century, it is certainly apposite to Ireland to consider aspects of his own output in this light. The little *Pastoral* fulfils most of Hatten's conditions for inhabiting this world, its title acting in the first instance as a code to direct the listener towards a scene of rural harmony, unsullied and picturesque. The piece satisfies Hatten's fundamental pastoral criteria in its overall mood and make-up, in that it is in compound time and utilizes mainly quiet dynamics, though the mode is minor, rather than the usual major indicated by Hatten, and there is a pervasive melancholy and pensiveness that was to become a feature of Ireland's nature pieces. The harmony is essentially consonant (though as this was such an early piece this would have been expected of Ireland). There is a simple melodic contour and a pervasive rocking motion (Example 4.1). In places Ireland uses the contrary, 'wedge' shape and melodic parallel thirds that Hatten (ibid.: 98) suggests are pastoral features.

Example 4.1

As it was initially from Beethoven (and presumably also from Handel) that Ireland learnt his pastoral conventions, it is unsurprising that it is easy to relate Hatten's findings in Beethoven to Ireland's derivations. Ireland's formative years as both pianist and composer were strongly influenced by Beethoven. In 1953 he wrote of the impact of hearing the finale of the Eighth Symphony as a student, 'the first shattering revelation to my adolescent mind of the real Beethoven':

> It was compelling, wild, free, full of a divine mirth, a new experience. I listened entranced, excited, led into a world new to me – a world of fauns, glancing sunlight, godlike mischief and joy... And to-day, fifty years later, I still think that Symphony (what the Master called his 'Little' Symphony) gives me more unalloyed pleasure than any other piece of music.

> (Herbage and Instone, 1953: 30)

Like Beethoven, Ireland was drawn to the countryside from an early age. Though he was born in the suburbs of one city and lived most of his life in the heart of another, he spent long periods of time on visits, most often alone, to rural areas. This was partly for the beauty of the landscape, but also for the escapism that this offered him. Just as he was writing 'pastoral' music very early in his life, so was he taking long holidays out of London. The earliest known letter from him, dated 30 August 1897 to a fellow RCM student and lodger, Mary Bentley, is written from Glenridding, in the Lake District. He was on his own, and had been away from London for five weeks. He wrote that he had 'become quite a recluse' and had been taking long walks, where he 'saw a few civilized people, which rather disgusted me' (MB: 30 Aug. 1897). Later in his life his desire for isolation in the countryside was satisfied through regular extended periods away from London, and the acquisition of permanent bolt holes to which he could escape.

Of all the ways in which Ireland produced musical responses to nature, the most unambiguous and straightforward is the 'pastoral' style that was begun in 1896. The works that can be classed as such are, with only one exception, one-sided studies of atmosphere without narrative. They are pastoral moods without complications, picturesque England at its most pleasing and safe. There are works bearing the title or the direction 'pastoral', and a great many part-songs in which the texts are rural. Several works have Hatten's pastoral features, and even more completely than did the early *Pastoral*. Thus the song 'Bed in summer' belongs to this pastoral subtopic because of its lilting, contained melody, unambiguous F major tonality and ⅜ time signature.

Of Ireland's pieces in this vein, his piano miniature, *The Towing Path* (1918) is both epitome and exception, and again fulfils Hatten's criteria for inhabiting the world of the pastoral. Like the 1896 *Pastoral*, its title suggests a country scene. The very fact that Ireland does not then add a poetic caption to the title might imply that he is aiming not to burden the image further, but is producing a serene tone poem in the manner of Handel's pastoral pieces, exuding Hatten's 'sturdily optimistic assurance' (ibid.: 83), without the layers of meaning that complicate some of his other works. *The Towing Path* is in compound time, a major mode and utilizes mainly quiet dynamics. It is in ternary form, and it is in the outer sections that Hatten's pastoral features can be seen. The harmony in bars 1–18 is essentially consonant, rooted firmly in C major. There is a simple melodic contour and a pervasive rocking accompaniment (Example 4.2).

Example 4.2

Ireland makes extensive use of the contrary motion that Hatten suggests is a pastoral feature, and the whole of the opening section uses mainly primary triads. This music is recapitulated in bar 49, and in the last part of the piece, from bar 67, the harmony becomes even more static, with the introduction of a repeating V–I pattern before the short four-bar C major coda. In the outer sections of *The Towing Path*, therefore, there is a strong sense of equilibrium, and a resolution of what are always consonant appoggiaturas.

Even in a piece as seemingly straightforward as this, there are other implications. Ireland's towing-path was a real one, in Pangbourne, Berkshire, and he was staying there at the time of writing. Though the central section, from bar 19 to bar 48, retains the rocking motion and the melodic emphasis, it moves away from C major clarity to a more chromatic and rhapsodic world that has echoes of other pieces. The bars that open this section are derived from the piano piece 'Chelsea Reach', written the previous year, the Thames here turned rural by the confined nature of the outer sections. The new accompaniment quaver-crotchet rhythm turns the sedate pastoral lilt into something more pensive. But there is no sense of action or event in this section, and the essential feel of the piece is one of serenity and tranquillity. The mood of calm is also enhanced by the use of *una corda* at two points (bars 46–52 and 75–8), a direction indicated by Ireland at particular points of repose in many of his piano miniatures with country associations.

Though it was most often a dreamscape or rhapsody, Ireland's countryside could also be a place of hearty pursuits: drinking, cavorting, hunting; and there are a number of songs in the jovial vein of 'Great things'. 'Hope the Hornblower' (1911) is in a convivial manner that has German origins. Its horn calls and harmonic language, namely the shifts from chord I to iii, and the modulation from tonic major to tonic minor, are directly derived from Schubert's huntsman songs. The pervasive piano accompaniment pattern uses rests and accents to enhance the depiction of the movement of the hunt.

In the same year Ireland wrote 'When lights go rolling round the sky', a song he shortly denounced as unsuitable for serious singers, saying that it was 'a ballad & might have been done by E. German' (GP: 13 Oct. 1918). It may be 'only' a rustic ballad, but it is a very good one, and despite Ireland's disclaimer there is no doubt that he was both skilled and natural at writing this sort of music, popular with a mass market at the time. Steadfastly tonal, 'When lights go rolling round the sky' (its title a reference to the different types of light; star, sun and moon) has a hearty piano accompaniment and a melody line that together exude joy (Example 4.3). Longmire thought it quite simply Ireland's '*jolliest* song' (Longmire, 1976: v).

Example 4.3

There are other songs of this type in Ireland's output, the texts of which are always concerned with rustic merry-making or maritime heartiness. There are several pieces in which the sea is a place of bluff encounters and salty sturdiness. Under the name Turlay Royce, Ireland wrote the rollicking ballad, 'Billee Bowline' (1911), and in 1920 set Eric Chilman's 'The East Riding'. His response to the poetry of Masefield was also part of this same sea spirit, but the two Masefield settings whose subject matter is the sea have a Dorian wistfulness in their contemplation. The strophic, modal setting, 'The bells of San Marie' (1918) is essentially a folk song. The most famous and popular of Ireland's songs, 'Sea fever' (1913) is a ballad in the tradition of Stanford's 1904 *Songs of the Sea*, in that its repeating stanzas set an unchanging vocal line over a varying accompaniment. Its impact is effected through a modal tune over simply placed piano chords (Example 4.4).

Example 4.4

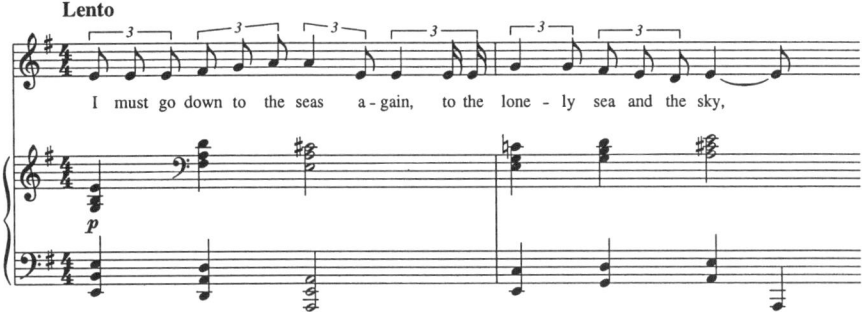

There are two other ballads with similarly affirmative mood and strophic construction. These are 'I have twelve oxen' and 'If there were dreams to sell', both, like 'The bells of San Marie', written in 1918. The 1922 piano *Soliloquy* is a wordless ballad in the same manner. 'This is one of the simplest and most characteristic of all Mr Ireland's short pieces ... It is an Andante in folk-song style, and the lyric form and poetic content are truly delightful' (*MMR*, Aug. 1922: 189).

Unlike most of his contemporaries, only rarely did Ireland associate nature with 'folk', in the sense of arranging English folk songs or incorporating existing folk melodies into his music. There is only one known arrangement of a traditional English folk song, 'The three ravens' (1920). This is a ballad in a different vein. It is a beautiful example, perfect in its textural simplicity. The increasingly poignant words are matched in a piano part of mounting turmoil, held together by the constancy of the melody and by a tiny piano ritornello.

Every one of the pieces discussed so far has structural correlatives, in that there is a sense of time and action standing still. There is a single mood captured in either a strophic or, more rarely, a ternary form. Both the pastoral and the ballad types are derivative of earlier models: Beethoven's merry-making peasants, Schubert's huntsmen, and the rustic or sea ditties of the Victorians. There are other nature tone poems in which the same sense of stasis is present, but which draw on quite different musical models. The evocation of spring in Ireland's output is a powerful one, and time, season and weather fascinated him. In his letters he often recorded weather conditions (as did Virginia Woolf in her diaries), sometimes in quite poetic terms. A fabulous spring could elevate other experiences, and nature, 'with its changing aspects & seasons, its sunrises and sunsets, & the life of the earth & trees' could also be a 'never-failing consolation' (KT: 16 Feb. 1943). The theme of season in Britain is a recurring one in his output, and in this sense he can be seen as having musical parallels with Constable. Like the painter he returned to the same landscapes in different aspects, and the same season in different places. His evocations of season are mainly confined to spring and summer, April and May specifically, and there are a handful of pieces that allude to time of day. These include works in which morning and place are entwined. 'Soho forenoons' falls into this category, but as a London work will be discussed in Chapter 5. There is also the part-song 'See how the morning smiles', mentioned in Chapter 1. In this work there are glimpses of the oscillating accompaniments that came to fruition in the later nature-ecstasy pieces such as 'Earth's call'. Two works have the title 'Aubade', implying a musical herald of dawn, one a part-song, the other a piano piece. There are also 'evening' pieces, again part-songs, including 'Twilight night' and 'Evening song'. The latter was a setting of words by James Vila Blake, a poet whose writing evidently appealed to Ireland during 1911 and 1912, primarily for its nature mysticism, as there are a number of settings from these two years. These include the aforementioned 'When lights go rolling round the sky', and the part-songs 'Spring' and 'In summer woods'. Many of J.V. Blake's words are translations of German poems, including those of Rückert, and perhaps for this reason Ireland's part-song settings tend to be derivative of Viennese models.

Spring evidently signified something quite specific to Ireland. Just as his musical places were a mixture of the real, the imagined and the literary, his spring was both reality and fantasy. It could either be the heady bliss of a glorious May day, love and warmth entwined in pieces such as 'In a May morning'; or it could be the unfulfilled promise of a grey English May, and he twice set poems with this disappointment at their heart. One of these songs has the title 'English May' and the other is a part-song, 'May flowers'. Spring was also a sexual metaphor, and many of Ireland's bigger spring pieces are linked with sexual experiences, again, both real and imagined.

One of the best of the springtime rhapsodies is the piano piece, 'April' (1925). This has shadowy associations with other pieces and places. An earlier, discarded title for the piece was 'The sweet season'. This was a reference to a poem by Richard Edwardes, set as a part-song by Ireland in 1920, called 'When May is in his prime'. The poem is a eulogy to the beauty of May. The part-song was written in Southwater, a village in West Sussex just north of Shipley. 'April', then, has connections with another expression of spring and with a place, even if only as a reminiscence. It was written as a pair with 'Bergomask', with which it shares motivic material. 'April' is yet another manifestation of 'country' in Ireland's output, but has the same sense of peacefulness and poise as *The Towing Path*. 'April' has a single melodic idea. The first fifteen bars constitute the first presentation, though within these fifteen bars there are smaller subsections, and in effect the work derives from the opening three bars. The fluid, 'rural' effect of the opening is created through the use of cross-rhythms, here the right-hand triplets against the left-hand quavers (Example 4.5). The very decorative nature of the melody line, and the frequent ornaments, form a different aspect of the topic.

Example 4.5

The phrase shown in Example 4.5 is repeated and modulates in bars 4–6. Bars 7–15 form the second half of the phrase and continue to develop the triplet pattern and the cross-rhythms. After this initial presentation, with its gently oscillating left hand and contained lyricism, Ireland repeats the idea, but subjects it to ever increasing elaboration. The second version starting at bar 16, for example, maintains the outline of the theme, but it is embellished with added notes, runs and a minim trill in bar 19 (the trill an overtly suggestive 'bird-like' aspect of Ireland's nature pieces). This is the melodious, major melody of nature, as opposed to the jarring, minor piping of 'Le Catioroc'.

Here the second half of the phrase moves away from the prevailing D major to a passage of chromatic wandering to arrive in E major in bar 36. In the new E major version of the theme, the first half of the phrase is decorated still further. This time there is no second half, but instead the first half is repeated again straight away in E flat major at bar 41. The notes of the original chordal accompaniment are still there, but have become a sextuplet/quintuplet figuration. Above this the melody takes off in a rippling flight of fancy in ever more complex cross-rhythms and more effusive trills, though it always retains the basic outline (Example 4.6).

Example 4.6

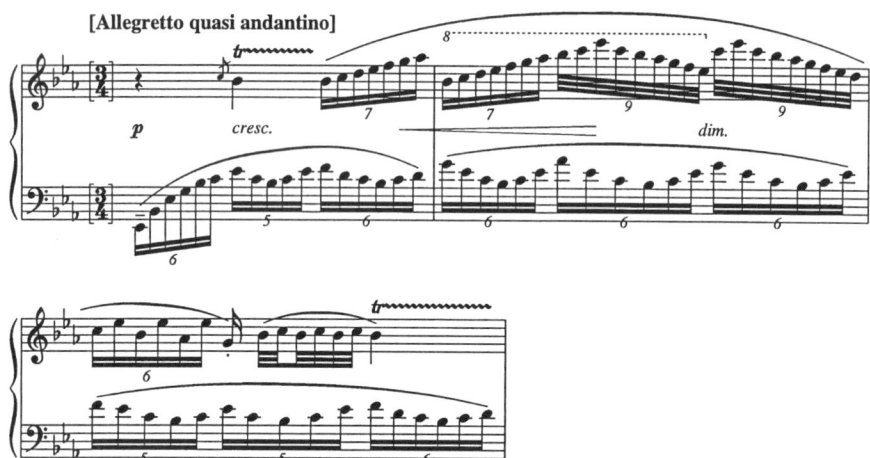

A version of the passage that was first heard in bar 25 leads the way back to a final version of the main theme in bar 57, in a mixture of its original and decorated presentations. There are a number of features of this piece that are typical of Ireland's response to place and season, most notably the overall structure, in which a single melodic idea is repeated and gradually made more intricate and complex. Within this, phrases end with an upward lilt (as in Example 4.5), and the fundamentally tonal base, as is often the case with Ireland, is clouded with modal drifts, such as the Dorian twist in bars 14 and 15.

The examples discussed so far are examples of the different ways in which a country topic is present in Ireland's music. There is a pastoral subtopic, there are ballads, both rollicking and lyrical, and lyrical single-theme pieces that rely on figuration, decoration and descriptively expressive suggestions of the sounds of the countryside. Another way in which Ireland responded to nature in his music was in a group of pieces that have strong French connections. One of the reasons for Ireland's propensity to produce nature pictures in music was his liking for the works of Debussy and Ravel, and it is evident that the whole Impressionist–Symbolist movement is a strong force in his music. According to Howes, what links Ireland's music to his French precursors and counterparts is 'the use of small forms for the piano to convey visual imagery, suggestions of place' (Howes, 1966: 222). It is an Impressionism that has links outside France, and once again with Machen. In *The Hill of Dreams* Lucian Taylor, the main protagonist, describes language as:

> ... chiefly important for the beauty of its sounds, by its possession of words resonant, glorious to the ear, by its capacity, when exquisitely arranged, of suggesting wonderful and indefinable impressions ... Here lay hidden the secret of the sensuous art of literature, it was the secret of suggestion, the art of causing delicious sensation by the use of words.
>
> (in Palmer, 1988: 234)

If Machen's description of the sensation of language is altered to focus on music, the following passage emerges, a passage that is applicable to Ireland's Symbolist mode, which is:

> ... chiefly important for the beauty of its sounds, by its possession of timbres and harmonies resonant, glorious to the ear, by its capacity, when exquisitely arranged, of suggesting wonderful and indefinable impressions ... Here lay hidden the secret of the sensuous art of music, it was the secret of suggestion, the art of causing delicious sensation by the use of sounds.

As was discussed by Banfield (1985: 164–5) with reference to the songs, Ireland's art is that of the 'indefinable impression' and in his music he creates a sensation or a state of mind. It is very much a music of suggestion. And there are a number of works that fall into this category. They are nature pieces, but not in the pastoral sense. Instead they are musical sensations that draw heavily on Debussy, in which the effect of musical indefiniteness is produced both by a confusion 'between the imaginary world and the real' (E. Wilson, 1993: 13), and by a focus on musical sensation. Ireland's favourite Symbolist was not a French, but an English one, Arthur Symons, who had been part of Mallarmé's coterie in Paris. Symons' writings first appear as an influence on Ireland in 1912, and recur periodically until *c.* 1930. There is also a very early dedication to the poet: the 1903 song, 'I was not sorrowful', carries the line 'For Arthur Symons'. Perhaps Ireland had met him; or perhaps it was a gesture of affinity in the dedication of a setting of Ernest Dowson to a fellow English Symbolist.

There are several instances of song settings of words by Symons, and in addition there are piano pieces that bear quotations from his poems. These are 'The island spell' and 'Moon-glade', the first two of the suite, *Decorations* (the third of which was 'The scarlet ceremonies'). The suite as a whole belongs to the same world as the Debussy Preludes for Piano, and in all three of the *Decorations* Ireland uses piano figuration extensively, as does Debussy. It is figuration for its own sake, as the essence of the music, and the textures are more limpid than those usually favoured by Ireland. A 1915 review of the set focused directly on the Impressionist influences:

These three pieces are well named, since they are the most successful pieces of pictorial writing we have encountered since the advent of Maurice Ravel, whose style they somewhat resemble as regards technique … Originality breathes in every bar of the 'Decorations', and the composer evidently possesses peculiar magic powers in the world of sound.

(*MMR*, Aug. 1915: 227)

'The island spell' was completed in August 1912, in Fauvic, Jersey, during a holiday on the island. The title is ambiguous, and like *The Forgotten Rite*, may have been associated with the excavations that were taking place on Jersey at the time. But this is an entirely idyllic piece, and its title more likely a reference to the beauty of the island. The attached quotation, from 'In the Wood of Finvara', one of Symons' Yeats-influenced poems, is an attempt to pin down the essence of the music, or at least the spirit behind it:

I would wash the dust of the world in a soft green flood:
Here, between sea and sea, in the fairy wood,
I have found a delicate, wave-green solitude …

Jersey remains a beautiful place, but in the early part of the century, without cars, would have been even more so. Ireland's holidays at this time were often taken as part of a group, and would presumably have involved communal seaside bathing and summer picnics. The island's miles of sandy beaches, with their different characteristics, were well known to Ireland. These included the stretches at St Ouen's Bay, on the west coast of the island, the rocky section at Corbière, and the north-west corner, its sea and sky brilliant blue on fine days, its coastal paths rich with wild flowers. In the north the beautiful and lush Mourier Valley leads down to the sea, and in the north-east the few cottages of the little fishing village of Rozel cluster round the harbour. Fauvic is on the east coast, with its vast swathes of sand at Grouville Bay. Jersey was popular as a tourist attraction in the first two decades of the century, and there were many passenger ships making the voyage from Southampton and Weymouth. In August 1912 entertainments on the island included the annual 'Battle of the Flowers', complete with military bands, fireworks and a 'great confetti battle'. There was an Opera House in the capital, St Helier, whose offerings for this month were performances of Franz Lehar's (1870–1948) *The Merry Widow* and for one night only an appearance by renowned violinist Marie Hall (1884–1956). There were grand dances in the Olympia Hall and twice nightly shows at the Alhambra Picture House (*The Evening Post*, 8 Aug. 1912). It was a blissful place and a blissful time, and it is clear that Ireland felt this way about the island.

'The island spell' is impressionistic in that it is an ethereal mood-picture. The pentatonic opening, with its 'delicate' oscillations (see Example 4.9b on p. 103) and chime-like melody picked out over the top, owes much to Debussy, and the blurring use of the pedal and acciaccaturas from bar 35 add to the hazy effect. The overt connections with 'La cathédrale engloutie' from bar 96, and the whole-tone scale then picked out in bar 101 (Example 4.7; bars 96–101), all serve to confirm that this is a deliberately French evocation befitting an island with a strong French culture: a piece about sensation in Symbolist tradition.

Example 4.7

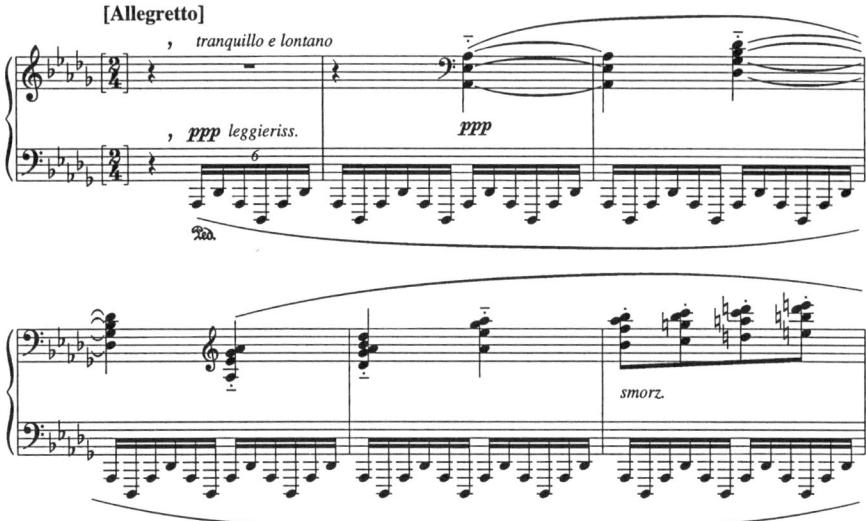

'Moon-glade', written the following year, explores a different aspect of the Symbolist approach to the entwining of nature and emotion. The attached Symons quotation reads:

> Why are you sorrowful in dreams?
> I am sad in the night;
> The hours till the morning are white,
> I hear the hours' flight
> All night in dreams …

The *MMR* review above described 'Moon-glade' as having a 'curious compelling charm and feeling of remoteness' (ibid.). This is the decadent, neurotic side of Symbolist poetry as captured in Ireland's obsessive, chromatically twisting quavers (Example 4.8).

Example 4.8

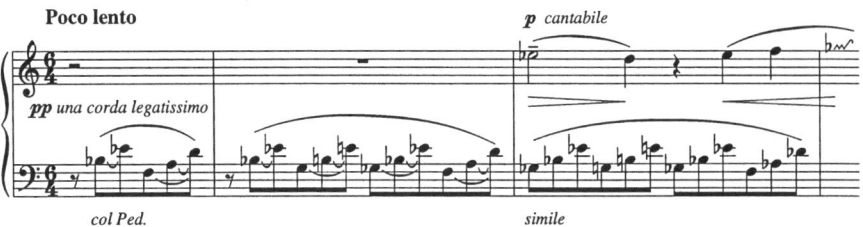

The piece closes with a rising, fading passage of single notes, 'so like the stuff dreams are made of' (ibid.). In the same year, 1913, Ireland wrote a short piano piece, *The Almond Tree*, which, though without the Symons associations, is in the same vein as 'The island spell', with its emphasis on figuration, delicate textures and pentatonic melodies. A feature of all three of these pieces, 'The island spell', 'Moon-glade' and *The Almond Tree*, is their common performance indications. They all have careful and atmospheric use of the pedal, with the instruction *una corda* a particular feature.

One aspect of Ireland's response to Symbolist literature was his attraction to the image of the sea as nature-ecstasy metaphor. 'The island spell' has obviously rhapsodic sea associations, as does the later song 'Santa Chiara' (1925). This is a setting of words by Symons, the sea here a metaphor for solitary contemplation. As was the case with the rural settings, Ireland's sea was a real location, a backdrop for personal experiences, but also a mythical or imagined place. 'Song of the springtides', for example, is both a real, known part of the Guernsey coast and a half-remembered Swinburnian fantasy, and as such, like 'Santa Chiara', carries the composer's musical ecstasy symbols. And on two occasions, the legend of Neptune, Roman god of the sea, was the subject of Ireland's works. One was the part-song, 'In praise of Neptune', the other a work for orchestra, *Tritons*.

The sea has been a lure for many British writers and composers, much as the forest is a part of the German psyche. In the twentieth century, attempts to depict the sea in music have ranged from impressionistic miniatures (the piano music of William Baines (1899–1922) to large-scale operas (Britten), song-cycles (Elgar), tone poems (Bax) and symphonies (Vaughan Williams). Many of Britain's coastlines and rivers ebb and flow through the oeuvre of the country's musicians. There are representations in sound of the cliffs of North Yorkshire and Cornwall, and of the bleak East Anglian and Northumbrian coasts. In a 1956 article, 'Baines and Britten: some affinities', Roger Carpenter looked at links between these two composers with regard to their sea music, finding common musical figurations on account of the shared impact of the 'surge of the waves, their soft splash against the hull of a boat, the approach of a storm, the sparkling sunlight, the mist with its seabirds and foghorn, and over and above it all the sense of vastness, of elemental fury, and of eerie desolation' (Carpenter, 1956: 187). Ireland belongs to the same school, and there are specific ways in which he draws on traits common to other British composers (though also common to contemporary French models). The most obvious is that he uses repeating figurations as a representational tool, constant movement as an analogy for water. In a very early work, the melodrama for voice and piano, 'Annabel Lee', Edgar Allan Poe's poem, set in a 'kingdom by the sea', is recited over a backdrop of a repeating motif (Example 4.9a) which has shared connotations with several other sea pieces, including the opening of 'The island spell' (Example 4.9b).

Example 4.9a

Example 4.9b

'Annabel Lee' also has a harmonic link with other of Ireland's sea pieces, in that it is in A flat major, the key used for two early piano works, 'Meridian' and *A Sea Idyll*.

With the exception of the *Three Songs* mentioned at the beginning of this chapter, the works discussed so far are short, single movements that belong to different 'subtopics' of Ireland's larger country topic. These are: pastoral pieces; simple strophic ballads; lyrical rhapsodies featuring cross-rhythms and florid melodic lines; and French-influenced impressions. In addition, there are song-cycles, solo piano pieces and suites of piano pieces that combine and contrast Ireland's different responses to nature, as was seen in the *Three Songs*. Often these more complex, or mixed, collections have literary slants. One such work was the 1937 set of three short piano pieces published under the title *Green Ways*, each of which has a descriptive title and an attached quotation.

These pieces bring together aspects of Ireland's musical responses to nature in a motivically unified set. The first piece, 'The cherry tree', was originally published in 1932 as *Indian Summer*. It was revised, and in its new version prefaced with a passage from A.E. Housman. Thematically, it belongs with 'April', in that it is a rhapsodic, lyrical miniature relying on decorative figuration. It has the same method of development of a single main theme, but is much shorter and simpler than the earlier work. It also has an introductory motif, featuring a falling octave (Example 4.10a) that recurs as a linking motif in the other works in the set.

Example 4.10a

The second, 'Cypress', was originally called 'The intruder'. In its 1937 version it was prefaced with Shakespeare's lines, 'Come away, come away, death, / and in sad cypress let me be laid'. 'Cypress' is in the 'Moon-glade' vein, with angular, chromatic lines and *una corda* markings. In this short, spare piece, the falling octave pattern set up in 'The cherry tree' becomes much more predominant (Example 4.10b).

Example 4.10b

The third of the set, 'The palm and may', quotes from a poem used previously by Ireland in the part-song 'Spring, the sweet spring', which deployed overt pictorial representations of birdsong. It opens with the falling octave pattern (Example 4.10c) and has the trills and decorative melodic lines of 'The cherry tree', but it also has whole-tone scales and elements of the pastoral Ireland, in dance-like passages (Example 4.11a; bar 10) that use the same patterns as 'A report song' (Example 4.11b), written slightly later in 1938.

Example 4.10c

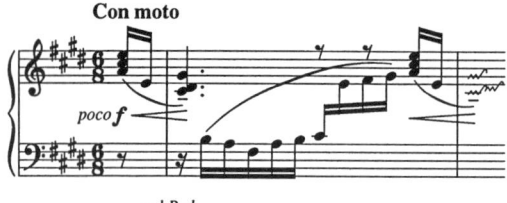

Example 4.11a

Example 4.11b

In 1938 Ireland wrote a set of country miniatures very similar to *Green Ways*. This was the group of songs, *Five Sixteenth-Century Poems*, in which spring is the connecting subject matter. An Elizabethan spring was a theme that surfaced in Ireland's output from time to time, as it did in the work of many of his contemporaries, though the Elizabethan poets never inspired his best work. Before this set of songs he had already set Campion's 'The peaceful western wind', his earliest surviving piece, which was discussed in Chapter 1. In *c.* 1905 he set Shakespeare's 'When daffodils begin to peer' as part of *Songs of a Wayfarer*; in *c.* 1908, Thomas Nashe's 'Spring, the sweet spring' for SATB, and in 1921 Thomas Dekker's 'The merry month of May' for voice and piano.

The first of the *Five Sixteenth-Century Songs*, 'A thanksgiving', is a paean to God, thanking him for nature, and as such is affirmative both in the D major tonality and in the positive melodic line that is passed between piano and voice. As in 'April', the notion of rural loveliness is conveyed through piano roulades, though here trills and mordents are more effusive in their depiction of hearing 'the birdès sing'. The second song, 'All in a garden green', is a lyrical ballad, and the third, 'An aside', is a jovial glance away from nature at the follies of women. 'A report song' is a simple pastoral piece (see Example 4.11b for its prevailing rhythmic pattern) and the last song, 'The sweet season', a joyous celebratory romp.

As well as the sets of country responses, there are two piano works that bring together in a single piece different aspects of nature. These are *Summer Evening* (1919) and 'Amberley Wild Brooks' (1921), the latter a reference to a part of Sussex. From early in his life, one of the most significant English landscapes for Ireland was the South Downs, as was seen with the orchestral work, *Legend*. Just as the Channel Islands prompted retrospective music when Ireland was not physically there, West Sussex was often the source of inspiration for a piece after Ireland had visited the county and returned to London. Once he moved to Sussex as his permanent home, it was no longer a creative stimulus, though admittedly this move came very late in his life, when he was producing very little music. West Sussex was a spiritual haven for Ireland, much as it was to Hilaire Belloc, who, like Ireland, wrote most of his Sussex-inspired works before he moved to live permanently in the village of Shipley. Ireland was by no means the only musician of his generation to find the county appealing. Albert Sammons lived in Middleton-on-Sea, and his pianist colleague William Murdoch in Bognor Regis in the 1920s, as did Albert Coates (1882–1953). Havergal Brian (1876–1972) lived in Shoreham, Parry maintained a house in Rustington, and Elgar spent some time at Brinkwells, Fittleworth, in the 1920s. Sussex was also attractive to writers at this time, with Eleanor Farjeon, D.H. Lawrence and Edward Thomas all drawn to the county.

It is impossible to date Ireland's first visit to West Sussex, though it was probably very early in the twentieth century. The first known visit was the St Luke's outing to Littlehampton in 1906, referred to in Chapter 2. Ireland's preferred part of West Sussex was the eastern end, near Steyning, and throughout the 1920s and 1930s he visited the area on a regular basis, all his major Sussex-inspired works dating from this time. Between *c.* 1920 and 1922 he maintained a pied-à-terre at Pound Farm, Stopham and then between *c.* 1922 and 1934 at Ivy Cottage, Ashington. In 1934 he gave up this cottage, and wrote to former pupil Horace Randerson that '"Legend" was evidently my farewell to the Downs' (HR: Sept. 1934). This was not the case, and Ireland renewed his acquaintance with the county in 1950, when he rented part of The Old Rectory, Meiros Farm, Ashington. He eventually settled at Rock Mill, Washington, in 1953. Rock Mill (see Plate 19) was a smock mill, dating from *c.* 1826, and had been converted into a house in 1919. Part of its appeal was that it stood just north of the Downs, opposite Chanctonbury Ring. This move had mixed consequences for Ireland. On the one hand, he was now living in a place that had been a big draw for many years, but the mill was cold, in an exposed spot, and soon after moving in he wrote that 'it was all we could do to keep this barrack-like place above freezing point' (KT: Feb. 1954). But equally he waxed lyrical about the beauty of springtime at the mill (KT: 4 May 1958).

In the 1920s and 1930s, Ireland's trips to Sussex were primarily in order to explore the landscape, and he frequently walked on the Downs. His regular eating and drinking haunts included the Swan Inn, Fittleworth, the Chequers, Steyning and the White Horse, Storrington, Bax's frequent stopping-place between 1939 and 1953. One of the attractions of Sussex was its many prehistoric sites, as was discussed in Chapter 3. The close proximity of such spots as Harrow Hill, the Devil's Jumps (a series of Bronze Age round barrows on Monkton Down, near Treyford), the Devil's Humps (striking round barrows at Kingley Vale) and Cissbury Ring, an Iron Age enclosure, was alluring.

However, as with the Channel Islands, there is a more gentle aspect of Sussex, and Ireland's depiction of the county was only partly concentrated in its pagan places. Sussex was also a place associated with good times, visited by Ireland with close friends when he was at his most prolific and successful, and as is the case with many of Ireland's places, it came to symbolize happier, lost days. In 1938, after spending Easter in the Horsham area, Ireland wrote to Thompson that he had 'covered a good deal of West Sussex, which has great charm for me and is full of memories of exciting times – now over, alas!' (KT: 1 May 1938). Some years later, while living in Ashington, Ireland used the word 'charm' again in reference to the county, which he described as 'rather relaxing', with 'a special charm of its own' (KT: 4 July 1951).

There are a number of works which are removed from the dark hill groves and barrows of the county, and are instead a more bucolic evocation of its woods and brooks. The title of 'Amberley Wild Brooks' refers to an area of low-lying wetland (Figure 4.1) contained by the Downs and the River Arun at Amberley, a village close to Arundel. Amberley is one of the jewels of West Sussex, an exquisite village with lavender-hedged thatched cottages, a castle and the 'wild brooks'. Ireland's piece is an amalgamation of the sentiments and construction of 'April' and the impressionist qualities of *Decorations*. Like 'April', it has a main theme that embraces a florid melody and a regular accompaniment pattern (Example 4.12a).

Example 4.12a

There are cross-rhythms, though these are here less striking than in 'April'. The main theme recurs in embellished forms, which are looser and more concealed than they were in 'April', dissolving more swiftly to heavily decorated versions. For example, the transformation of the opening four bars starting at bar 30, though opening in the same key as bars 1–4, is adorned with new figuration and rapidly moves away from the melodic and harmonic foundation. In this first part of the piece there are the ornaments that are associated with nature in Ireland's works, including trills and runs, and air breathed into the music through the use of rests, such as those in bars 5 and 6. There are also moments, for example at bar 15, of static oscillations. The central part of the piece, from bar 41, moves to a new idea combining a modal melody with implied pentatonic figuration (Example 4.12b).

Example 4.12b

This dissolves into brilliant, rapid figuration leading to a dramatic climax and a cadenza-like passage in bar 80. The return of the main theme at bar 82 has a pagan note inserted into the rural elegy, in that it has alterations to imply a changed state. This is not simply because of the different left-hand accompaniment, but in the new and potent C natural that occurs in bar 85. But this closing section somehow retains its tranquillity through the use of *una corda*, the *lontano* marking at bar 92 and the shimmering semiquavers in bars 96–9. *Summer Evening* is a much simpler, but similar work, which juxtaposes the lyrical ballad side of Ireland with brief Dorian excursions into a more ecstatic world, once again ending with the *una corda* and *lontano* indications.

The two works above belong to the period of Ireland's most vivid nature music, *c.* 1912–25. In particular, the years 1918–20 were a time of sharp focus on this topic, embracing such pieces as *The Towing Path*, 'The bells of San Marie' and *Summer Evening*. Evidently 1918 was a year of emphasis on place, both country and city. In addition to the ballads and *The Towing Path*,

4.1 Amberley Wild Brooks

Ireland wrote another 'country' work that is of a very different nature. The song 'Earth's call (A sylvan rhapsody)' is the quintessential example of Ireland's musical representations of an experience in a landscape. It is a setting of No. VII of Harold Monro's sonnets from his set, 'Week-End', in *Strange Meetings* (Monro, 1917). The poem sits within the collection as an expression of a weekend idyll away in the country before the protagonists return to London. According to Ireland, Monro was 'livid with fury' (H.Rutland: 14 Oct. 1951) when he heard the setting, perhaps because it goes so completely against the sonnet structure of the poem, imbuing it with an overtly sexual meaning removed from the irony of Monro's cycle of poems.

This song and others, such as 'Youth's spring-tribute' and 'The trellis', are difficult to place within a single topic. They are about nature, but they are also about love. They are songs with words that describe an idyll for two people in a rural setting. The emphasis on nature itself is stronger in 'Earth's call' than in its counterparts, such as 'Youth's spring-tribute', hence the decision to include it in this chapter, and not in Chapter 6.

Banfield wrote of 'Earth's call' that when Ireland set a pastoral poem to music he was 'expressing not the beauty of nature but the personal ecstasy of which the beauty of nature, part cause, is the corollary or symbol' (Banfield, 1985: 165). 'Earth's call' is Ireland at his most ecstatic. The work falls into sections which explore changing human emotions alongside the different aspects of nature that emerge as the poem progresses. Thus the first section (bars 1–27), which ends at the Meno mosso, establishes a scene and a mood of ecstatic contemplation. There are specific ways in which Ireland's music attempts to express this country ecstasy. The first is a feature explored by Banfield, which he describes as Ireland's nature 'coruscations' (ibid.). This is where an accompaniment pattern sets up a shimmering effect, with oscillating intervals, as seen for example, in bar 3, and developed more fully in the descending patterns of bar 15 (Example 4.13a).

Example 4.13a

[Con moto moderato]

This particular pattern is developed in the opening section of the song, and dominates the whole of the passage from bar 15 to bar 24, before settling down to a more static 'in tempo tranquillo' in bar 25. The effect is of a place, a moment, frozen in time, where a constant bass note – the E♭ – serves as the anchor over which these coruscations are allowed to float. Added to this is a vocal part whose outline is also typically used in Ireland's expressions of ecstasy. This is a Dorian melody in which the emphasis is on the natural sixth (Example 4.13b). Towards the end of this opening section, in bar 25, the cuckoo makes a first, fleeting appearance, its call at this point a minor third.

Example 4.13b

The fresh air moves like wa-ter round a boat.

There follows a seven-bar interlude at bars 28–34, which serves as a bridge to a new section. The first bars of this passage have the thick, parallel chords of the second movement of the First Violin Sonata, marked 'solenne'. The question that follows, 'What are the great trees calling?' is a reference back, both textually and melodically, to material from a very early song cycle, *Songs of a Wayfarer*.

The new scene from bar 35 has Ireland's pastoral tonal rocking accompaniment, as the emphasis shifts from contemplation of the countryside to the two protagonists' contemplation of one another against the rural backdrop. The way in which Ireland does this is simple. What begins as a level lyricism, at the words 'Just come a little farther', turns to increasing intensity. The vocal line and the piano part slowly rise in pitch, the drawn-out F♯ at 'Give me your hand' (bar 55) betraying the mounting emotion. To what are the people listening? To the sounds of the landscape? Or to their own outpourings? At the words 'Let us both listen till we understand, / Each through the other, ev'ry natural sound', the vocal line is marked 'appass.', the melodic outline in bars 69–70 one that recurs in Ireland's music about love. Now the piano takes over, the intensity mounting further, symbolic surely of an act of passion in this rural setting. The ecstasy is expressed through a series of rising parallel chords, until the E flat rhapsody of bar 15 returns in bar 87. The moment of physical pleasure past, the cuckoo call is heard again in bar 89, now a major third, symbolizing fulfilment, arrival. The protagonists are sated, reflective, tranquil. In this piece, and typically in Ireland's passionate idylls that will be discussed in Chapter 6, there is always a single moment of climax, after which the music is changed in some way. This work is about nature, but it is also about a powerful sexual experience, and as such there are motivic and harmonic links with other works such as 'The trellis'. It is an example of a piece in which nature is significant both for itself and for its qualities as a backdrop against which passion is enacted.

Every work discussed so far deals with an emotion or a single place, or an emotion experienced within a particular, fixed setting. The mood is contained within one location. To end this chapter, there is also a section of Ireland's nature music that focuses on the symbol of the traveller on a personal journey, idylls with a passage from one place to another, and Ireland was certainly drawn to the image of the tramp figure, whether city beggar, busker or country traveller. This was a preoccupation of the late Victorians and Edwardians, who idealized the tramp figure (see Crowther, 1993: 91–113), seeing him as a symbol of freedom of movement, sexual liberation, almost as a guardian of the countryside; a rather, unkempt, human equivalent to the Pan figure. The romanticizing of vagrant life in George Borrow's *Lavengro* (1851) and *Romany Rye* (1857) was continued by John Drinkwater, Lionel Johnson and E.V. Lucas, whose 1899 anthology, *The Open Road*, was 'a garland of good or enkindling poetry and prose fitted to urge folk into the open air' (Crowther, 1994: 107). Robert Louis Stevenson's *Songs of Travel* embodied the spirit of the Edwardian Wanderlust.

The appeal of the tramp figure to Ireland was multifold. As a solitary figure given to countryside escapism, he was drawn to the image of the solitary individual on a personal quest into the wilderness. He was also attracted to the urban vagrant exploring the city (as will be discussed in Chapter 5). And he would have found the rough, wild nature of the beggar or tramp appealing. But Ireland was also drawn to the symbolic traveller's journey simply because it was part of the spirit of the age. It was not an idea that always brought out the best in him. Although the London character pieces, such as 'Ragamuffin' and *Merry Andrew*, are successful, piquant exercises in capturing the vernacular in music, the musical journeys can be rather clumsy and unconvincing, unlike Vaughan Williams' essays in this genre. The 1920 setting of 'The journey' by the obscure poet, Ernest Blake, makes use of repetitive figurations in the tradition of Vaughan Williams' *Songs of Travel*, but whereas in the former they became the undercurrent for the whole cycle, here they are merely trite.

Ireland's setting of Masefield's 'The vagabond', in 1922, is retrospective in mood and style. Masefield's colloquial words have only the barest of piano accompaniments, somewhat similar in style to that of 'Sea fever' (and the poem came from the same *Saltwater Ballads*). Chordal textures and plain harmonies act as a sentimentalizing of the words.

The biggest of Ireland's journeys was his *Songs of a Wayfarer*, which span the period *c.* 1903–11. There is no common poet within the set, but the words of the songs, four of which were written before 1905, are linked in spirit. In the first song, 'Memory', the journey is as much of the mind as of the body. A solitary figure dreams by day in the countryside, where memories and sensations mingle. Night-time is a shift to darkness and 'Melancholy'. This song is strophic, clearly drawing on Ireland's musical inheritance, with its simple, assured, chordal style. There is a single, overt attempt at picture-painting at the words 'linnet's song' (bar 23), where Ireland deploys a minim trill. Even at this early stage in his career there are hints of his ability to move between worlds. The musical twist in bar 30, at the words 'Walking along the darken'd valley' is simply a chromatic A♯ appoggiatura and a move to the relative minor, yet coming after music of such a positive, sanguine nature, the twist is effective in evoking the darkness of night-time reflection. The second song, 'When daffodils begin to peer', heralds spring and a more physical wandering in the countryside. It contains obvious nature images such as ornaments to invoke bird-song, for example at 'The lark, that tirra-lyra chants' (bars 29–30), heralding the more sophisticated language of 'April'. In 'English May', the third song, the spirit wishes for a better, sunnier May. While in the ballad vein of Ireland's country topic, this, too, pre-empts 'April', with its upward lilting phrases, and its last section, with its 'spirit at rest' which walks 'unseen', looks back at 'Memory'. The fourth song, 'I was not sorrowful', uses a rather different, much more dream-like, musical language. It is a setting of Dowson, and the Symbolist text provokes the usual French-influenced response. In this poem a solitary figure sits and watches the weather while the memory wanders to thoughts of old desires. The piano part uses a pattern that is constant until the last few bars, a rippling arpeggio figure, against pointed chords, with the familiar markings *lontano* and *una corda* (Example 4.14). Over this a static voice line expresses the sorrow denied in the words.

Example 4.14

Thus the recurring subject matter of these first four songs is a wayfaring of the mind. The theme is private contemplation, set against the landscape. The fifth song, written later, in 1911, is rather different, more of a pantheistic engagement with the landscape. The first song of *Songs of a Wayfarer* ends with the words 'Walking along the darken'd valley, / With silent melancholy.' The 'darken'd valley' is both a place by night and a country of the mind. In 1920 Ireland used the same words as a prefix to his piano piece *The Darkened Valley*. In 1941 he described this piece as being a 'a little mood-picture, called forth by Blake's lines beginning "Memory, hither come" … In those days I certainly had nothing to feel "melancholy" about: I had every reason to go on my way rejoicing, had I only known it' (KT: 25 Nov. 1941).

The year 1920 was a significant one for Ireland, and in terms of its date of composition, *The Darkened Valley* is sandwiched between powerful songs. 'The Trellis' and 'My true love hath my heart' were written in January and February, and work started on *The Land of Lost Content* later that year. These songs are about love, war, passion, repression. Despite Ireland's 1941 declaration that in 1920 he should have gone on his way rejoicing, much of this music is imbued with a sense of melancholy, a melancholy that pervaded his output. *The Darkened Valley* is a realization for piano of the sentiments of the Blake poem, intertwining memory and landscape, and it seems also very likely that there was a real darkened valley visited by Ireland, given that there were real scenes behind so many of his works. The piece deploys a ternary structure. The contemplation of the opening G minor section is created through a clear tonal centre, above which the impulse is a melodic one. The liquid nature of the right-hand melody (Example 4.15a) is created by ties, rests and slightly ambiguous cadences, against which inner lines meander, all ultimately coming to rest in G minor.

Example 4.15a

The central section, starting at bar 21, shifts to the relative major for a static, almost ecstatic, *una corda* state of reverie (Example 4.15b) before the return to the now altered opening music. It is a journey, hence the changed state at the end.

Example 4.15b

Ireland's solitary traveller did not only take his walks in the countryside, but was also an explorer of the unknown aspects of the city. Symons inspired London as well as country pieces, and the sense of security and belonging inherent in the country pieces also pervades Ireland's city music. As part of a long tradition, Ireland identifies the countryside with romantic yearning, beauty and ecstasy. But his city is no less romantic than his countryside, and there are a number of ways in which things rural and things urban have shared concerns.

Chapter 5

City

'For if you think of it, there is a London *cognita* and a London *incognita*' (Machen, 1924: 60). Arthur Machen's known and unknown city was a recurring theme in John Ireland's music. For the composer, 'the city' meant London. It was a real place, where he lived for most of his life: an amalgam of houses, churches, streets, the RCM, cafés, squares and bridges, with the Thames at its heart. But it was also an invented cityscape derived from memory and from literary evocations, an idea, a fantasy, an image in his mind. London was a city that became far more important to Ireland than the very different city suburbs of Manchester and Leeds where he spent his youth, and there was as much an urban John Ireland as a rural one. He derived pleasure from city as well as from country pursuits, and was a frequenter of cinemas and shops, pubs and clubs.

The first of Ireland's six 'London' pieces, five of which are for solo piano, appeared in 1917, and the last in 1936. Four of them were written in close succession between 1917 and 1920. These works, every one of which has a descriptive title, act as an indicator of the London both of Ireland's mind and of his experience. Three of the pieces, 'Chelsea Reach' (1917), 'Ragamuffin' (1917) and 'Soho forenoons' (1920), are grouped together as *London Pieces* (originally *London: Impressions for Piano*). The others are *Merry Andrew* (1918), *Ballade of London Nights* (*c.* 1930) and *A London Overture* (1936). In terms of their musical connections, there are also glimmerings of the city in other works, such as the Second Violin Sonata, the Piano Sonata, which was composed between the first and last of the *London Pieces*, and *Epic March*.

London has always been a city that has both beguiled and repelled. Ireland's own fascination with the capital as a source of inspiration occurred at a time when the city, as a metaphor for complexity, innovation and liberation, was at the centre of Modernist writing. London, as the largest city in the world at that time, was depicted (by Americans T.S. Eliot and Ezra Pound, but also by English poets writing in the early decades of the twentieth century) as a city of darkness, sterility and ruin. At the same time the insular, parochial and domestic aspects of the city were developing, with a huge suburban sprawl from about 1919. Though Ireland was hardly a Modernist, his very engagement with the notion of the city, and its representation in his music as a series of impressions moving backwards and forwards across time, shares some of the characteristic features of the Modernist movement in literature. He liked the miscellany and variety of London: its greyness and stateliness, the elements of wilderness in the city and its mixture of the international and the parochial.

Ireland's real, located London was the city in which he lived for most of his life, from his student days at the RCM, beginning in 1893, until 1953, though he did spend spells away from the city, some of them quite lengthy, within this period. From as early as 1896 he was living in Chelsea, the area that was to be his base for the next fifty-seven years. Ireland's unreal, dislocated London was a literary landscape, an amalgam of the myriad images of the city produced by writers including Charles Dickens, Dowson, Conan Doyle, Eliot, le Gallienne (whom Ireland had met while living in Bowdon), Machen, Symons and Wilde. Ireland was also drawn to pictorial representations of London, and prints by Chelsea artists including Walter Greaves, Hamilton Hay and James McNeill Whistler hung on his walls. From the surviving books belonging to Ireland it is evident that the whole concept of the city fascinated him. In addition to the writers above, he read James Boswell and Leigh Hunt on London, and books about Chelsea, including Reginald Blunt's *Red Anchor Pieces* (1928).

At the time of writing his first London piece, in 1917, Ireland was living through the First World War. He had already witnessed the decadent face of the 1890s London of Wilde and *The Yellow Book*, had seen Victorian London give way to Edwardianism, and the hansom cabs and horse-drawn buses of the 1890s superseded by electric trams and cars. He had lived through the heyday of the music hall and the emergence of jazz, had seen Mühlfeld performing Brahms in 1898 and the *Ballets Russes* on their visit to London in 1912. By 1917, therefore, he already had his own nostalgic memories of an older London, when 'in those long-off, misty days, then the lamps glittered, then the bells rang sweetly, gaily, then the horses' hoofs beat music from the road' (Machen, 1912, in Palmer, 1988: 327). These memories became part of his conception of 'London', and found their way into his music.

Ireland's musical representations of London are imbued with history and tradition, but at the same time are always personal to him. Much more obviously than was the case in the country evocations, characters, real and fictitious, including Ireland himself, invade these works. Of the six works, two are depictions of location, two are character pieces, in the light music genre, and two are more complex mixings of people and places.

There are two main ways in which Ireland forms his London. It is either a progressively shifting panorama, a journey around the capital, effected through a succession of new sections of music, as in *Ballade of London Nights*, or it is a more confined sketch of a corporate image, as in the character pieces. There are links with the country pieces, in that Ireland's London can be a hazy reverie in the Symbolist tradition, in which there is a sense of looking beyond the visible to the invisible, clothed in remote references. The new, distinct feature of this topic is the inclusion of the carnivalesque in the Bakhtinian sense, in that musical expressions of the festive, vulgar aspects of the city are located against a historical background which is both literary and musical. This was not a trait exclusive to Ireland: Elgar's 1900–01 overture, *Cockaigne*, was also part of this tradition, in that its title refers both to London and to the mythical, Utopian Land of Cockaigne, its roots medieval, its manifestations far-reaching. Fairground, music hall and pantomime sensibilities are essential to Ireland's London, and indeed there are many traces of light music connotations across his output, from early works such as the 1904 violin Cavatina to the late waltz, *Columbine* (1949).

Chelsea was Ireland's home for the greater part of his life, and so for him this was the central focus of London. Historically, Chelsea was an artistic haven, a community of painters, writers and musicians. D.G. Rossetti had lived there, as had Carlyle, George Meredith, Swinburne and Whistler, all of whom played a role in the creation of Ireland's personal style. And other composers, including Vaughan Williams and Warlock, also spent periods of time in the area. Before moving to Chelsea, Ireland first lodged with his sister in Paddington. Although full details of all the expected student moves from lodgings to lodgings do not survive, there are four known early addresses between 1893 and 1897. These included rented rooms in Paddington and Kilburn, after which he moved closer to the RCM, to 10 Sunningdale Gardens, Stratford Road, Kensington (*c.* 1896) and 46 Winchendon Road, Fulham. His first Chelsea address was in about 1896, at 43 Markham Square, after which he moved to lodgings in 62 Limerston Street, next door to musician contemporary Cecil Forsyth. The first home in which he lived for any length of time, from *c.* 1904 until 1915, was 54 Elm Park Mansions, Park Walk. In 1915 Ireland purchased 14A Gunter Grove, the studio at the back of a big house owned by the sculptor father of St Luke's choirboy, Robert Glassby. In 1923 Ireland bought the whole house from the boy's mother, Agnes Glassby, and it remained his base for the next thirty years. Every one of Ireland's Chelsea addresses was a road leading off the Kings Road. This road was the main artery that connected his homes and other significant places such as St Luke's, Holy Trinity and Chelsea Arts Club.

Ireland was a member of the Chelsea Arts Club, founded in 1891 as a place in which artists could eat, talk and promote exhibitions. The early meetings were held in premises in the Kings Road, and visited by such eminent figures as Monet and Pissarro. In 1901 the Club moved to 143–5 Old Church Street, where it has remained ever since, providing its members with bedrooms for overnight visits, and maintaining a library, billiard room and garden. Augustus John was a member from 1909 until his death in 1961, and other members included Jacob Epstein and John Singer Sargent. In the 1920s the club began to extend membership to figures outside the visual arts, creating honorary positions for some actors and musicians, among them Thomas Beecham (1879–1961), oboist Leon Goossens (1897–1988) and Ireland, for whom the club was an important place. Ireland was an honorary member for many years, from 1925 to at least 1941, and he used the club as a stopping-place on several

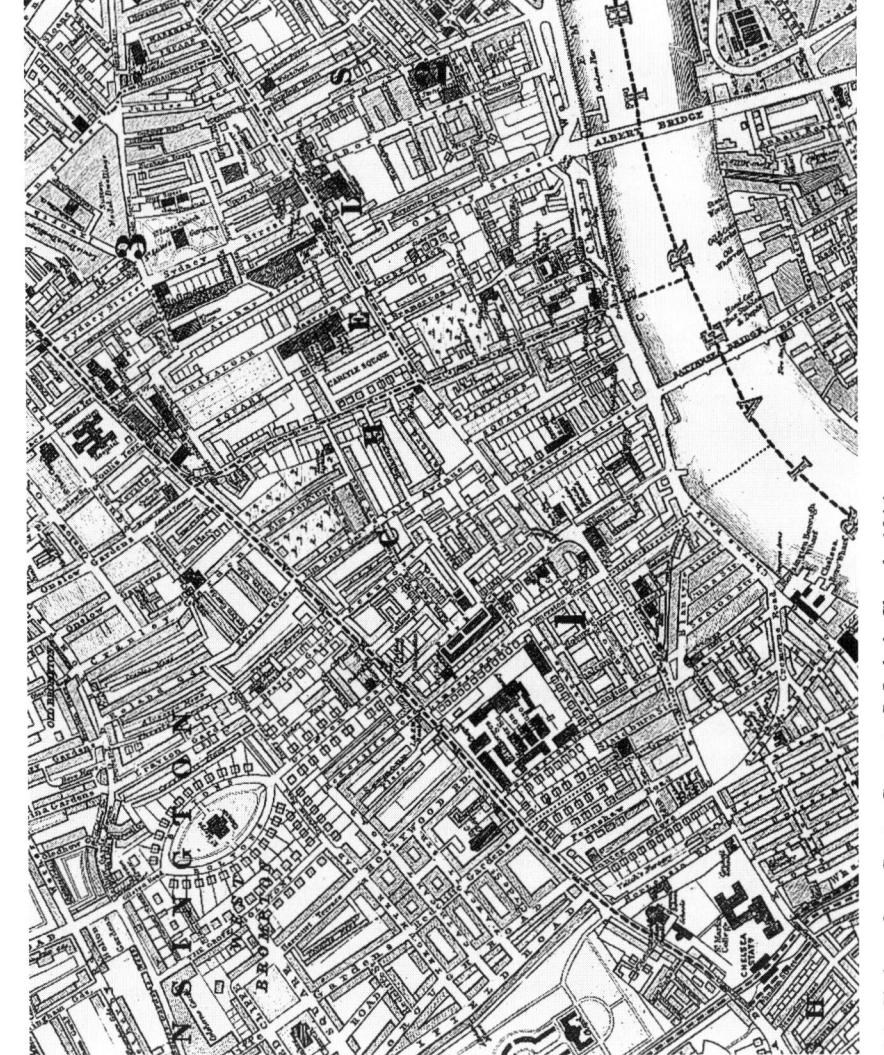

5.1 Chelsea, from Gunter Grove to St Luke's Church, 1914

occasions. Evidently he was a frequent user of the club's dining and drinking facilities, as he appears in Thomas Dugdale's 1933 painting, 'Lunch at the Chelsea Arts Club' (Plate 14). This shows the Club as a comfortable, male, meeting-place, in which John Ireland is seen talking to his sculptor friend Percy Bentham, who had himself become a member in 1931.

Chelsea was the inspiration for the first of Ireland's designated 'London' works. This was the piano piece, 'Chelsea Reach', the first of the *London Pieces*, described by Evans as a 'reverie in which the sentimental side of the Londoner – the side that takes "ballads" seriously – comes uppermost' (Evans, 1919a: 219). The title of the work refers to the part of the Thames Embankment closest to Gunter Grove, and the piece was purportedly the expression of a particularly beautiful evening view from Battersea Bridge (Searle, 1979: 51). In that sense the work is simply an impressionistic picture of Ireland's 'real' London, but it is the closest of all his London pieces to his country pieces in that it shares some features with his other waterscapes and with his pastoral works, and is therefore not exclusive to the Thames.

Ireland's indication that the piece should be in the 'Tempo di Barcarole' sets it within a particular musical tradition: the river is located historically as well as geographically, though it is shifted from eighteenth-century Venice via nineteenth-century France to twentieth-century London. Given that so many of Ireland's works have complex and sometimes distant connections with other works, it seems very likely that this piece was also affiliated to the images of Chelsea that Ireland knew and loved. An early review of the piece commented on 'something in common between Ireland's poetic pictorialness and the London water-colours of Yusi Markino' (*MMR*, April 1918: 84). More obviously, Whistler's 'Nocturne in Blue and Green' (1871) is a view from Battersea of Chelsea Reach, with the tower of Old Chelsea Church faintly visible. Whistler was friendly with the Greaves brothers, who were professional boatmen and artists with a profound knowledge of the river Thames, and this may be one reason for the piece being labelled a barcarolle, implying the stroke of a rowing-boat on the river.

The main features of the piano barcarolles of Chopin and Fauré are maintained, namely the $\frac{6}{8}$ time signature, the prevailing pulsing rhythm and a tendency towards sentimentality in the harmonies and tempo markings. Ireland also gives directions that point to the background of the barcarola as an Italian rowing-song, notably the instruction 'ben cantando il melodia', just as he had signalled 'il melodia' in the earlier 'Meridian'. There are other links with 'Meridian', and a path can be traced through the three earlier piano miniatures mentioned in Chapter 4, 'Meridian' (1895), *A Sea Idyll* (1899–1900) and 'The island spell' (1912), showing the composer's gradually shifting perceptions of the sea. There are also connections with the middle movement of the Second Violin Sonata, completed earlier in the year, and with *The Towing Path* (1918).

It seems that the key of A flat major was for Ireland in some sense associated with waterscapes: 'Meridian', *A Sea Idyll* and 'Chelsea Reach' are all situated in A flat, and all have compound time signatures (Examples 5.1a–c).

Example 5.1a 'Meridian'

Example 5.1b *A Sea Idyll*

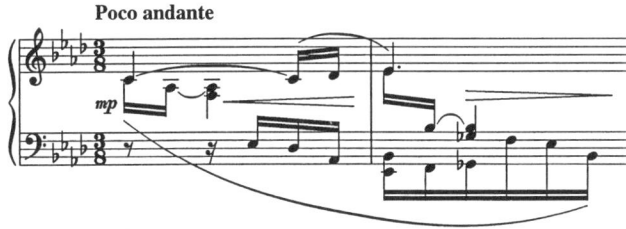

Example 5.1c 'Chelsea Reach'

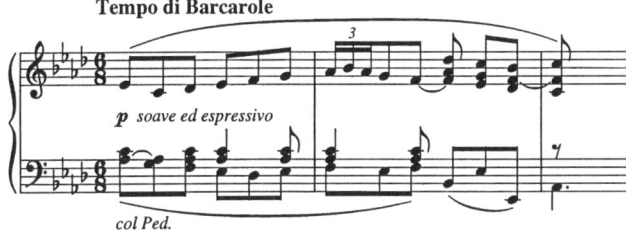

These works have other shared sensibilities: all three have strong melodies and lilting bass lines, they make extensive use of a triplet rhythm, and they have comparably calm closing bars. In 'Chelsea Reach' the water idea is more extensively explored and Ireland makes subtle use of ties and rests to create the impression of movement and of ebb and flow.

What marks 'Chelsea Reach' as something different from the enclosed, static, country pieces is its more extended structure, greater development of the melodic material and much richer chords. Structurally, 'Chelsea Reach' builds on the forms of the two violin sonatas in that it is an amalgam of modified sonata principle and an organically evolving rhapsody. Aspects of sonata principle can be seen in the tonalities and in the presentation of thematic material. The outer parts of the work, the exposition and the short recapitulation (starting at bar 103), are firmly rooted in A flat major, with the rich, chromatic excursions always contained. There are two main themes presented early in the piece, the first more fundamental to the evolution of the piece than the second. This emanates from the ^5^3^4^5 pattern much used by Ireland (Example 5.2).

Example 5.2

The second theme is one that belongs to Ireland's pastoral: an expansive, lilting melodic pattern with an anacrusis, similar to melodies appearing in *The Towing Path* and the Second Violin Sonata (Example 5.3).

Example 5.3

But the first part of the piece is not just an exposition. The first subject is really a little two-bar motif that is developed and developed again, either in its entirety or fragmented: the descending parallel chords of bar 2 (at this point first inversions) become a significant feature. Ireland prepares the way to the middle part of the piece by way of more repeating parallel triads in bars 60–61, now root position chords, used previously in a different format in 'The island spell'.

The development section (from bar 68 to bar 102) is much freer and less controlled, its function to rhapsodize, to move from repose and solemnity to ecstatic reverie. Here the opening theme is shifted to the middle of the texture and transformed into a Mixolydian tune, first on B, in bar 78 on D♭ and in bar 88 on B again. Freely moving parallel chords, for example at bar 74, separate these presentations, and perhaps have affiliations with the impressionistic qualities in the works of the Chelsea artists with whom Ireland empathized. This central section concludes with a descending bass line (from bar 99) that leads the way to a short recapitulation and brief six-bar coda, in which the main theme is presented one last time in the tonic key.

As a way of enhancing the barcarolle effect, throughout 'Chelsea Reach' Ireland inserts moments of stasis, where oscillations and repetitions check the harmonic movement of the work, while maintaining the pulsing of the oar (Example 5.4).

Example 5.4

These moments of stasis are a feature of the London works, and give a sense of repose, of location, of belonging. But unlike the country pieces, points of rest are just that – brief and ephemeral – rather than complete periods of repose in one place. It is perhaps the sense of expansiveness and power, created through the use of thick chords and spacious textures, that makes the Thames different from and grander than places in Ireland's other water pieces.

The second movement of the *London Pieces* was 'Ragamuffin', and then, in 1920, Ireland added a third piece, 'Soho forenoons'. Time as well as place is specified in 'Soho forenoons', in a complex maze of meanings. The piece is located in London, but it is not a very English Soho. The very title, with its substitution of 'forenoon' for 'morning' displaces and estranges. 'Forenoon' was a word much used by poets writing in the second half of the nineteenth and early part of the twentieth centuries, and it is likely that Ireland's use of the term is a literary reference of some sort. The most plausible link is with Walt Whitman, who used the term extensively in *Leaves of Grass*, a work that Ireland was reading in February 1920, the month in which he wrote 'Soho forenoons'.

The subsequent instruction 'quasi Tambourine' is a further signal, this time that this is a Soho viewed as a French quarter, a composite of myriad images, gaiety tinged with wistfulness, reality with unreality. When Ireland first came to live in London, Soho maintained a number of French restaurants and cafés, and supported French pharmacies, grocery shops, bakeries and patisseries. The area had had a strong French history, ever since French Huguenots settled in the area in the 1680s, opening many French chapels, including *L'Église des Grecs* in Hog Lane and *La Patente* in Berwick Street. By the early part of the seventeenth century, 40 per cent of Soho's residents were French. This trend continued, and in the eighteenth century it became a centre for craftsmen, among them Augustin Courtauld. In the nineteenth century yet more French refugees fled to Soho.

Ireland would not only have known this French aspect of the area, but would also have read some of the evocations of a French Soho in literature. In the latter part of the nineteenth century and early part of the twentieth, there were many poems and other writings about the place, including the first of Verlaine's 'Streets', published in 1874 after journeys to London in the company of Rimbaud, during which he visited Soho. This poem is ambiguous, a song of a Soho street-woman, with the recurring refrain 'Dansons la gigue!' ('Let's dance the jig!'), but it also has personal overtones. While French writers were visiting London and capturing in verse the images they saw, English writers were superimposing an ambience of Frenchness on to their capital, in works such as Lord Alfred Douglas' 'Impression de Nuit', a celebration of the glittering aspects of the city. Ireland must also have been once again influenced by the work of Arthur Machen. From his early days living in London, Machen regularly walked in Soho, exploring its private as well as its public face. His relationship with the place is complex, and for him, too, it was both a place of reality and a place of fiction. Thomas de Quincey wrote his *Confessions of an English Opium Eater* in Soho, a work read by Machen and featured in his *Hill of Dreams*. For Machen, writing in 1895, Soho was a magical, foreign quarter, which might provoke an encounter or reveal marvellous secrets:

> They walked down a sober street and turned into what seemed a narrow passage past an iron-barred gate thrown back. The passage was paved with flagstones, and decorated with handsome shrubs in pots on either side, and the shadow of the high walls made a coolness which was very agreeable after the hot breath of the sunny street. Presently the passage opened out into a tiny square, a charming place, a morsel of France transplanted into the heart of London. High walls rose on every side, covered with glossy creepers, flower-beds beneath were gay with nasturtiums, and marigolds, and odorous mignonette, and in the centre of the square a fountain, hidden by greenery, sent a cool shower continually plashing into the basin beneath.

(Machen, 1926: 27–8)

Similarly for Ireland, Soho was a place of the imagination as well as of reality, and there were many historical and literary reasons why he should have been inclined to think of it as French. 'Soho forenoons' also has French musical links, and the piece is permeated with tinges of Debussy. Most apparent are the connections with Debussy's piano prelude with the English title 'Minstrels'. Ireland's instruction 'quasi Tambourine', is possibly a reference to Debussy's own 'quasi tambouro' in 'Minstrels', but could equally imply a transformation of the French dance, the 'tambourin'. Perhaps somewhat obscurely, there are also connections with Debussy's *Gigues* (1909–12), which was inspired by memories of visits to England, and which quotes from the Northumbrian folk song, 'The Keel Row'. This tune had already been used by Debussy's friend Charles Bordes (1863–1909) in his 1890 setting of Verlaine's 'Streets': so we have a Frenchman setting a French poem about an English city, taking an

English (Tyneside) folk melody to enhance the image. With Ireland we have an Englishman writing a piano piece about an English city, using French references to turn it into a foreign place.

'Soho forenoons' uses a ternary structure to contain a sequence of images of aspects of Soho, rather as 'Minstrels' is a succession of images of aspects of the characters it invokes. This is a morning perambulation around the area, its passing sights and sounds drifting in and out of the piece. The outer A sections (1–31 and 58–106) first establish and then return to the central face of Soho, a quarter in which reverie and gaiety co-exist. The air of dislocation and evasiveness is created by the opening Dorian modality on A and by the haunting melodic qualities of the main theme (Example 5.5a). This theme is a Dorian tune with a very simple, contrary-moving bass line. The emphasis on the F♯ creates a mood of wistfulness. There are two parts to this tune, the second (5.5b) derived from the first, but with the melancholy lightened, primarily through the use of offbeat accompaniment patterns in the manner of Ireland's vernacular character pieces, to replace the opening ebbing accompaniment.

Example 5.5a

Example 5.5b

The notion of moving images is enhanced by the use of marked, but subtle harmonic twists away from the opening modality, such as the augmented chord in bar 5 and the passage in bar 14, which shares features with Debussy's alternating major / minor thirds in 'Minstrels'. Ireland's own Soho 'minstrels' (Soho also had a strong history as an area where street musicians, instrument makers and music printers settled, particularly in Golden Square) appear in the opening A section. These are characterized through a hurdy-gurdy drone figure that appears at bar 16 (Example 5.6) and also through mimetic movement in a staccato offbeat motif featuring acciaccaturas, again influenced by Debussy (Example 5.7).

Example 5.6

Example 5.7

The central B section (bars 32–57) moves to Ireland's favoured diminished fifth key relationship, in this case E flat, and differs from its enclosing sections in that it contains new motifs, none of which appear in the outer A sections. It opens with a moment of stasis, with repeated bass chords under minor sixths (Example 5.8).

Example 5.8

The person at walk has stopped for a moment, and faint sounds and glimpses of the essence of this Soho mingle at the start of this section. Bars 35–7 hint at the minstrels, before the climax of the work occurs in bar 43. This bar contains the kernels of a motif (Example 5.9) that was soon developed by Ireland and used as a musical symbol of Passion. At this stage it is a new part of his technical vocabulary, its rather muted appearance here just a part of the Soho saunter.

Example 5.9

The other motif in this section is a vernacular theme similar to that of *Merry Andrew* (Example 5.10), its repeated, drum-like bass pattern akin to the bass of the French tambourin.

Example 5.10

At the return of the A music, the main theme is first on A♭, returning to A for its second half, in bar 67. It is repeated in bar 74, but is now transformed into something more ardent, the melancholy accented and combined with the offbeats and staccato street musician elements. The latter part of the piece is a wonderful kaleidoscope of images, starting with a single repeated bass note (bar 90), again in the spirit of 'Minstrels', parallel chords referring back to 'Chelsea Reach' and the minstrels taking over to end definitively in A major.

In 1922, two years after Ireland wrote 'Soho forenoons', Machen's book *The Secret Glory* was published, after a wait of some fifteen years. In this work Machen expanded on the image of Soho as an unreal, French place, with a vivid description of an adventure in Soho, in which the real Café de l'Europe, where Machen was a regular diner, was transformed into the 'Café Restaurant: au château de Chinon'. It is quite possible that Ireland had already read some of this work, as it was published in instalments much earlier. Ireland himself continued to view Soho as a strange place, and there is a mysterious reference in one of the Thompson letters to a 'pilgrimage in the West End, & the vision (Satanic or otherwise) which attracted us both' (KT: 1 March 1940).

Having a base in the city for sixty years meant that many of Ireland's closest friends were London dwellers. While his circle revolved mainly around the obvious musician acquaintances, it also included sculptors, such as Percy Bentham, and people associated with the church (those mentioned in Chapter 2, including Bobby Glassby, Charlie Markes, Kenneth Thompson and Arthur Miller). Some of these London acquaintances are embodied in Ireland's music.

There is a vernacular strand in Ireland's output that is present in 'Soho forenoons', *Ballade of London Nights* and *A London Overture*, but which is manifest most completely in 'Ragamuffin' and *Merry Andrew*, which are both in the same key of E major. These two works belong to the light music tradition of portraying town people, people of the street, in vignettes of a jaunty, cocky nature. Ireland's ability to understand and depict London characters in this way was partly influenced by his professional connections with the music hall. One of his first part-time jobs was as accompanist to Charles Coborn (1852–1945), famous for 'Two lovely black eyes', and renowned for his 'character' performances as cabby, waterman, costermonger and 'French reciter'. It appears that Ireland played for some of these performances at the Holborn Restaurant, though there is little information on this association.

'Ragamuffin' is the central number of *London Pieces*. Its anecdotal origins lie in an actual encounter with a dirty but swaggering urchin, who 'jauntily whistled a perky tune' in Chelsea's streets (Searle, 1979: 51–2). However, Ireland's urchin is also part of a London tradition, and in particular the tradition of Dickens. Ireland read much Dickens, including *Dombey and Son*, *Nicholas Nickleby* and *Oliver Twist*, and the boys of the streets portrayed in these novels, above all the Artful Dodger, share the jaunty characteristics of Ireland's ragamuffin:

> He was a snub-nosed, flat-browed, common-faced boy enough; and as dirty a juvenile as one would wish to see; but he had about him all the airs and manners of a man. He was short of his age, with rather bow legs, and little, sharp, ugly eyes. His hat was stuck on the top of his head so lightly, that it threatened to fall off every moment – and would have done so, very often, if the wearer had not had a knack of every now and then giving his head a sudden twitch, which brought it back to its old place again. He wore a man's coat, which reached nearly to his heels. He had turned the cuffs back, half-way up his arm, to get his hands out of the sleeves: apparently with the ultimate view of thrusting them into the pockets of his corduroy trousers; for there he kept them. He was, altogether, as roystering and swaggering a young gentleman as ever stood four feet six, or something less, in his bluchers.
>
> (Dickens, 1975: 100)

The basis of 'Ragamuffin' is mimetic. It is music about movement: a compact character sketch introduced with an upward flourish, heralding the entrance of the ragamuffin. The whole piece stems from one tiny two-bar motif, which has the same melodic outline as opened 'Chelsea Reach' (Example 5.11).

Example 5.11

The sixteen bars that make up the first section of the piece are about anticipation and resolution, question and answer, one gesture followed by another. The two-bar motif is used to create layers of antecedent and consequent phrases, cameos within cameos. This section of the work could be seen as one sixteen-bar phrase, but it is also two eight-bar phrases, four four-bar phrases and eight two-bar phrases (Example 5.12).

Example 5.12

The piece evolves through the extension and repetition of phrases, and by the transformation of the melody into an inner tune with a brittle accompaniment (bar 25). The harmonic basis of Ireland's vernacular style is diatonicism coloured with lush romantic chords, and here the strong key centres are spiced with added sixths and dominant ninths. The detailed characterization of the ragamuffin is through carefully pointed articulations and a certain pertness in the way in which phrases are shaped (the chromatic twist in bar 5, the cheek of the inverted interval in bar 12 and the contrast between staccato and legato in bars 13 and 14, for example). This piece again has connections with Debussy's

'Minstrels', such as the abundant presence of staccato markings, the use of contrary motion and parallel chords (bars 53–6) and the repeated minor seconds (Example 5.13, bars 73–5). The coda (the last eight bars of the piece) cocks a musical snook by introducing a new, frivolous idea, a brilliant glissando and a pianissimo final chord.

Example 5.13

This ragamuffin may have been real, but he was also part of a historical and literary tradition. Ireland's interest in the lived past of the streets of London took him back from the contemporary music hall to its roots in the much older street-cry tradition, dating from about 1600, when vendors and itinerants were first depicted on broadsheets. For artists such as Marcellus Laroon, whose *Cryes of the City of London Drawne after the Life* appeared in 1687, pictures of the various criers were not just of 'types', but were based on actual known figures. Although there is no record of Ireland reading about street criers or studying relevant pictures, he must have known something of the tradition to have produced his short piano piece, *Merry Andrew*, in 1918, occupying the same part of London as his 'Ragamuffin', though this time the figure is entirely historical:

> Then entered the Conjurer of the whole Company, Merry *Andrew* ... the first thing that he undertook to give a singular Instance of his Cleanliness was by blowing his Nose upon the People, who were mightily pleas'd, and Laugh'd heartily at the Jest. Then, after he had pick'd out from the whole *Dramatick* Assembly a Man of most admirable Acquirements in the Art of *Tittle-Tattle*, and fit to Confabulate with the Witty and Intelligible Mr. *Andrews*, he begins a *Tale of a Tub*, which he Illustrates with abundance of Ugly Faces, and Mimical Actions; for in that lay the chief of the Comedy ... The Epilogue of Merry *Andrew's* Farce, was, *Walk in Gentlemen, and take your places whilst you may have 'em; the Candles are all Lighted, and we are just a going to begin*: Then Screwing his Body into an ill-Favour'd Posture, agreeable to his Intellects, he struts along.
>
> (Shesgreen, 1990: 180)

During the seventeenth century, London's markets and fairs attracted a vast array of hawkers and popular entertainers who performed on the streets alongside the sellers. Merry Andrews were the descendants of court jesters and jugglers, travelling entertainers earning their living in the London

53

5.2 Merry Andrew, as depicted by Marcellus Laroon, 1687

markets and at special gatherings such as Bartholomew Fair, their role eventually to be displaced from the streets to the stage of the music hall. They worked primarily as clowns and fools, drawing an audience by gesturing and distorting their bodies. Sometimes dressed as Punch or as an ass, and they performed extravagant, menacing facial contortions. The other function of the Merry Andrew was to act as musician to rope dancers and the like, in this role behaving more as a benevolent buffoon than a gyrating grotesque. Traditionally the Merry Andrew had a split personality, the happy outside masking a sad inside, rather like an English Pierrot figure. He went by other names, including Zany, Jack Pudding, Pickle Herring and Tom Fool.

An interest in everyday life and especially that which tends toward the lowlife, is a peculiarly English trait, finding expression in Hogarth's engravings, Dickens' novels and in church misericords, intricately carved corbels depicting characters, animals and plants. Certain of Ireland's works, and particularly the London pieces, are part of this historical tradition. His *Merry Andrew* is a detailed sketch of a carnivalesque character, located within a popular culture.

The piece is in a ternary format, and is essentially monothematic, with the B material derived from A, the coda alternating music from both A and B. This *Merry Andrew* does not seem to have a split personality, appearing quite definitely in jesting mode. Ireland's disjointed, gesticulating clown is clearly recognizable, characterized through signs peculiar to the Merry Andrew, but also shares some traits (a simple harmonic language, a situation primarily within a sharp major tonality and an abundance of staccato, offbeat patterns) with the London 'Ragamuffin' and the Puck of a later piano piece, 'Puck's birthday'.

The pivotal and most extensively worked theme is the opening motif, the face of the Merry Andrew (Example 5.14). Although the face remains constant, its contortions are effected through a series of subtle and detailed changes, in which pitches, rhythms and articulation markings are altered, two examples of which are shown in Example 5.15.

Example 5.14

Example 5.15

In the C major B section (bars 36–79) the gaps in the melody are filled in, the brittle buoyancy turned into a mesmeric undulation (Example 5.16).

Example 5.16

There are also smaller patterns affiliated to the Merry Andrew's antics. Skips are characterized by staccato notes and offbeat chords (bar 5), slides by an upward slur with hands in octaves (bar 9) and puppet-like oscillations by repeating, rocking, legato patterns (Example 5.17; bars 54–5). These oscillations have the same sense of stasis as the moments of rest in 'Chelsea Reach' and 'Soho forenoons'.

Example 5.17

Merry Andrew and the three *London Pieces* were all written within a three-year period. These four works included two straightforward characterizations and two representations of place. The 1920s saw Ireland move away from the London theme, but in the 1930s he returned to the subject, and produced two larger, narratological works, both of which consisted of more than one image. These two pieces, *Ballade of London Nights* and *A London Overture*, combine city and citizen, extroversion and introversion. Both have overt connections with other musical works, and both have a cloudy history.

Any analysis of *A London Overture* is complicated by the existence of an earlier piece. In 1934 Ireland wrote a work for brass band with the title *Comedy Overture*, commissioned by Herbert Whitely and John Henry Iles for that year's National Brass Band Championships. In 1936 he reworked this music for orchestra, giving it the new title *A London Overture*. Perhaps here, more than with any other work, the evolution of the piece and its title present ambiguities. Did Ireland write a piece for brass band with an orchestral work in mind? Or is *A London Overture* simply a reworking of the earlier piece? What is certain is that the two works are extremely similar. Although the scoring, and thus textures and musical detail, underwent radical alterations, they share the same structure, the same harmonic scheme and the same melodic material. The fact that the brass band parts were written in B flat, for B flat instruments, and that the new piece remained written at the same pitches might imply that Ireland conceived the work as *sounding* in B flat; in other words, that the band piece was an early version of a piece that was forming in Ireland's mind. A letter written to Edwin Evans (Figure 5.3) also carries the implication that *A London Overture* replaced the *Comedy Overture*.

With Ireland, it was often the case that a piece was completed before being given a title, although a specific meaning underlay the compositional process. This was seen with the naming of the three movements of *Sarnia*, the meaning of each of which was quite clear in Ireland's mind, though the titles underwent changes and all came after the music. In the case of *Comedy Overture* and *A London Overture*, it would seem likely that the music, whether in brass band or orchestral versions, was connected with London; there are simply two manifestations of the same vernacular substance. This is borne out by Ireland's statement that he wished *A London Overture* to be considered as one of his London pieces, but more obviously by the fact that this piece, with its contrasting moods of gaiety and sentimental lyricism and its major tonality, has similarities with aspects of his other London works.

A London Overture also shares sensibilities with London works by other composers, notably with Elgar's *Cockaigne*. At the time of writing *A London Overture*, the London theme was certainly topical, especially with writers of light music, and with American as well as English composers. There were new editions of Elizabethan street cries published in the 1920s and 1930s, and songs, including Edward German's (1862–1936) 'London town' (1926). There were dance numbers such as Tot Seymour's foxtrot *London Bridge is falling down* (1938), orchestral works such as Albert Ketèlbey's (1875–1959) *Cockney Suite* (1924) and show scores such as Ord Hamilton's *Bow Bells* (1932). But most significantly there were the works of Ireland's contemporary, Eric Coates (1886–1957), notably his three orchestral pieces, the *London Suite* (1933), the *London Bridge* march (1934) and *London Again* (1936). The Coates pieces in particular, given their appeal and their popular success, must have been tremendously influential. Ireland's work sits in the midst of all these works, and is thus part of a culture of 1920s and 1930s London-inspired musical expressions. But it is also the last of his own London pieces, the culmination of an interest that began in 1917, and it is a bringing together of different eras: the city of the turn of the century on to which he superimposes personal experiences of 1936.

5.3 Letter from Ireland to Edwin Evans, 11 October 1937

A London Overture opens with one of the thumbprints of Ireland's music, an upward flourish, of the type that heralded the entrance of the 'Ragamuffin'. The music which follows in this opening Andante moderato is introductory because of its unresolved harmonies and short motifs, notably the interval of a third, major or minor, which are developed as the piece unfolds. This material recurs during the course of the piece, used to separate the three main sections of the overture.

The two outer sections (bars 33–215 and 288–401), which are the main body of the piece, deploy sonata principle in terms of the melodic material and key schemes. The first theme, which dominates the piece, opens the Allegro brioso in bar 33. An early review of the work spent some time on the nature of this theme:

> The result is, if not a new 'Cockaigne', an attractive piece of music with a genuine Cockney tang about its main theme, of which Mr. Ireland writes, with the customary timidity of composers when avowing the source of their inspiration: 'It has been stated that the first four notes of the prinicipal theme were based on the word "Piccadilly" as called out by a bus conductor.'

> (*The Times*, 24 Sept. 1936: 10)

The vernacular, jaunty mood of this motif (Example 5.18), which really does seem to delineate the words 'Piccadilly', accords with the vernacular aspect of Ireland's music, as found in his other London works.

Example 5.18

The scoring of this section utilizes some of the classic hallmarks of British light music. Though Ireland's London feels less busy than that of Eric Coates, the influence of Coates is apparent in the bowed offbeats in the lower strings, the twinkling woodwind interjections, the prominent percussion, namely the jingles, all combined with a jaunty string melody emphasized with an acciacciatura (Figure 5.4). The scoring of this tune is highly effective, and the the woodwind ornaments (for example in bar 70), the repeating patterns that start at bar 290, and the pointed use of xylophone in bars 372–4, all serve to create an air of exuberance, similar to that of the 1930 Piano Concerto.

The juxtaposition of the raffish and the lyrical had already been seen in the piano *London Pieces*, and thus the second theme of *A London Overture*, starting at bar 136, by contrast with the jauntiness of the first, is an expansive outpouring, a nostalgic reminder of a bygone London (Example 5.19).

Example 5.19

The presentation of first, 'vernacular' subject and second, 'affirmative', rather hymn-like subject is followed by a brief reference to the 'Piccadilly' theme and then a return to the transitional, dividing material, which takes the piece into a new section.

There are complex, personal associations at play in *A London Overture*. This piece is not just about the city as a place, but also about the people of London. The central section of the work moves to an entirely different plane. In both the brass band and orchestral versions this central section quotes from Schumann's song 'Widmung', which, in a sense, is a *donné* introduced into the work in the light music tradition. As with 'Soho forenoons' the layers of meaning are difficult to unpick. Schumann's song opens with the words 'Du meine Seele, du mein Herz' ('You my soul, you my heart'). Ireland quotes the melody of these words directly, using Schumann's key of A flat (Example 5.20).

Example 5.20 (above) Melody of Schumann's 'Widmung'
              (below) The 'Widmung' tune in *A London Overture*

[Innig, lebhaft]

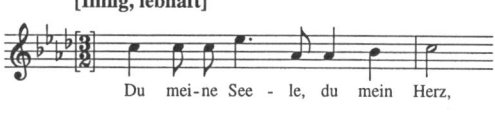

Du mei-ne See - le, du mein Herz,

Meno mosso

5.4 The opening of the Allegro brioso section of *A London Overture*, bars 33–44

It would seem strange to quote music from such a passionate, personal song, were it not to have some associated meaning. There is also another motif that permeates this section of both *Comedy Overture* and *A London Overture*, a little four-note pattern that was prevalent in the second movement of the Piano Concerto (Example 5.21).

Example 5.21

In 1934, three months before the first performance of *Comedy Overture*, Ireland suffered a rift with his protégée and friend, Helen Perkin (1909–96), dedicatee of the Piano Concerto, and it may well be that this section was some sort of reference to this loss. However, Lewis Foreman (1990: 3–4) has also remarked on the fact that the quotation may have been a reference to a popular hit that singer Richard Tauber (1891–1948) had with Schumann's song under the title *Hearts Desire*; 'The heart's desire' itself the title of one of Ireland's most poignant Housman settings.

There are further layers of complication. The score of *A London Overture* bears the dedication, 'In memory of Percy G. Bentham, Sculptor and Friend – died June 1936'. Bentham was one of many professional sculptors working in Chelsea and a close friend of Ireland (as seen in Plate 14). He moved into The Studio, 8 Gunter Grove, in 1926, a few doors away from Ireland, and knew the composer from this time. During this period, according to Ireland, they 'met almost daily' (EI: 17 June 1936). His early, futile death affected Ireland deeply, as expressed at some length in a letter to Thompson:

> It is perfectly appalling, and even terrifying, how, when one is in the fifties, one's whole world so badly goes to pieces. People die – I have just lost my very best & most intimate friend – a man several years younger than myself – you met him – Bentham, the Sculptor … he was one of the most vital & energetic people I have ever met – & the finest companion – a real man, & a true friend – well, he died, in a few days, of blood poison … I have not yet got over it & shall never get over the loss of this friend. The loss of him is inconceivable to me – & so far as I can see, his death was absolutely casual & unnecessary …
>
> (KT: 16 July 1936)

The central section of *A London Overture* may thus also be an elegy for Percy Bentham. To mark this, Ireland superimposed on to his Schumannscape a grieving horn solo. While the greater part of this was not present in the *Comedy Overture*, the latter part of the solo itself picks up more of Schumann's song, as did a similar horn line in the *Comedy Overture*, adding the music that accompanied the words 'du meine Wonn', – o du mein Schmerz' ('you my bliss, o you my pain') (Example 5.22).

Example 5.22   'Widmung', followed by the horn solo from *A London Overture*

This central elegy is followed by a further version of the transitional material and a recapitulation of the two main themes, ending with a joyous rout. *A London Overture* is a complex mixing of ideas, and the last of Ireland's London pieces. There was one other, earlier, 'London' work, which has an equally enigmatic genesis and which also mixes ideas. This is the unfinished, and tougher work, *Ballade of London Nights*. The date of composition of this piece is unknown. It is catalogued as 1930, though Norah Kirby claimed that it was written in 1913 (NK to GD: 6 March 1969). Quite possibly neither of these dates is correct, as the piece is really an amalgamation of the essential characteristics of the three *London Pieces*, drawing together the shadowy morning scene of 'Soho forenoons', the vernacular aspects of 'Ragamuffin' and the barcarolle elements of 'Chelsea Reach'. More than any other of Ireland's city pieces, this is a real mixing of reality and fantasy, a dreamscape in the tradition of the Symbolist writings of Le Gallienne, Symons and James Thomson. Ireland was an avid reader of those poets who depicted London in verse, in particular Dowson and Symons. The latter's relationship with Ireland is far-reaching. He was acquainted with Alexander Ireland, when John Ireland was a young boy, and his verse permeates the composer's output, as has already been seen in Chapter 4.

Symons travelled to France in 1889, and in the 1890s met Mallarmé and Verlaine. Like them, he used contemplative, atmospheric, impressionistic and shadowy language. As an Englishman he was a frequenter of the music hall, and in *London: A Book of Aspects* (1909) he wrote of the appeal of London lying in its sensation and artifice, mentioning the ballet at the Alhambra and the Empire, music hall and the world of illusion. His poems capture the immediate and the tacky, but also the distant impression: while 'The Street-Singer' portrays a ballad-singer, 'Nocturne' is a Whistlerian impression of the river.

While there are clearly connections between *Ballade of London Nights* and Symons' writings, these are elusive. Ireland had read Symons' *Days and Nights*, and very likely other of his works, so it is quite possible that Symons' 1895 collection of poems, *London Nights*, may have influenced Ireland's choice of title for his piece. *Ballade of London Nights* emanates from the same school as Symons' poetry. The themes of wandering in the city – tawdry contrasted with fresh – occur in both figures' works: Symons' poem 'April Midnight' is Ireland-like in its notion of being lost in the London night:

> Side by side through the streets at midnight,
> Roaming together,
> > Through the tumultuous night of London,
> > In the miraculous April weather.

(in Holdsworth, 1989: 35)

Ballade of London Nights was published posthumously, with the opening section repeated as an ending for the work, as advocated by Alan Rowlands. It is a mingling of images, a song of London nights spent both in Chelsea and in Soho, nights which move from tranquillity into chaos. As in 'Chelsea Reach', the opening bars, with their lilting rhythms and repeating patterns, play out a barcarolle, though this one is more contemplative and wistful, without the rich spaciousness of 'Chelsea Reach' (Example 5.23).

   Although the piece starts in B minor, there are modal implications from the outset, in that the dominant chord appears in its minor format, and there are Dorian hints in the manner of 'Soho forenoons' from the G♯s in bars 5 and 6. With its oscillations and repetitions, as in the opening left-hand ostinato (bars 1–10) and the passage from bars 22–8, for example, this opening section has the same sense of location as the other London pieces, until the repose is upset, most conclusively by a C minor[7] chord with an appoggiatura (bar 42), precipitating movement towards disturbance. By bar 80 there is an actual, distorted reference to 'Chelsea Reach' (Example 5.24), followed by further rhythmic disequilibrium and an eventual shift away from barcarolle.

   From bar 98 there is a movement away from Chelsea to Soho. By bar 108 the material of 'Soho forenoons' is echoed, in that the music is modal (Dorian), there is the same contrary motion between melody and bass line, and there is an oscillating inner line, here picking out a pentatonic scale (Example 5.25).

   However, this Soho is swiftly transfigured into a wild place of brilliant piano figurations and further references to the distorted 'Chelsea Reach'. In bars 139–40, two bars of Dorian scales are followed in bars 141–2 by two bars of contrary motion triads, which lead to a passage fusing the vernacular staccato rhythms of 'Ragamuffin' with modal delineations (Example 5.26).

Example 5.23

Example 5.24

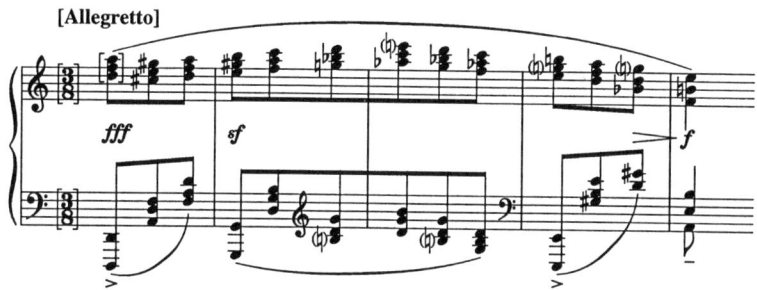

Example 5.25

Example 5.26

The piece disintegrates into a simultaneous sounding of pentatonic and whole-tone scales. From bar 161 there is a reiteration of the 'warped' barcarolle that was heard from bar 42, though here the warping is much more comprehensive. Over first a C pedal, and then an F♯ pedal, the barcarolle theme appears with melodic and harmonic twists. It was at the end of this page that Ireland's manuscript stopped. Rowlands' decision to complete the work with a return to the opening material was entirely apposite. Aside from the fact that the F♯ pedal suggests this, and that in any case Ireland often chose to return to his opening material, in this particular piece the arch shape suggests this move. The only problem with this interpretation is the literal repetition of the A section, as Ireland would undoubtedly have made transformations in his recapitulation.

Ireland's London was a real, experienced place, and it is evident from the music that this was a city for which he felt deep affection. But it was also a fictional and remembered city of multiple impressions, of gaslight, hansom cabs, spattering hoofs and street urchins. The city is as much a romanticized place as was Ireland's country. It is Machen's city in that it yields surprises, Dickens' in that it is a landscape inhabited by urban types. It has the shifting Soho skyline and memories of Bartholomew Fair. It is the magical city of Peter Pan, the unreal aesthete and the Alhambra, but also a place of real human joy and despair. Whereas Ireland's country has clearly defined seasons, his city does not, and instead has only night and day. In some ways it is a denser, more difficult place to penetrate, in that the music is laden with associations. Whereas in the country it was the landscape itself with which Ireland felt affinity, in London it was primarily to people that he was drawn, and where he met those who were to become his personal passions.

Chapter 6

Love

The prevailing image of John Ireland is that preserved in portrait photographs: an old man, sedate, formal and living with his housekeeper, 'a modest English gentleman, retiring and reticent' (Pirie, 1979b: 18). But this is an image of a man in the latter years of his life. There was a younger Ireland, who loved ardently yet without ultimate fulfilment, and whose personal passions remain elusive. His music expresses a gamut of emotions associated with love, from hedonistic, ecstatic outpourings to a cramped, tortured angst. As with most of Ireland's works, the music about love is autobiographical, linked to people, places and literature.

Ireland had a handful of close friends, to whom he revealed the more private side of his nature. His lonely childhood must have contributed to his later difficulties with forging attachments, and his siblings appear to have had similar problems: his elder brother Alleyne remained single, and his sister Ethel married, but was divorced, and spent her last years as a gambler and drinker. Ireland had relationships with women, and was even married, albeit briefly and unsuccessfully. But throughout his life his involvement with women was problematical. Sometimes his feelings towards them were merely ambivalent, but he could also be positively vitriolic. Of his three sisters he remained in touch only with Ethel: in all the surviving archive material there are no references of any note to either Lucy or Alice, and it is almost as though they never existed. With Ethel, however, he certainly enjoyed a warm friendship. They lodged together in London as students, and exchanged letters over many years, in which Ireland was clearly prepared to reveal some of his more intimate thoughts. He had very few women friends, and those with whom he did have some sort of rapport, such as Sylvia Townsend Warner and Anna Instone, the one-time head of BBC gramophone programmes, and those to whom he dedicated pieces, such as Mrs Mignot, a Guernsey friend, never seemed to have played a major part in his life. His greater desires were for other men, and particularly for much younger men.

Just as the letters to Kenneth Thompson reveal Ireland's fluctuating and contradictory relationship with the Anglican Church, so they contain allusions, both veiled and explicit, to his homosexuality. In the latter part of his life Ireland made increasing reference to lost opportunities, fantasies and retrospective longings, with his yearnings for beautiful youths ever more clearly formulated, both in words and in music. There are also affirmations of homosexual leanings in his choice of reading matter, and in fact Ireland's homosexuality appears to have been played out as much through literature and in fantasy as in reality. It appears that for him, the essence of love was infatuation with someone much younger and impressionable, who in turn had an adulatory infatuation with him. Thus Ireland could maintain a degree of independence in the knowledge that alliances of this type were unlikely to be sustained. We do not know if his relationships with his closest companions were sexual ones. And there is no evidence of his having had a sexual relationship with another man, though this would in any case have been prohibited in his day, secrets closely guarded, confessions never committed to paper.

Ireland's loves and friendships permeate his music. The poems he set were often about hidden or frustrated love: for example, Samuel Daniels' 'Love is a sickness full of woes', which he set to music in 1921, talks of love as 'a torment of the mind, / A tempest everlasting'. The theme of reminiscence is strongest in this area of Ireland's output, with aptly titled works such as the piano piece 'For remembrance' and the song 'Remember'. His ballad-like setting of Dowson's 'When I am old' begs the former lover to remember 'nothing of you and me but yesterday'. The church works are a curious mixture of the erotic and the chaste, and homoerotic associations inevitably colour Ireland's pagan works, linked as they were to a *fin-de-siècle* movement that linked homosexuality with paganism, with Pan as a figurehead and symbol of repressed desire. The nature poems also have sexual connotations. They are often solitary dreams played out against a rural backdrop, but there are also shared idylls, as in 'Earth's call'. And then there are works that are overtly about love in its various manifestations: sentiment and nostalgia, pain and denial, joy and achievement. These are mainly the songs of the period 1920–27, which, as Banfield has pointed out, are a 'personal testament' (Banfield, 1985: 167), their meaning conveyed through consistent musical responses and through motivic symbols.

In terms of modes of expressions of love, probably the most significant of the poets favoured by Ireland was A.E. Housman, whose works he set as songs and also used as a source of quotations to attach to piano pieces. Although by dint of his lyrical verse Housman's poems had already proved a popular stimulus for other English composers, his writings held a particularly personal appeal for Ireland. Housman's own complex character has similarities with that of the composer. Both men grew up in a comfortable middle-class family, and both lost their mother at a young age; Ireland at fourteen, Housman at twelve. Housman was a private figure with few close friends and as with Ireland, his homosexuality was concealed. Ireland's music is autobiographical in the sense that Housman's poetry 'has tended to become a kind of cryptic diary, as important for its gaps and omissions as for anything it actually does say' (Jebb, 1992: 12). Housman's poetic world is an imaginary landscape inhabited by dream figures, but it is also a real place. Similarly, Ireland's world mixes imagined and real elements.

Ireland's settings of Housman's verse are among his most highly charged, intimate works. His first use of Housman's verse was in 1917, when he set no. X of *A Shropshire Lad,* omitting the first two stanzas and altering the title from 'March' to 'The heart's desire'. The song is one of his most perfect in structural and lyrical terms. The gently contained, yearning elements of the song, as expressed in the melody's flattened sevenths and appoggiaturas, yield to outpourings of passion, with strings of four-note chords at the words 'the heart's desire' and again at 'Ah, let not only mine be vain'. The mood here is confident, the conclusion a positive one. The next Housman setting came two years later, in 1919, when he used in its entirety another poem from *A Shropshire Lad*, no. XXXIX, giving it the title 'Hawthorn time'. The last Housman piece was 'A Grecian lad', a 1941 piano piece rewritten from an early work of *c.* 1906, and prefaced with a quotation from *A Shropshire Lad.* Between these first and last works there were two major song-cycles, which will be discussed within this chapter.

Another recurring literary influence was the poetry of William Blake, whose words appear in solo song as prefatory material, and in unison songs and SATB part-songs. One of the early part-songs, in *c.* 1910, was an setting of Blake's 'Cupid', the words of which encapsulate Ireland's complex sexual personality. Cupid, the beautiful boy, induces both ecstasy and pain in those whom he hits with his arrows, while woman is quite definitely depicted in the poem as 'other', a separate entity. The last four lines of the poem, within which man is described as being 'pierced with cares and wounded with arrowy smarts' has resonances with Ireland's own personal torments.

Despite the problems and ambiguities outlined above, Ireland had a deep affection for the mother–child relationship, and for children generally, perhaps because of his own curtailed childhood, his long periods away from home while very young and the early death of his mother. Reminiscences and anecdotes portray him as someone who liked young children, with whom he had a rapport. Like Britten, though on a much less ambitious scale, Ireland wrote a number of short, functional songs for children's voices. These were lyrical works, popular with those for whom they were intended. He also set words whose subject matter was childhood, such as 'Bed in summer' (1912–13), the first of Robert Louis Stevenson's *Child's Garden of Verses*, a volume of poems for and about children. Ireland's version was published both as a unison song, and for voice and piano. As was mentioned in Chapter 4, it has the characteristics of Ireland's pastoral pieces, and is musically among the simplest of Ireland's works, with its straightforward three-stanza format, diatonic harmonies and restricted melodic line. The same deliberate simplicity imbues the two sets of piano pieces written for children, the *Three Dances* (1913) and *Leaves from a Child's Sketchbook* (1918), and the same artless quality pervades the song-cycle *Mother and Child.*

Mother and Child (1918) is a collection of eight settings of poems from Christina Rossetti's *Sing-Song: A Nursery Rhyme Book.* The directness of Rossetti's poetic language and the simple rhyming schemes appealed to Ireland, as did the images of domesticity which pepper her poetry, the antithetical representations of control and passion and the frequently dreamy tone. This was the first time he set her poetry. The eight short songs chart the passage from birth to death in a sequence of simple, lilting pieces. Ireland was to return to words by Rossetti several times. In January of the following year he wrote 'May flowers', a song for two voice parts and piano, for Thomas Dunhill's niece, Lillian Dunhill, who died of pneumonia at the age of twelve. One of Ireland's finest responses to a Rossetti text was in 1925, 'What are you thinking of', a setting of a poem from her *Mother and Child* collection.

Besides the recurring literary expressions of sentiments associated with love, there are strong autobiographical undercurrents in Ireland's music. His attraction to the beauty of youth found an obvious outlet in his connections with the Church. His posts as organist brought him in contact with young men and boys who, in a number of cases, had a significant impact on his life and output. The first of the important choirboys was Charles (Charlie) Stafford Markes (see Plate 5). The son of an alcoholic, living in very poor circumstances, he joined St Luke's as a chorister in 1908, exchanging singing for duties as Ireland's deputy at the organ when his voice broke in 1915. Markes, whose uncle was a chorister at Southwark Cathedral and at St Anne's, Soho, was a natural musician, and was taken on as a piano pupil by Ireland *c.* 1911 (GD, 1). Ireland, with assistance from St Luke's, also contributed to Markes' school fees. The two gradually developed a close friendship, and the boy spent much time in his teacher's company. There were many evenings when Markes listened to what Ireland had composed that day, and commented on its effectiveness. This role was particularly important in the years 1915–18, with Markes having an input into the Rhapsody and 'Spring sorrow'.

Markes was called up in 1918. On his return to London in 1919 he found employment as a music hall artist. In 1920 a misunderstanding (a moment of misinterpretation as Ireland appeared to cut Markes in the street) led to the end of his friendship with Ireland, and this was not renewed until 1948. The rediscovered intimacy saw Markes once again working closely with Ireland, correcting the proofs of the score of *Satyricon* and preparing the editions of the early string quartets.

One of Markes' boyhood friends was Bobby Glassby (Robert McLean Glassby), a youth who joined St Luke's choir in about 1911 at the instigation of Markes. A few years later Ireland wrote what has become one of his most frequently performed pieces, 'The holy boy', ambiguous both in its conception and in its subsequent transformations. Ireland composed the piece in Chelsea in 1913, and it was originally published as the third of a set of four piano *Preludes,*

Plate 1   Alexander Ireland and John Ireland, Blackpool, 1886

Plate 2   Annie Nicholson Ireland

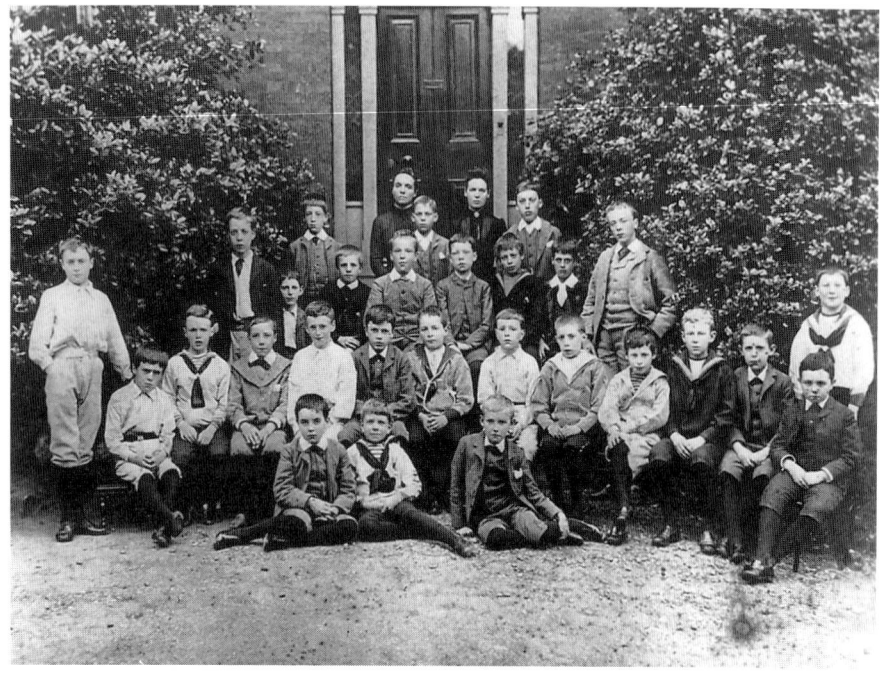

Plate 3 John Ireland at dame school, *c.* 1887. John Ireland seated front left.

Plate 4 John Ireland in his studio, Gunter Grove

Key: 4 Merly; 7 Charles Hindes (vestry clerk); 8 Hugh Otter-Barry (preacher); 13 W.H. Stewart; 14 A.R.L. Gardner (cleric); 15 Banting (caretaker); 17 Scarborough (I); 19 Carpenter (solo boy); 21 Hugh Bevan (eldest son of 32); 24 Crowe; 25 Motley (I); 26 Charles Markes; 27 Robert Glassby; 28 Lester (caretaker); 29 Beck (organ blower); 30 Capel C. Peacey (cleric); 31 Robinson (Chelsea solicitor and sidesman); 32 H. Bevan (Rector of Chelsea and Arch-Deacon of Middlesex); 35 John Ireland; 36 Scarborough (II); 37 Greenwood; 40 Bunce; 41 Motley (II).

Plate 5 St Luke's choir, *c.* 1908

Plate 6 Bobby Glassby, 1920

Plate 7 Arthur Miller, Norfolk, 1922

Plate 8 John Ireland, Norfolk Broads, 26 August 1922

Plate 9 John Ireland, Norfolk, 20 August 1922

Plate 10 Maiden Castle, Dorset, 1923

Plate 11 John Ireland, St Augustine's Well, Cerne Abbas, 1923

Plate 12 Arthur Miller in John Ireland's car, Dorset or Wiltshire, 1923

Plate 13 Thomas Dunhill, John Ireland, Lionel Tertis, Broadstairs, 1930s

Plate 14 Thomas Dugdale's painting, 'Lunch at the Chelsea Arts Club', 1933. John Ireland and Percy Bentham seated back left.

Plate 15 Helen Perkin, 1930s

Plate 16 Le Trépied dolmen, Le Catioroc, Guernsey

Ealing Studios present a great romantic adventure

"CHIPS" RAFFERTY & DAPHNE CAMPBELL in

The OVERLANDERS

Produced by MICHAEL BALCON   Written and Directed by HARRY WATT

Distributed by Eagle-Lion

Plate 17 Poster for *The Overlanders*, 1946

Plate 18 John Ireland in his studio, Rock Mill, *c.* 1955

Plate 19 Rock Mill, 1950s

Plate 20 Kenneth Thompson, John Ireland, Norah Kirby, c. late 1950s

between 'Obsession' and 'Fire of spring'. At first glance the piece is about Christmas and the birth of Christ, the 'holy boy'. It was written on Christmas Day and published in an early edition as a 'carol'. This meaning was perpetuated by Ireland in that he transcribed it for organ in 1919, making very few alterations to the notes, but giving it the fuller title *The Holy Boy (A Carol of the Nativity)* thus rendering it suitable for church performance. In 1938 he took the church association a stage further, when he turned it into a song with words by his friend Herbert Brown; and in 1941 transformed it again into its final form, an unaccompanied choral setting of Brown's poem, which is an unambiguous Christmas text, a simple carol about the 'Heav'nly Child'.

On one level, then, the piece is a Christmas piece of the utmost simplicity, vocal in its conception in that it is melody driven and falls into three distinct, related 'stanzas', which are themselves constructed from clear-cut modal phrases. However, there are other meanings at work here. 1913 was a significant year for Ireland, in which he produced a number of major works, visited Jersey and was in his most Utopian period at St Luke's. Muriel Searle (Searle, 1979: 37) has suggested that a real 'holy boy' lay behind the work, this being the young Bobby Glassby, a sculpted head of whom was a treasured possession of the composer. The piece may therefore also be a tribute to the innocence and beauty of a young choirboy. Glassby was certainly attractive, as the signed photograph that he gave to Ireland in 1920 testifies (Plate 6). He died in tragic circumstances: his body was recovered from the River Ouse in 1934.

There are yet more complications, and there is a further possible stimulus that lies behind this work. There exists a poem by Harold Monro with the title, 'Children of Love', its opening lines 'The holy boy / Went from his mother out in the cool of the day'. This holy boy, the young Jesus, meets Cupid, who draws his bow and shoots an arrow at him. Although this poem was not published until November 1914, Monro held twice-weekly public readings at his Poetry Bookshop in Great Russell Street from 1913, and it is possible that Ireland may have known the poem at the time of writing 'The holy boy'. Perhaps the composer's musical 'holy boy' is a composite figure: a sort of tribute to all these choirboys and literary youths.

The year 1913 was a landmark year in Ireland's development. Aside from significant works such as the set of piano preludes to which 'The holy boy' belongs, there was *The Forgotten Rite* and a song-cycle, *Marigold: An Impression*. It is in this work that we first really encounter Ireland's different responses to love. *Marigold* is an ambitious project, in which 'song' is much more than a setting of words. It is a world in which poems are subjected to an expansive treatment, and the piano's role is crucial to the personal emotional landscape, as it is here that the song's meaning is communicated. The three songs in this cycle reveal contrasting facets of love (as discussed in some detail in Banfield, 1985: 167–9). It is apparent in this cycle that Ireland had the capacity to experience utterly magical, 'fulfilled' moments, but also to feel a real anguish and 'unfulfilment'.

The first of the set, 'Youth's spring-tribute', is an earlier manifestation of the laden atmosphere of 'Earth's call', in which two people experience a very physical consciousness, both of one another and of the rural backdrop. As in 'Earth's call', a musical ecstasy underpins the whole song. Here this is effected through the opening bars, where the static chords are unresolved beneath a falling fourth in the melody line. There is a deliciously swooning, yet controlled, feel to the first part of the song, where the words 'On this sweet bank your head thrice sweet and dear I lay' are intoned over the static chords. In the central part of the song consciousness moves away from self to surroundings before a return to the opening chords in bar 40. The passage from rural ecstasy to physical consummation is effected in a similar manner to that of 'Earth's call'. There is a gradual movement towards a moment of self-knowledge in bar 50. The second song, 'Penumbra', tells a very different story, and is an expression of the other side of Ireland, love denied, turned cold. This is reflected through a modal, speech-like, angular manner to which Ireland returned many times as a means of detached musing. Though there is a reference to the ecstatic opening chords of 'Youth's spring-tribute' at bar 44, these are no longer warm and static, but ugly and shifting. The latter part of the song dissolves into a passage of nature worship in which there is no longer a second player. The main protagonist now alone, the music mixes ecstasy symbols with references to *Songs of a Wayfarer*. The third song, 'Spleen', is a setting of Dowson's translation of words by Verlaine, its melodic lines again angular as a musical response to an expression of pain. It ends on a positive note. At memories of the loved one, there is a return to the commencing chord sequence of 'Youth's spring-tribute'. A similar contrasting of the delirious and tortured emotions of love was the focus of the later *Three Songs* (1918–19), to words by Symons.

In the opening song of *Marigold*, Ireland used a motif that was developed as a recurrent symbol of Passion. This was the bar of piano chords that followed the words 'your warm lips': the moment of self-knowledge in bar 50.

Example 6.1a

At this stage the motif was not an overt climax, and consisted merely of a hushed sequence of chords in octaves, as shown in Example 6.1a.

The germs of this motif had also been used in the First Violin Sonata. In the second movement of this work, at bar 58, a descending scale in octaves marked a climactic point in the melody. The pattern was refined, its meaning consolidated some years later, in 1920. It is always associated with love, and usually occurs only once within a piece, at a moment of great intensity.

In the first two months of 1920 Ireland wrote two songs, 'The trellis' and 'My true love hath my heart', which embody his positive musical declarations of love during the first part of this decade. By now, the Passion motif had become one of the most dramatically powerful and immediately recognizable of Ireland's musical gestures. It has been identified by previous writers on Ireland, first by Peter Pears (1910–86) in 1964, and its meaning developed by Longmire (1976), Banfield and Rowlands. Rowlands (1993: 10–11) viewed it as a signifier of intense emotion. Drawing on Longmire's unformulated belief (1976: iii) that this pattern might have been influenced by the music of Richard Strauss, Rowlands suggested that Ireland's motif may have been derived from the moment in *Salome* when she confesses her love for Jochanaan the prophet (significantly, a love that cannot come to fruition). This proposition seems quite plausible. As Salome first begins to sing of the allure of Jochanaan, a motif appears at the words 'music to my ears'. This is a three-note falling scale in octaves (the first of Example 6.1b). This falling octave pattern recurs throughout Salome's descriptions of Jochanaan's white body, black hair and red lips. During her praise of his body a second motif appears (the second of Example 6.1b). Rowlands suggested that these two germs together formed Ireland's motif, and its manifestation in 1920, at the heart of the *Two Songs* of this year, could certainly be viewed as deriving from Strauss.

Example 6.1b

The first of these songs, 'The trellis', is one of the most idyllic and rapturous of all Ireland's works. Like 'Youth's spring-tribute' and 'Earth's call', and to a certain extent the 1918 song, 'The sacred flame', this is a piece whose concerns are love and nature, in which passions are dreamt of or enacted in a tranquil setting, though here the emphasis is more on love than on its rural backdrop. The tone of all of these songs is positive, passionate, but also dreamy. Shared musical traits are triple metre, static harmony and shifting parallel chords. 'The trellis' is an early poem by Aldous Huxley, the subject of which is secret love, the trellis shielding 'silent kisses', 'white caresses' and 'whisper'd words' from 'prying eyes'. The opening oscillating, pulsing, parallel chords (Example 6.2) set an ecstatic scene, the same scene as that of 'Earth's call', hinting at an idyllic dreamworld. Against the A flat major tonality, the D♭ minor ninth chord in bar 2 has a strong sensory effect.

Example 6.2

In this song the act of love is not played out as a single moment in time, as it was in 'Earth's call', but is rather described as something that happens more regularly behind the trellis. Here the Passion motif has become a more overt symbol of sexual fulfilment. It appears early in the song, in bar 16, a sudden huge outburst (Example 6.3a).

Example 6.3a

The remainder of the song is spent reflecting on the secret nature of this love. Whereas 'The trellis' has a single, brief flowering of Passion, 'My true love hath my heart' is exclusively about consummation. Here the dreamy euphoria of 'The trellis' gives way to absolute affirmation of love. The sonnet comes from Sir Philip Sidney's sequence, *The Countess of Pembroke's Arcadia*. A young maid, Chorita, holds a shepherd, Dametas, in her lap and sings to him. Although this is a love poem from a woman to a man, it also makes perfect sense as a love song from a man to another man, given the non-specific nature of the words and Ireland's own sexuality. The Passion motif is now an essential part of the song, and unusually appears more than once, introducing the piece 'con calore' (with fervour) (Example 6.3b), concluding it and dividing it into two halves.

Example 6.3b

Con anima ma non troppo mosso

Both these songs, 'The trellis' and 'My true love hath my heart', portray a mood of utter fulfilment, with twisting chromaticisms and appoggiaturas always resolving. The implication is that 1920 was a year of personal rapture, though whether this was in hope or in reality remains a mystery. Soon after this date Ireland must have begun to experience a different type of love, one that was to cause him anguish, and which was not to be fulfilled, as he never again wrote a song in such affirmative and passionate vein.

Later in the same year Ireland started work on his Housman cycle, *The Land of Lost Content*, completing it in 1921. This was a selection of six poems from *A Shropshire Lad*, nos XXIX, XV, XVII, XXXIII, XXII and LVII. Of these, only one bore a title. Ireland kept the existing title, 'The Lent lily' and created five new ones: 'Ladslove', 'Goal and wicket', 'The vain desire', 'The encounter' and 'Epilogue'. This song-cycle is a mixing of topics within a topic, with a range of musical ideas. The theme of the cycle is Housman's lissom world of love, springtime and soldiers. Ireland's responses form a tightly knit song-cycle, musically connected by the interval of a falling fifth and Dorian melodies. The opening of 'The Lent lily' suggests that the world is the same as that of 'The trellis', with the similarly oscillating parallel thirds, but in 'The Lent lily' these never develop into passion. The emotional climate is much more confined, and the piano's modal quavers, with the same Dorian inflection, and by implication the same wistfulness as 'Soho forenoons', move inexorably from start to finish. 'Ladslove' is the first of two pieces by Ireland with the subject of the youth Narcissus at their heart, but the most interesting of the set in terms of Ireland's later development is the soliloquy, 'The vain desire'. The speech-like vocal writing in this song, where a melody line twists in an angular manner over pointedly placed piano chords, is pared down still further by the time of Ireland's next Housman cycle. The 'Epilogue' has a version of the Passion motif after the words 'happy is the lover'. This is the only use of the motif in the song-cycle, and its position in the song is not at a moment of musical climax. Here it is not a symbol of Passion achieved within this song, but rather a fleeting reference to a previous experience.

It is apparent that the years 1920–21 were a time when Ireland consolidated and extended his compositional technique. It was the start of a period of creative intensity, and a time when his personal passions were most obviously played out in his music. There were further hints of the Passion motif in 'For remembrance' (1921), and then in 1922 Ireland wrote the piano solo *On a Birthday Morning*. This bore the dedication 'Pro amicitia' ('for friendship'), and was dated 22 February 1922. It was a present for another St Luke's choirboy, Arthur George Miller, who was seventeen on that day. Between 1922 and 1929 Ireland dedicated a series of works to Miller, most of which were intended as birthday gifts, dated 22 February. This young man was a central figure in Ireland's life, and because of this, the period provoked the composer's most intense music. Born in 1905, Miller was the eldest son of Arthur Miller and Maud Major. There were three younger siblings: Ruby, Charles and Rene. According to Markes, Miller 'became a choirboy at St Luke's towards the end of my years there. He was the son of an antique dealer who had a small "antique" shop a few doors from where the Chelsea Palace used to be' (CM to GD: 2 Nov. 1974). Miller probably joined the choir in about 1915.

The initial St Luke's connection swiftly flowered into a much closer companionship, with Miller spending much time with the composer. In 1922, the year of the first dedication, for example, they holidayed together in Norfolk (see Miller in Plate 7), a habit that was continued over the next few years. It is unclear exactly what was the nature of the Ireland–Miller relationship. There are no known extant letters from Ireland to Miller, only one from Miller to Ireland, and very few surviving details of this friendship. It is not known whether Miller was aware what Ireland felt for him, and there is no evidence that their relationship was a sexual one. But it is clear from the recurrence of the dedications to Miller and the intense nature of the works that, for Ireland at least, this relationship was of the utmost significance. And, as Keith Jebb wrote of Housman, and his elusive relationships, there is an 'uncertainty principle: it sets up a set of circumstances that strongly suggest a certain conclusion, but denies you anything like proof' (Jebb, 1992: 69).

On a Birthday Morning is the first of four piano works dedicated to Miller. Musically, it is a bridge between the unassigned works of the early months of 1920, the *Two Songs* and 'Soho forenoons', and the Miller series that followed. Of all the Miller pieces this is the most optimistic, revealed in the performance indications and in the musical material, with the opening marked 'gaily' and the Poco più mosso at bar 67 'fresh and joyous'. There are close links with 'Ragamuffin' and *Merry Andrew*, the former in that they share clear-cut melodic phrases, the latter in that they both utilize a structure derived from one main idea, and within which there are moments of stasis. This is a character sketch in the same tradition, with the same jaunty briskness, but here it is keener, with a prevailing modality. As in 'Soho forenoons', a French breeze blows through the work, most noticeably in the modal cadences derived from Ravel (bars 15–16, for example). There are also resonances of the parallel thirds of 'The Lent lily', such as in bars 17–19. Sudden dramatic outbursts (the '*f subito*' in bar 20) are juxtaposed with playful little motifs. The climax of the work comes with an impassioned presentation of the Passion motif in bar 114, after which a few dormant bars of E major suddenly give way to an eight-bar concluding Vivace whose 'con calore' and rich chromatic chords recall 'My true love hath my heart'.

There was no work specifically dedicated to Miller in 1923, and Ireland spent much of this year working on his large-scale Cello Sonata. There are, however, musical links between this sonata and the pieces written for Miller, and these will be addressed in Chapter 8. In this year the two men travelled together to Dorset, Somerset and Wiltshire, visiting the type of historic sites that interested Ireland, including Avebury, Maiden Castle, Abbotsbury Castle and Cerne Abbas (see Miller in Ireland's car in Plate 12). In 1924 Ireland dedicated another piano piece, Prelude, to Miller, and the year after that, 'Bergomask'. The latter work was published as a pair with 'April'. On two occasions a Miller-dedicated work was published as a pair alongside an undedicated piece, seeming to link the second by implication to Arthur. But additionally, although 'Bergomask' is paired with 'April', the three piano solos of 1922, 1924 and 1925, *On a Birthday Morning*, Prelude and 'Bergomask' work together as a set of 'movements'. This is not only because of their dedications, but also because of the thematic links between them, and it would be perfectly plausible to perform them as a group in the same way that *Sarnia* and the 1941 *Three Pastels* are a set. The 1924 Prelude is essentially the slow movement of the three, its title an ambiguous choice after two earlier attempts. On the manuscript the word 'Penumbra' has been crossed out. There are also fainter pencil markings, which read 'Long Dawn' and also 'Before Sunrise'. Maybe the innocuous 'Prelude' was chosen because it is a prelude in the sense of the Debussy piano preludes, in that it explores a mood. But there may be a literary link, in that there is a poem by Swinburne bearing the title 'Prelude', contained within his *Songs before Sunrise*. This poem is about youth, and the passing of pleasure and passion. Ireland's piece is a processional, ritualistic by reason of its stately chords, repetitions and phrasing. The opening four bars (Example 6.4) contain the kernels of the whole piece.

Example 6.4

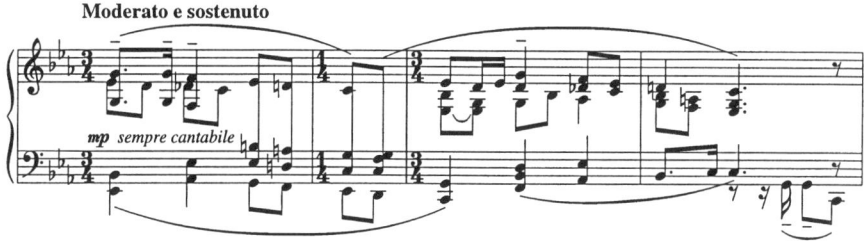

The initial melodic idea is simply a falling minor scale, ^5^4^3^2^1, the bass line presenting the notes in imitation, after which the right hand repeats the five notes, the phrase ending with a falling fifth. This interval pervades the work, and the very deliberate manner of its presentation sets a tone of formality. While the Prelude is modal, there are numerous harmonic ambiguities: bar 6 is an example of the way in which melodic lines, bass lines and inner parts pursue their own course. The second main idea comes in bar 18, imbued, as the first, with a sense of ritual. Here a Dorian melody twists and turns over a two-chord ostinato, a sequence of chords then leading the way back to the first idea in bar 35, now made ever more laden by the new offbeat accompaniment. This re-statement is followed by a reference to the opening of *On a Birthday Morning* (bar 45), Ireland's climax a frustrated one here. What the ear longs for is culmination, and a presentation of the Passion motif, but this does not happen. Instead the rather tortured reference to *On a Birthday Morning* leads simply to repetitions of the two main melodic ideas and a closing E♭ major chord, the desires in this piece remaining frustrated. Although 'Bergomask' is derived from the same four notes as its publication partner, 'April', it could equally belong as a conclusion to the Prelude. As its title suggests, it is a dance, and thus also has an air of formality, though its playful moments and grand climax (a somewhat different version of the Passion motif at bar 80) situate it with *On a Birthday Morning* as a character piece.

'Bergomask' was not the only piece dedicated to Miller in 1925. In 1924 Ireland had returned to Christina Rossetti's verse to set the frequently used poem, 'When I am dead, my dearest', a passage from 'Song' in *Goblin Market and other poems*. This was doubtless popular with composers for its lyrical, pensive tone. Like Ireland's earlier Rossetti settings this one is of the utmost simplicity, with a very restricted, lucid melody and clean, uncluttered piano harmonies and textures. The following year he inscribed the song 'To A.G.M.: Cerne Abbas, June, 1925'. Presumably a trip to the pagan site at Cerne Abbas had been a memorable one, and the wistful nostalgia of Rossetti's words must have been in some way connected to the feelings kindled at this time.

This was the first song that Ireland dedicated to Miller. In the following year, 1926, Ireland produced a cycle of *Three Songs*. Completed in July, the work was then retrospectively headed 'for February 22, 1926'. The first poem, Emily Brontë's 'Love and friendship', likens friendship to the evergreen hollybush, love to the ephemeral wild rose-briar. Ireland's setting is a musical corollary to these words. There is a constant 'evergreen' aspect in the piano ritornello (Example 6.5). Its opening melody has strong connections with the simple folk opening of 'Soho forenoons'. Against this pattern there is a bass ostinato. (These opening two bars also recur much later in Ireland's life as an integral part of the Fantasy-Sonata.)

Example 6.5

With moderate movement

Over the constant, inexorably moving piano writing, the voice has a more ephemeral role, interjecting with short, mainly two- or three-bar phrases. These emerge and disappear, reflecting, commenting, while the piano ploughs its course. The second song, the anonymous 'Friendship in misfortune', is a slow, sentimental reflection, another of Ireland's 'middle' movements. The third song, 'The one hope', is a blend of the pathetic and the sublime. Its opening chords, dominated by the interval of the perfect fourth, set a tone of bleakness, deepened by the A♭ pedal that appears after the words 'And teach the unforgetful to forget?'. Yet at the words 'flowering amulet' there is a direct quotation of the opening bars of 'The trellis' (another hint that 'The trellis' is in some way itself connected with Arthur Miller or at least with the sentiments involved), and a clear, but pianissimo reference to the Passion motif in bar 44. Its concluding falling phrases are a transformation of those that closed 'Friendship in misfortune'.

1926 was a momentous year for Ireland, and the start of a period of bleak despair, reflected in his music. In October he left St Luke's. On 17 December he married a seventeen-year-old pianist and student at the Royal Academy of Music, Dorothy Phillips (*b.* 1909), Arthur Miller acting as his witness. This turned out to be a disastrous move, and Ireland developed an extreme antipathy for the girl, two years later recounting to Townsend Warner that they had quarrelled violently. Why Ireland ever chose to marry Phillips remains open to question. Searle (1979: 72) suggested that he wished to act as the girl's guardian, given her difficult family life, Longmire (1969: 26) that he was 'obsessed by thoughts of this young girl'. Both of these interpretations seem most unlikely, given Ireland's situation with Miller at this time. Perhaps he was going through some sort of mid-life crisis, and saw marriage as a conventional and proper thing to do, a way of presenting himself to the public as a respectable married man. It could also have been a challenge to Arthur that backfired.

The Miller work of two months later, February 1927, was the song-cycle *We'll to the Woods no more*. The dedication in the printed music merely says 'To Arthur', with the additional inscription 'for February 22 1927' at the end of the work. The manuscript version offers a fuller dedication, reading 'To Arthur: in memory of the darkest days', with some further words heavily scratched out. The cycle is axiomatic of the problems surrounding Ireland's sexuality: there are many ambiguities and subtle connections at play here. The work is a collection of three pieces, unusual among Ireland's output in that the first two numbers, 'We'll to the woods no more' and 'In boyhood' are settings for voice and piano and the third, 'Spring will not wait', is a piano solo.

We'll to the Woods no more is a tightly integrated work, with motivic links between its three parts. The songs are settings of two of Housman's *Last Poems* of 1922. The first is not a numbered poem within *Last Poems*, but the introductory lines to the collection, and a translation of the French poem 'Nous n'irons plus au bois' ('We'll go to the woods no more'), adapted from an old nursery rhyme by Théodore de Banville. The piano epilogue both takes its title from and is prefaced with a quotation from no. XXXIX of *A Shropshire Lad*, the poem Ireland had set some years earlier as 'Hawthorn time'. The three items are thus a collection linked by poet and by the aura of nostalgia running through the three poems. As a group, they are also connected thematically and harmonically. Each piece begins with harmonic stability and swiftly dissolves into instability. The gently pulsing opening of 'We'll to the woods no more' is, like 'The Lent lily', also Dorian (Example 6.6), but unlike the earlier song the modal base is almost immediately relinquished for a chromatic wandering.

Example 6.6

The song ends with a D minor chord with an added minor sixth. 'In boyhood' opens with a D minor chord, this time without the sixth, but with an added minor seventh. The structure and mood of this song are derived from 'The vain desire', the melodic material from 'We'll to the woods no more', in that the opening melody is taken from the first appearance of the lines, 'the bow'rs are bare of bay'. Once again, the straightforward opening piano accompaniment soon gives way to chromatic explorations. 'Spring will not wait' opens in D major, but its brighter tonality is almost immediately clouded with the insertion of a C natural, and it ends with the same chord that closed 'We'll to the woods no more'. The final bars of each of the three pieces use the same format (Examples 6.7a, 6.7b, 6.7c): a held chord, against which single notes are picked out, in the case of

'We'll to the woods no more' a falling fifth followed by a rising arpeggio. 'In boyhood' merely has the falling fifth as does 'Spring will not wait'.

Example 6.7a

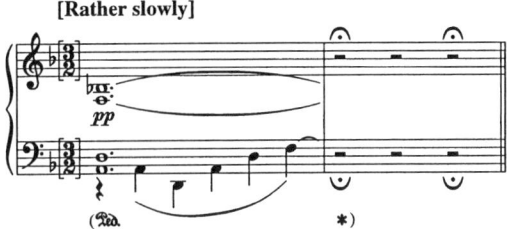

Example 6.7b

Example 6.7c

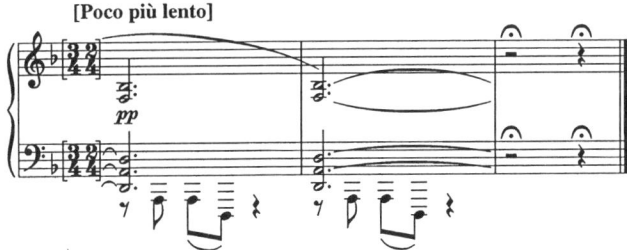

There are other thematic links between the pieces. One of the most potent moments of 'We'll to the woods no more' features a passage of major thirds whose notes outline a whole-tone scale (Example 6.8).

Example 6.8

This becomes an integral part of 'Spring will not wait', in which the last six bars of the first song are quoted three times. The first reference is in bars 21–3, the next starting in bar 31. From the Poco più lento in bar 53 the quotation is used, almost exactly, to close the work. The first song and the piano epilogue thus form a tightly linked pair straddling the central song.

The melodic, harmonic and poetic coherence of the three pieces thus signifies their common meaning. Banfield speaks of the work as expressing pain and personal loss, with backward glances at other works (1985: 177). The sparse nature of the piano writing, the simple, almost declamatory, angular vocal lines and the dissonant harmonic language seem to confirm this interpretation. Ireland's choice of texts by Housman, and particularly poignant ones at that, also denote the work as being about longing and nostalgia. Ireland, at a time of emotional turbulence in 1927, evidently heard an empathetic voice in the poet's writings. Signs of this impending crisis had already been present in his music of the previous year, in the setting of *Five Poems* by Thomas Hardy.

The theme of this cycle is unrequited love, futile, but inescapable adoration. As in *We'll to the Woods no more*, the initial lyricism of the first song, 'Beckon to me to come', soon gives way to twisting chromatic lines. The words of the second song, 'In my sage moments', ponder the possibility of turning away from the loved one, in order to once again be 'serene and clear'. This is another of the declamatory songs, in the vein of 'In boyhood' and 'The vain desire', and the characteristic, recurring melodic pattern of bar 2 was also an integral part of 'The vain desire'. The third song, 'It was what you bore with you, woman', moves to a more rhapsodic state, with the cross-rhythms and fluid figurations of the country pieces, and ecstatic oscillations (for example, in bars 15 and 16). This is followed by another, even more sparse, declamation, 'The tragedy of that moment', and to end the cycle, the musing 'Dear, think not that they will forget you'.

The composer's disastrous marriage in 1926 was shortly followed by Miller's own marriage to a twenty-one-year-old Chelsea girl, Emmeline Orriss, which took place in St Luke's Church on 26 June 1927, this time with Ireland acting as witness. No compositions were dedicated to Miller in 1928, and in March of that year Ireland's marriage ended. There is virtually nothing known of his relationship with Phillips in the intervening months, and again this has been open to interpretation. Townsend Warner, who spent the evening of 31 March 1928 with him, going for dinner and then to his studio, recalled in her diary entry of that night:

> He was about to play me his sonatina when he suddenly went off into what a devil of a time he'd had. First a boy growing up and marrying, then his own reaction of marrying a girl of seventeen. They quarrelled horribly; and with a ghastly exactitude he recalled one quarrel, the girl sitting on the piano and swinging her legs, and singing a rag-time – he stopped, musicianly, to give a rather incorrect musician's rendering of 'I want to be happy', and how he had

wanted to strangle her. He raged across the room strangling a ghost, and then when I jumped up and told him to have done with such tormenting nonsense, he stood quite still and dazed.

(Harman, 1995: 16)

This diary entry both clarifies and confuses the picture of Ireland's marriage. It makes it very clear that it was a disaster for Ireland, but implies that there was some sort of relationship between him and Phillips after the marriage took place. This goes against popular belief. Carpenter (1992: 37) wrote that Phillips left Ireland, Longmire (1969: 26) that they had 'separated on their bridal night', and both Longmire and Searle stated that the marriage was annulled. Ireland himself wrote to singer George Parker later that year of his private affairs involving him in 'endless worry' (GP: 17 Oct. 1928), and much later spoke of the situation to Arthur Gardner: 'my marriage was annulled, & therefore never was a "marriage"' (ARLG: 22 Aug. 1954). It may have been unconsummated, but in fact there was a divorce, which was made absolute on 19 September 1928. In this year Ireland wrote only the *Two Songs*: 'Tryst' and 'During music'. The first of these, 'Tryst', is a setting of words by Symons. The words describe a hazy June evening, as the lover waits. But there is not the ecstatic sense of reverie of 'The trellis', and the secret assignation does not come to fruition.

In 1929 and 1930 Ireland wrote *Two Pieces* for piano: 'February's child' and 'Aubade'. To the first of these, the ravishingly lovely 'February's child', were appended the words 'To AGM for 22 February, 1929'. This is a different manifestation of the sentiments of 'April'. As with *We'll to the Woods no more*, the manuscript carries a fuller dedication, deleted by another hand. However, it is possible to read through the obliteration to find these words, those marked in square brackets showing alternatives at the points where the words are difficult to discern:

... whatsoever things are grave [gone] ...
whatsoever things are lovely ...
So [I'll] think on these things.
[End: [date]]

These words are a personal eulogy to Miller, but are also a transformation of a biblical text. The Letter of Paul to the Philippians, 4: 8, reads: 'Whatsoever things are true, whatsoever things are honest, whatsoever things are just, whatsoever things are pure, whatsoever things are lovely, whatsoever things are of good report; if there be any virtue, and if there be any praise, think on these things.'

There are three other pieces that seem to belong to this sequence of Miller works, and which are expressions of Ireland's state of mind at this time. One bears no dedication, but just the words 'for 25 July 1929'. The implication that 25 July 1929 was a date of particular significance to Ireland is furthered by the piece's title, 'If we must part'. This song is a setting of Dowson's conversational, musing words about the sorrow, but also the acceptance, of parting. It is another of the soliloquy songs, the piano chords leaner than in the earlier songs of this type. The chromatic sliding, tonal uncertainties and rather uncomfortable melodic line, combined with the sometimes soupy, sentimental harmonies, add up to a rather unappealing, tortuous piece of music, surely redolent of some personal loss. July 1929 was also the date of the song 'My fair', which, though not dedicated to Arthur, like many of the known Miller pieces, bears a heavily deleted inscription.

In August Ireland wrote to Randerson from his Sussex retreat of 'the worst worries which have confronted me (an aftermath of previous disturbances)' (HR: 29 Aug. 1929). The piece of this year that is perhaps the strongest utterance of a state of crisis is the Ballade for piano. This is one of the grimmest of Ireland's works, with stark melodic lines, obsessive ostinati and an ever-present sense of menace. The purpose of the work seems to be to present a sequence of 'warped' quotations from other of his pieces. The tune starting at bar 14 is a distorted version of 'The Lent lily', and there are also references to 'The trellis' (bar 47) and the first movement of the Piano Sonata (bar 61), all of these works dating from 1920. From the pieces of 1929, it might have seemed that this year would mark the end of this period in Ireland's life, and the end of his relationship with Miller, but this was not to be the case.

In the meantime, Ireland had acquired another beautiful young protégée, this time a woman, with whom he enjoyed a happier and much more productive relationship than he had with his wife, albeit temporarily. This was the pianist, Helen Perkin (1909–96). As with Miller, it is difficult to ascertain the nature of Ireland's relationship with Helen Perkin. Longmire saw it as 'devoted and disinterested love' (1969: 29), saying that Perkin was 'his muse, his inspiration, and his constant companion' (ibid.: 27). Thompson repudiated Longmire's account, on the grounds that he believed Ireland could not possibly have had an intense personal relationship with a woman, and that his interests in her were purely musical (KT to CSS: 20 Sept. 1976). Perkin herself said that they were inseparable between 1928 and 1930, and that their relationship was 'one of the highest forms of love that I have ever known' (JIT, 7). Despite Thompson's reservations, it does seem that Perkin was more than just a professional concern to Ireland, and the early 1930s were certainly a happy time for him: for example, the short piano piece 'Aubade', written in 1930, is a much more cheerful proposition than the previous year's Ballade.

Perkin had first studied the piano with her mother Nellie, daughter of a music-hall entertainer, George Garlick. At the age of 16, in 1925, a year after her mother had died in a car crash, she entered the Royal College on a scholarship, enrolling as a piano student of Arthur Alexander, from whom she had already taken some lessons. Two years later, in 1927, she was assigned to Ireland as a composition pupil. His first report of her work, in December 1927, read: 'Good: has talent & invention – must guard against being misled by her facility.' Evidently she showed ability in this area, or at least captured Ireland's attention, as her next term's report, in April 1928, was: 'Excellent: has made a decisive step forwards – her work is fresh & interesting.' Composition continued to be an important aspect of her musical career, but it was as a pianist that Helen Perkin first made her name, and as a pianist that she captivated Ireland. She soon became a close companion of the composer, spending much time in his company and accompanying him to concerts and dinners. Townsend Warner's diaries (as quoted in Chapter 3) mention Perkin's involvement at a BBC evening devoted to Ireland's music as early as April 1928, just a few months after her lessons with him had begun:

> A very beautiful serious child named Perkins [*sic*] ... turned over, tense with anxiety to turn over right. Her hands were ice-cold with nervous exhaustion when I talked to her afterwards. She, I, Ireland and Edward Clark went on to a late dinner.

> (Harman, 1995: 15–16)

By 1929 Perkin was beginning to include Ireland's piano works in her recital programmes, and at about this time a song that eventually became one of *Songs Sacred and Profane*, 'Hymn for a child', was dedicated 'To Helen'. In addition to her developing personal and professional relationship with Ireland, Perkin spent time studying major works, including Prokofiev's Third Piano Concerto, which she performed at the RCM on 4 April 1930, with Malcolm Sargent (1895–1967) conducting the students' orchestra. Reviews of the concert praised her playing, and in July of that year she broadcast on the National Programme. 1930, an important year in the advancement of her career, was also significant for her association with Ireland.

The evening of 2 October 1930 saw the last concert of a series called 'British Composers' Nights', which formed part of the Promenade Concerts of that year, and which had been conceived in conjunction with the first season for the recently formed BBC Symphony Orchestra. This was the concert in which Ireland's new Piano Concerto received its first performance. It was dedicated to Helen Perkin, who was also the work's soloist in this concert. She had already given the first performances of the short works, 'February's child' and 'Aubade', but here he was entrusting responsibility for a big new piece to a virtually unknown music student. The concert finished with Elgar conducting his Second Symphony, which rather detracted from Ireland's concerto, though reviews praised both the piece and the performer.

The Piano Concerto is closely and irrevocably linked with Perkin. Ireland knew her as a young and very striking woman: slender, blonde and solemn-eyed, a figure who commanded attention (Plate 15). As other of his works are concerned with a 'whole experience', so this concerto is about the whole experience of knowing Helen Perkin. It marks a crossroads for the composer; the end of a phase of music of great intimacy and intensity, a period in which songs and piano music predominate. It heralds a decade in which Ireland went on to produce a variety of works in different genres and radically different from one another in musical substance and topical associations.

In terms of its construction the concerto displays Ireland's now customary coherent, organic structure, with the three movements all interrelated. The first movement has two principal subjects, from which smaller fragments are derived and developed. The slow movement presents new lyrical themes, but also refers to three of the motifs from the first movement. The finale is based on two new themes, and additionally quotes from both of the preceding movements. The three movements are based in E flat major, B major and E flat major, possibly a deliberate reference to Beethoven's Fifth Piano Concerto, as there are other Beethoven influences at work. The overall structure is essentially traditional: a modified sonata form movement, a slow movement and a modified rondo, but like so many of Ireland's works it captures a particular moment in time. The piano writing is more sparkling than anything he had produced in the previous years. The virtuosic piano part was designed to suit Perkin's small hands, and the dependence on brilliant figuration, though itself a typical concerto trait, was a new side to Ireland's piano writing. The straightforward tonal language signifies happier times than those implied by the sparse, acerbic harmonies of *We'll to the Woods no more* and the Ballade, and the obvious Russian influences must also have been due to the impact of Perkin. In the first and last movements there are striking similarities to Prokofiev's Third Piano Concerto, the work that Perkin had performed earlier in the year.

On a number of occasions writers have identified a solo violin passage in the last movement of the concerto as a quotation from a string quartet by Helen Perkin. This is not the case: no such passage, or anything remotely like it, appears in any of Perkin's works. However, it may be that there was a quotation of her music, or rather a discreet remoulding and assimilating, in the first movement of Ireland's concerto. In 1930 Perkin won the Cobbett Prize for her Phantasy Quartet for string quartet, completed in December 1929, and later broadcast in 1931 by the Spencer Dyke String Quartet. According to Perkin, writing to Longmire in 1962, the 'reference to a theme in my String Quartet is more a reminiscence than a direct quotation' (HP to JL: 25 Oct. 1962). She quoted the melody from the first movement of the quartet (Example 6.9), transposing it into Ireland's E flat major, saying that Ireland had incorporated a reference to this into the first movement of the concerto. She then made excuses for this, saying it was

> ... perhaps rather too vague to mention. He has even reversed the 1st bar as you see, but I remember his telling me what he had done, but I could not remember, when I told you, exactly where it was, & I thought it was the solo violin passage in the last movement, but I see there is no resemblance there at all. I have tried very hard not to invent anything in the material I have given you, and I leave it to you how you deal with this point, if at all.

(ibid.)

It is likely that Perkin's explanation of the relationship between the two works was, in fact, correct, as there are other, smaller motivic links between the pieces.

Example 6.9

Example 6.10

Ireland's first movement opens with an orchestral passage of four bars in which the interval of a perfect fourth occurs four times (Example 6.10). This melodic idea, the one that may have been derived from Perkin's Phantasy, is the germ of the whole movement. The perfect fourth is then featured as a recurrent motif in the work as a whole. Very soon after this introduction the piano enters, with a rhapsodic, musing presentation of the first subject (Ia), derived and expanded from the opening four bars. The next section, up to Figure 5, develops the falling fourth motif. At Figure 5 the second subject (Ib) is introduced in the same way as was the first: the germ of the subject is heard in the orchestra, now as clarinet and trumpet solos, before the piano introduces the theme proper. The culmination of the 'exposition' is an expanded version of the Passion motif, now in the orchestra (two bars after Figure 13). Ireland was not to use this motif again for another thirteen years. There is no clearly demarcated development and recapitulation: instead the evolution and transformation of the two subjects continues, the movement ending with an exuberant tutti fanfare at Figure 30, in which the two main melodic ideas are combined with the oscillating major second that had earlier been earlier developed as an ostinato figure.

Like some of Ireland's other three-movement works, including the Piano Sonata and *Sarnia*, the slow movement is essentially a love song, the falling sevenths and thick string textures of the opening creating a lushly romantic backdrop for the entry of the new piano theme, one of the sunniest and most lyrical of all Ireland's second movement themes. This is the movement in which the impact of Beethoven is most apparent, in that it is a dialogue between piano and orchestra. Where the orchestra starts by reflecting on what is past (the second subject of the first movement), the piano introduces a new lyrical idea (Example 6.11) that is then taken up by the strings at Figure 33. The piano now reverts back to reflect on Ib. Figure 37 sees the culmination of this reflection and transformation. Here the piano plays a version of Ia, after which the orchestra turn Ia and Ib into a single melodic idea. The introduction of a quiet drum ostinato and then the trumpet version of Ia gradually propels the movement forward to a brief piano cadenza and the final 'Allegretto giocoso'.

Example 6.11

The third movement is perhaps the most enigmatic of the three. On the surface it is one of Ireland's jubilant declarations, like the last movement of the Second Violin Sonata, opening with repeating tonic-dominant chords that outline the ever-present perfect fourth. There are two main themes, the first buoyant and perky, in vernacular vein (Example 6.12), and again derived from the first movement; the second more lyrical and expansive. The harmonic journey through the movement is absolutely clear, opening and closing in E flat, with sections in E Dorian (as in the first movement) and in A flat.

Example 6.12

There are two significant quotations within this movement. The first concerns the second subject (Example 6.13a). This incorporates a passage from, and even using the same key as, 'Spring will not wait' (Example 6.13b) which itself quoted from 'We'll to the woods no more', surely here a dramatic reference to love and Miller. And at Figure 67 a short violin solo is combined with a reference back to the slow movement of the concerto. The coda is a brilliant development of IIIa, now rhythmically transformed.

Example 6.13a

Example 6.13b

The concerto was one of Ireland's most successful works, swiftly taken up by many eminent performers, including Artur Rubinstein (1887–1982), Gina Bachauer (1914–76) and Clifford Curzon (1907–82). Its success was due not only to its sympathetic piano writing, but also to its brilliant orchestration. The orchestral scoring is mainly quite sparse, with solos and duos emerging, fine chord interjections and the string section often used minus one or two of its parts. A good example of this can be seen at Figure 15, where muted upper strings and piano play an ostinato pattern, against which a single horn note intones, and a clarinet melody reflects. Ireland's use of percussion in the piece, notably Chinese block, is particularly pointed. Another innovative feature was the use of trumpet with fibre mute, an effect more commonly used in the dance band. Advertised in advance, this attracted a large audience, who were expecting to hear a jazz concerto.

Further performances soon followed, with Helen Perkin again performing the work at the Proms in 1931. It is probably true that of all the many pianists who tackled the concerto, Ireland most admired the original dedicatee's performances of the work, describing her playing in almost rapturous terms after her second Proms appearance in this year:

> Believe me or not, what carried the whole thing thro' ... was the outstanding quality of Helen's playing. She held the audience in a way I have seldom known even with pianists of twice her age & fame ... the slow movement was absolutely electrifying, Helen playing the long phrases in the most intimate way, long drawn out, & holding the audience by the short hairs, in a way I have heard many pianists fail over – & pianists with very big names, too. I

have known her for nearly four years & any time she plays in public (the bigger the occasion the better) the more she surprises & astounds me.

(EClark: 30 Sept. 1931)

As had happened with Arthur Miller, the friendship with Helen Perkin came to a bitter end, though unlike that with Miller, it was never really resumed. In 1932 Perkin travelled to Vienna to study with Anton Webern (1884–1945) and Edward Steuermann (1892–1964). She began to forge an international performing career, and broadcasts from all over Europe became a special feature. In May 1933 she was performing in France, playing works by Frederick Delius (1862–1934), Ireland and her own piano trio, and also broadcasting her compositions from Vienna. Time abroad meant enforced estrangement from Ireland, but despite this, in January 1934 she gave the first performance of *Legend* at Queen's Hall, and several performances of the concerto in Europe in January and February 1934.

In June 1934 Helen Perkin married an affluent architect, George Adie. Ireland was deeply shocked by the marriage, as his friendship with Perkin had been an intense, possessive one. Equally, Perkin's new husband was jealous of her former partnership with Ireland. That the marriage came as a severe blow to the composer, and caused him anguish is evident from his letters of the next two years. In 1935 he wrote to his sister Ethel of 'the terrific shock I had last June', and the actual physical manifestation of this in a skin condition, going on to say that 'she has detached herself from me entirely, & I do not blame her – circumstances probably dictated her actions, & she probably was not able to consider what effect on me her rather ruthless behaviour might have' (EI: 5 April 1935). The following year he wrote again to his sister, after Percy Bentham's death, of the part Bentham had played in helping him to come to terms with this: 'Had it not been for him, the apparently worthless Helen's actions in 1934, might have ended in my death. Yet he very rightly held some brief for her, & pointed out how impossible the situation between me & Helen would have become' (EI: 17 June 1936).

What might have been a temporary quarrel turned into a complete rift. Writing retrospectively in 1962, Perkin said that 'although every effort was made on the part of all concerned to have a friendly relation, it was too difficult, and the situation became so impossible that a complete break had to be made' (*JIT*, 7). The two ceased to communicate, and when, in 1936, Perkin broadcast English music from Frankfurt, Leipzig and Hamburg, there was no Ireland in the programme, but rather works by William Sterndale Bennett (1816–75) and Moeran and her own *Episode*. Her career continued to develop, and in 1937 she was featured in a television series, *Music-Makers*.

In 1939 Perkin attempted to resume the relationship, and wrote to Ireland. Though he did not want to meet her, Ireland was happy that she wished to perform his music again, and wrote: 'it will be a fresh impulse to my work to know that you will no longer feel obliged to exclude it' (*JIT*, 7). Unfortunately the outbreak of war and the birth of three sons brought what had promised to be a dazzling career to an end, and although Perkin resumed concert-giving after 1945, opportunities were never the same again. There was some correspondence between Ireland and Perkin during the war, and this was always friendly and positive:

> Should you feel inclined to write with some news of yourself, etc, I should welcome it ... Whatever occurred between the end of the last war & the beginning of the new war, almost finished, seems shadowy and vague ... I trust you are happy, and rolling in money and rejoicing in your family.
>
> (HP: Oct. 1945, in *JIT*, 7)

In the early 1950s Perkin began to broadcast again, but for unknown reasons, Ireland's letters to her had now become increasingly vitriolic, telling her that she was 'intensely ego-centric' and saying how totally she lacked 'self-criticism in [her] activities as a musician'. In this same letter Ireland was quite dictatorial on the subject of which of his pieces were suitable for her to play:

> If you have any intention of considering my wishes & judgment ... you will definitely cut out 'Ragamuffin'. And on recollecting the character of 'Spring Will Not Wait', that, too, is totally unsuitable for you ... The Sonatina, of course, suits you very well, except that you always hurry the Rondo, & fail to make it really satisfactory & coherent as regards its rhythm & construction.
>
> (HP: 21 Oct. 1954)

This tone is unusual in Ireland's letters, and the dictate surprising, given that 'Ragamuffin' was one of the first of his pieces performed in public by Perkin, in January 1929, and that the Piano Concerto dedicated to her quoted from 'Spring will not wait'. It was also a great shock to Perkin to find that Ireland had, in 1950, removed the dedication from the score of the concerto and had taken steps to prevent her playing the work for the BBC. Perkin herself said that she never understood why he had done this, given the friendly correspondence of the previous eleven years. Possibly it was the outcome of a suggestion from other sources, perhaps the protective housekeeper, Norah Kirby (1898–1982), who had been with him since 1947 (see Plate 20).

Ireland's association with Helen Perkin appears to have been his last important relationship with a woman until his latter years in the company of Norah Kirby. Although he thought so highly of Perkin's playing, Ireland was often critical of performances of his music undertaken by women, and after the demise of his friendship with Perkin he increasingly expressed a dislike for women performers, although he must at some point have admired Harriet Cohen's playing, as she performed his music from about 1919, and works of 1931 and 1937 are dedicated to her. After his friendship with Perkin came to an end, Ireland was not closely involved with any single individual, male or female, for some time. His disastrous marriage and the rifts with Arthur Miller and Helen

Perkin were so traumatic that Ireland retreated into a more solitary existence, producing works that were not concerned with love. There was, however, one person who was to prove enduring, and this was Kenneth Thompson.

In addition to the discussion of religious and literary issues, the tone and content of Ireland's letters to him revealed aspects of his most private side. Thompson's own sympathies with Ireland's sexuality and his position as a cleric seemed to enable Ireland to offload some of his desires and fantasies. There is an informality and an honesty about these letters that is rarely seen elsewhere. Those of the 1930s already show a willingness to speak with Thompson on the subject of young boys: in 1936 Ireland was reading works by Forrest Reid, including the newly published *The Retreat*, and *Uncle Stephen*, in which the subject is comradeship between an older man and a youth. The admiration for Greek platonic love and the depiction of the beauty and comradeship of young males, which pervades many literary works of the early part of the twentieth century, was alluring for Ireland. At about this time a group of writers were producing romantic works concerned with the beauty and attraction of young boys. The literature produced by writers such as Lord Alfred Douglas, Horatio Forbes Brown and Charles Kains Jackson came to be termed 'Uranian', the word taken from Plato's Uranos of the *Symposium* (a work Ireland knew well), and used to denote 'Uranian', or 'heavenly', pederasty in the Greek sense. The theme of comradeship between a middle-class man and a youth, usually a working-class youth, with implicit sexual overtones, was central to the work of the Uranian poets, and other common subjects were the evanescence of boyhood, the angelic face of youth, and guilt at a forbidden passion. While there is no evidence that Ireland read any of the specifically (usually privately printed) Uranian works, he did read Edward Carpenter's *Iolaus*, a collection of poetry and other writings about Greek friendship and other man–boy relationships. He was also certainly aware of the use and meaning of the word, as evinced from a letter to Thompson, in which he suggests that marriage 'is not for Uranians', advising Thompson against taking this step, clarifying his position with the statement that it 'only creates the most ghastly strife and horrible unhappiness, for both parties, believe me' (KT: 25 Nov. 1943). Ireland also wrote to Thompson of homoerotic literature that he enjoyed, in 1938 mentioning that he had come across 'an interesting poem by Martin Armstrong, called "The Young Bather"', also a 'remarkable story – Death in Venice', which he described as a 'forbidden subject … treated with great beauty and skill' (KT: 1 May 1938). This book was read and re-read, and discussed many times with Thompson. The latter wrote of Ireland's music in 1976 that 'romantic love of a homosexual inspiration is everywhere … John was a romantic Invert … of an undeveloped, almost schoolboy type … i.e. without any general indulgence, if any, of an immoral kind' (KT to CSS: 20 Sept. 1976). This 'homosexual inspiration' was most often a fantasy, a yearning after the beauty and perfection of youth.

In June 1939 Ireland moved to Guernsey. His sojourn there was to act as a major stimulus, and an affirmation of his interest in young boys. One of the reasons for this was his renewed involvement with a church choir, that of St Stephen's. In April 1940 Ireland moved from the west coast of the island to the Birnam Court Hotel in St Peter Port, owned by an ex-naval man, George Davy Rayson, and his wife, Margaret. They had a nine-year-old son, Michael (*b.* 1930), described by Ireland as 'beautiful, clever & alert, with perfect manners – & being well educated at one of the best schools here. Not, alas, musical. But lovely, long, curling eyelashes. Here comes out the stifled paternal instinct' (KT: 29 April 1940). In a slightly later letter Ireland enclosed a photograph of the boy, saying that he was 'attractive, but not at all affectionate, wh: is perhaps as well!' (KT: 18 May 1940). Thompson's reply to all this (KT to JI: 27 May 1940) was to say 'how happy I am at the way in which your spiritual needs are now satisfied'. Just over a month later Ireland was forced to leave Guernsey.

For Ireland, the beauty of this boy, together with the aura of the island in the spring of 1940, with its idyllic small bays and sheltered inland lanes, was a heady mixture. He had already written one Guernsey piece, 'Le Catioroc', and on his return to England worked on the other two movements of *Sarnia*. The second movement of the work was closely associated with Michael Rayson. Ireland originally wanted to call it 'Boyslove', which is a name of the plant Southernwood (a word much used by the Uranian poets as a way of obscuring meaning), but eventually settled on 'In a May morning', dedicating the piece to Michael. He wrote to Thompson a year after his departure from the island:

> I think you referred to Michael, in connection with my new piano pieces. Well of course he was just a part of the whole flood of beauty in Guernsey – those last 6 or 7 weeks were really an extraordinary revelation – there was everything at once – the unbelievable beauty of the Channel Islands in Spring, the delightful surroundings and feeling of heart's ease – the joy of that lovely Church where I played the organ – and Michael constantly about the house and garden, fitting in so well with everything – it was almost too wonderful to be true & certainly far too wonderful to last … alas, how fragile, how transitory! And yet, how eternal & true! Well, I have expressed some of it in my new piano work, 'SARNIA'.

(KT: 26 June 1941)

In September 1941 Ireland played the piece to Thompson, with a picture of Michael Rayson on the piano. Thompson had by now become a chaplain in the Navy, and meetings took place when he had periods of leave. There were a number of wistful reminiscences of Rayson and Guernsey on Ireland's part throughout the war years, and on a November evening in 1945 Ireland played the piece to Thompson again, along with a selection of boy-love-nature works which included 'April', 'Bergomask', 'The boy bishop' and 'Puck's birthday'. In 1946 there were further retrospective musings on the intoxicating atmosphere of the Channel Islands, causing Ireland to write:

Yes, the little snapshot you returned to me arouses some poignant memories
of a happy and very vivid time – a combination of various factors, including
Spring in the Channel Islands, which is more violent than English Spring –
constant attendances at a Catholic Church – all pervaded by the glamour of
Contact with Beauty in its finest human form. Too good, alas, to last –
excellent in memory. Imperfectly recorded, maybe, in music.

(KT: 15 Nov. 1946)

'In a May morning' is this imperfect record, an attempt to capture in music the
atmosphere of a person, a place and a time. The work is prefaced by a quotation
from Victor Hugo's novel of 1866, *Les Travailleurs de la Mer*. Hugo spent
some time living in exile on Guernsey, where he wrote and located this work.
Ireland wrote to Evans that the quotation 'is not intended to describe the music,
which contains some elements of regret or wistfulness, but rather the unalloyed
beauty to which the music is my reaction' (EE: 1 Dec. 1941). To do this he
selected several sentences, not consecutive, from a passage near the end of the
novel, in which a day in May is described in sensuous terms. May pours forth
its beauty, signalling the first appearance of roses, butterflies and fledglings. It
is a day of freshness, the aura pagan, and most importantly, 'Qui brillait,
brillait plus; qui aimait, aimait mieux' ('What shone, shone more fully; who
loved, loved better'). The piece is thus about a particular experience in a
specific landscape, but as is so often the case, it is also a fantasy with literary
associations.

The movement has three main parts. The outer sections feature one
principal melodic idea, developed in ballad-like fashion. This is Ireland in
sentimental mode: a slowly-moving lyrical idea rests on thick chords and rich
appoggiaturas. The central section is more rhapsodic, and moves away from
the opening material to an expression of ecstasy.

Michael Rayson was not the only Guernsey youth to have an impact on
Ireland. In 1941–42 he made a number of settings for equal voices and piano of
verse from Eleanor Farjeon's children's book, *Over the Garden Wall* (1933).
These included 'The boy', 'Boys' names', 'Joseph fell a-dreaming', 'The bell
in the leaves' and 'Here be naked boys'. Of these, 'Boys' names' was
dedicated to another Guernsey boy, Peter Lihou, who had been in the St
Stephen's choir for only a short time. Although like all the other Farjeon
settings, this has a simple, artless quality, the words can be read as ambiguous.
They are ruminations on boys' names, but it is possible to construct Uranian
resonances here, in that the poet John Gambril Nicholson, in 1892, had
produced a Ballade with the title 'Of Boys' Names', a remarkably similar
exposition to that of Farjeon, but intended for a quite different readership.

These 'boy' songs were followed in 1941 by a set of pieces for piano,
Three Pastels, miniature pictures which share the same topical concerns. The
connections, as ever with Ireland, are complex, but it is in this set of pieces that
Ireland's fascination with boys comes to musical fruition. Each work bears a

title suggesting a mythical or historical youth: 'A Grecian lad' (Narcissus), 'The boy bishop' and 'Puck's birthday' (Puck), each in some way subversive. Narcissus falls in love with himself, and the other two generate misrule. Each work has a literary descriptor added by Ireland, and in accordance with the fact that this was a time of retrospection in the composer's life, they are all in some sense backward-looking. The first two are reworkings of very early piano pieces dating from some time between 1896 and 1906, and each of the three bears hints of previous works. Although this time there are no motivic links between the three pieces, and each portrays a different type of character through contrasting tempi, themes and harmonies, they belong as a set by way of their shared meanings.

'A Grecian lad' bears an inscription from *A Shropshire Lad*, the same words set by Ireland in 1921 as part of *The Land of Lost Content*, and there is a continued engagement with Narcissus. The youth who falls in love with his own beautiful image, and who is therefore a symbol of homoerotic love, was of long-standing interest to Ireland. At one point he was uncertain whether to call the piece Hyacinthus, an equally appropriate choice, as he, too, was a patron of same-sex love, the beloved of both Apollo and Zephyr. In order to write the work, Ireland contacted his friend Paul Walde, from his St Luke's days. He mentioned a former holiday in Jersey, where a picture was taken of a youth called 'Fred', and asked if Walde still had this in his possession, as he needed it as a musical stimulant:

> I wish I could revive old memories by means of some of the <u>Jersey</u> photos taken by you, particularly those of <u>Fred</u>, or <u>including</u> him. I really am anxious to recapture some of the essence of those days – it would help my work, the basis of which is becoming more and more retrospective in its inspiration.
>
> (PW: 9 Sept. 1941)

'A Grecian lad' is a modal song without words (Example 6.14), melody driven, and with a repeating, evolving verse and chorus format.

Example 6.14

'The boy bishop' is musically more complex and carries a multitude of meanings. As in *Month's Mind*, the source of the title was Brand's *Observations on Popular Antiquities*, this particular observation a description of an ancient custom, dating back to the tenth century. On 6 December, St

Nicholas' Day, in cathedrals and parish churches, one of the choirboys was chosen to be a counterfeit 'boy bishop'. On 28 December, Innocents' Day, he reigned supreme, taking the main part in the services, wearing bishop's robes, with the clergy demoted to the role of choirboys. The boy bishop was allowed to preach, but not to celebrate Mass, and there was always an associated period of misrule on this day. The tradition had distant connections with the Merry Andrew, whose ass costume derived from the Feast of Fools, which was a New Year celebration in which the lower clergy dressed up as asses to usurp the priest and bishops for a day. In addition to the evocative title Ireland added a brief, highly suggestive inscription: 'diffusa est gratia in labiis tuis' ('full of grace are thy lips'). The modality of 'A Grecian lad' continues in this ternary piece, which is fundamentally Æolian. There is no misrule in this interpretation of the custom, but instead a sense of profound melancholy in the bleakness of the melodic lines (Example 6.15), and these two of the *Three Pastels* affirm that Ireland reserved the Æolian mode for moments of detachment. The solemnity of the ornate opening of 'The boy bishop' is maintained in the processional central section.

Example 6.15

The poise of the first two pastels is shattered by 'Puck's birthday', its vernacular character (Example 6.16) a continuation of the musical language of the 1925 'Bergomask'. This Puck is a relation of the 'Ragamuffin' and the *Merry Andrew*.

Example 6.16

Ireland's return to Greek subject matter in this set of pieces demonstrated a continued interest in a subject that had always lurked behind his music, a subject there for its homoerotic, more specifically pederastic connotations. 'Greek love' became progressively more present in his thoughts, as expressed in the later letters to and from Thompson. In 1949 Thompson sent Ireland a photograph of a statue of Hermes, the winged messenger, associated with homoerotic love, with the words 'A picture of, surely, an old friend of yours' (KT to JI: 31 Aug. 1949). Later in the year Thompson sent Ireland a card from Italy, saying 'I think it will amuse you – & the subject, the boy Corybantes (I suppose) certainly suits you' (KT to JI: 22 Dec. 1949). Another friend of the 1940s was Arthur Lee Gardner. A handful of letters from him to Ireland survive. Gardner was the former cleric at St Luke's (see Plate 5), mentioned in Chapter 2, who gave up holy orders later in his life and became a crime writer. Though neither so wide-ranging nor so personal, these letters have similarities with those to Thompson, in that Ireland makes reference to Greek influences and to his attraction to boys, and talks of the two of them (that is, Gardner and Ireland) as being of the same persuasion. In 1944, for example, he wrote of the first performance of *Ex ore innocentium* that 'age is no cure for deeply-rooted passions & enchantments, given the magical material' (ARLG: 23 July 1944).

Throughout this time, and despite the anguish expressed in *We'll to the Woods no more*, Ireland had maintained his relationship with Arthur Miller. In 1940 Miller had married for a second time, to Rita. He already had one child from his first marriage, and the second produced two sons and two daughters. Miller and Ireland continued to stay in touch, and during the 1940s and 1950s Ireland lent him sums of money on several occasions, purchased businesses for him (a practice that had begun some years earlier) and acted as mortgage guarantor for a family home in 1948. Ireland's solicitor friend, Herbert Brown, was closely involved with the financial dealings between Miller and Ireland. There no longer appeared to be any trauma in the relationship between the two men, as the only extant letter from Miller to Ireland (AGM to JI: 29 Dec. 1949) seems to testify. In this Miller thanks him for money and tells him that he is about to sail either to Australia or to Singapore, Hong Kong and Japan in his new P. & O. job. Miller then goes on to describe his financial problems and to ask for more money. In 1952 Ireland was again bailing out Miller, clearing his debts, as a bank note of this year indicates (*JIT*, 8). Astonishingly, Ireland's letters to Thompson never mention Miller, perhaps because the reality of the relationship was too far removed from the fantasies that Ireland preferred to impart to his friend.

During the 1950s, Ireland's letters to Thompson become more explicit and increasingly acerbic on the subject of women. The composer had never liked the sound of women's voices in church, a dislike that was extended to other areas of his output. In 1954 he stated that 'very few of my 70-odd songs are suitable for female singers' (KT: Feb. 1954), and in 1955 that 'experience has taught me that my music is seldom understood by women performers' (KT: 15 May 1955). This attitude was closely tied up with a distaste for women generally, and in the letters to Kenneth Thompson there are many references to this aversion. On reading Alberto Moravia, Ireland remarked that he found the writing 'quite horrid in places, where the sensuality of the females is described' (KT: 24 March 1953). In 1956 Thompson was evidently thinking once more about marriage, and over the next three years Ireland wrote a number of letters to him urging caution, saying 'if you cannot see how disastrous it would be (for you or anyone of our temperament) nothing I could say would convince you' (KT: 4 May 1958). Eventually Thompson decided that he would marry, and Ireland wrote, somewhat belatedly, in formal mode, to 'congratulate [him] on [his] engagement & approaching marriage, and to wish [him] every happiness therein' (KT: 17 July 1960). Thompson's wedding took place on 5 September 1960.

At one point Thompson had been involved in the drafting of Ireland's will, and here there are yet more uncertainties and ambiguities. It was suggested by Muriel Searle (1979: 149) that a will was drawn up in 1932, in favour of Arthur Miller. This may have been the case, but there is no supporting evidence. However, there is a surviving document in the hand of Ireland's solicitor, Herbert Brown, dating from *c.* 1940–42 (*JIT*, 9). This is a piece of paper listing the proposed recipients of Ireland's estate. In it £1500 is left to his sister Ethel, small sums to several other people and the residue to Arthur G. Miller. At about this time Brown referred to Miller as being Ireland's legatee (HB to JI: 8 Dec. 1940). In 1952, largely on account of Ethel's death in 1948, Ireland wrote to Thompson that he was thinking of making a new will, and asked him to help deal with things, as he would 'hate the idea of all my papers, letters, etc. passing through the hands of a normal (heterosexual) person' (KT: 30 Dec. 1952). In 1953 Ireland was clearly thinking about his family and his will, as he wrote to a number of distant relatives asking them for biographical information. On 17 July 1953 Ireland drew up his new will, leaving everything bar a small sum of money to Norah Kirby, his housekeeper, whom he had known for only six years. Perhaps this was a curious decision given that he had two living nephews with whom he stayed in touch, and that there were also Arthur Miller (though he had received substantial sums of money over the previous years, and especially in 1952) and Kenneth Thompson. However, Norah Kirby was a woman who was plainly devoted to the composer, and who cared for him as a frail, virtually blind man in the latter part of his life. She is buried beside him.

Chapter 7

War

In February 1916 Professor S.D. Adshead described the function of the war memorial as neither the celebration of victory, nor the commemoration of peace, but as 'prophetic and inspiring, as well as retrospective; if it is both it will be sublime' (Bushaway, 1993: 143). The First World War memorial symbolized the glorification of the sacrifice of man for his country, with the emphasis placed firmly on the individual, the British hero. By the start of the Second World War, collective stoicism and determination had replaced the idealized conception of honour through death.

Many British composers, including Rutland Boughton (1878–1960) and Havergal Brian (1876–1972), were actively engaged in these conflicts. In the First World War, Arthur Bliss (1891–1975) was in the Royal Fusiliers, and then in the Grenadier Guards along with Sammons and Murdoch. Edgar Bainton (1880–1956), Benjamin Dale (1885–1943) and Frederick Keel (1871–1954), holidaying in Germany in August 1914, were interned for the duration of the war. Ivor Gurney and Moeran fought in the Great War, and survived with injuries, while former RCM students George Butterworth (1885–1916) and Ernest Farrar (1885–1918) died in service in this same war. Vaughan Williams served as an orderly in the First World War, and in the Second World War was involved with the organization of National Gallery concerts and directing the work of the Home Office Committee for the release of Interned Alien Musicians. Others, including Bridge, renounced war by embracing pacifism, while Bax in 1915 wrote:

> For my own part I have been swaying backwards and forwards between two courses – that of entering the army (and becoming bold and British thereby, or pretending to be) and that of plunging into a narcotic ocean of creative work.
>
> (Foreman, 1987: 79)

As Ireland fought in neither war, the impact on him was as a civilian, suffering the loss of friends and material discomforts. He may have been physically more removed from the situations than a number of his musician contemporaries, but like most composers he was profoundly affected, both emotionally and practically.

The two conflicts were reflected and foreshadowed in his 'war' pieces. This small but significant body of works was written immediately before, during and shortly after the dates of the two world wars, and the content and purpose of the pieces accord with the prevailing national sentiments. Ireland's First World War works mirror the spirit of the age, the prophecy and inspiration described by Professor Adshead, and the notion of individual sacrifice – the 'hero', as opposed to the 'people'. His music of these years, most notably the Second Violin Sonata and the Second Piano Trio, is of a deeply personal, reflective nature, just as much of the poetry of this war is a meditation on the situation. In contrast, the change from a romanticized vision of brave heroes to the Second World War mood of stoicism, patriotism and aspiration inspired music of a more public, functional nature, using bigger orchestral genres. As a generalization, Ireland's music of the Great War is personal, intimate and radical; that of the next war more clichéd, full-blown and traditional.

But despite the dissimilarities, there are very clear topical links between the musics of the two wars. Although they provoked two distinct reactions, there are strong correlatives between the works of the two conflicts. There are two main types of response: the first an emotional outpouring that is particularly seen in the music of the First World War, and the second a prevalent use of march genre and 'military' motifs. Specifically, and at the most fundamental level, these include pounding pedals, left-hand octaves in piano parts, repeating scale patterns and driving upbeats (such as opens the piano Rhapsody). Common to both periods is that Ireland produced significant chamber works.

In the year before the outbreak of the First World War, Ireland produced some of his most hedonistic, Jersey-inspired works such as *Decorations* and *The Forgotten Rite*, and other important works including *Marigold*. These pieces show him on the verge of developing his own distinctive musical language, in which there are no signs of the impending war. In 1914, at the age of thirty-five, Ireland offered his services, but was turned down, as he recalled in 1950: 'Why was I not in the British Army fighting for my country? My health and physique failed to reach the standard required, and after several medical examinations I was rejected for any form of military service' (*JIT*, 1). He therefore spent the years 1914–18 working in London, based in Chelsea. There is little documentary information regarding Ireland's activities during the First World War, save for details of his work at St Luke's and of performances of his music. The way in which Ireland responded to the conflict of the First World War has to be gleaned mainly from the music itself, and occasionally from his retrospective writings. Until 1917, this was not a prolific period, which is perhaps surprising after the productivity of 1913, and a signal that the war was stifling, but nevertheless it was a time when he wrote a number of significant works. Ireland seemed to be preoccupied with the war, and almost every piece from the years 1914–17 has some obvious connection, either in the poems he chose to set, the purpose for which the music was intended or in shared thematic material.

In many ways the backdrop against which Ireland was writing during the Great War was valuable as far as the promotion of his own music was concerned. From 1915 public anti-German sentiments triggered a number of populist anti-war pieces on the part of several composers (although these were not commissioned works). While there was no official government policy to use music for propaganda purposes, a short-lived decision to ban performances of German music was in itself a form of propaganda, leading as it did to a greatly improved platform for new British music, and Ireland certainly benefited from this. From Elgar there were works such as *Carillon*, celebrating the resistance of Belgium to the German invasion, *Polonia*, *The Spirit of England* and *The Fringes of the Fleet*. Parry's reactionary works included *From Death to Life*, which was a response to outbreak of hostilities, *A Hymn for Aviators*, 'Jerusalem', and the *Naval Ode*. Many composers, particularly of this earlier generation, sympathized with nationalistic sentiments, but there were also younger dissenters. One of the most vehement was Peter Warlock, who wrote to Delius in October 1914:

> I have never been able to understand the sentiment of patriotism, the love of empire: it has always seemed to me so empty and intangible an idea, so impersonal and so supremely unimportant as regards the things that really matter – which are all the common heritage of humanity, without distinction of race or nationality.

> (Smith, 1994: 64)

Rather like Herbert Howells, who was also working at home during the war, Ireland sits between the sentiments of patriotism and aversion. For him, the First World War inspired no overtly propagandist work. Instead his intensely personal reflection on the war helped him to formulate his mature musical voice and to move right away from the German influences and Brahmsian inheritance which had coloured earlier pieces. An increasing independence of musical thought occurred in his work in 1913, with the composition of *The Forgotten Rite*, and by 1917 this was consolidated in the Second Violin Sonata, composed during the years 1915–17.

Most of Ireland's energies during the First World War were channelled into two big chamber works and a few songs. But while he set the emotive poetry of the day, it was in the field of chamber music that he found a more instinctive musical response to the war spirit. As was described in Chapter 1, the first performance of the Second Violin Sonata in 1917 was peculiarly potent. Its association with young men in uniform imbued the work with the spirit of a particular time and place, Ireland's work the musical equivalent of the prevailing vogue for a literary embalming of the war. Ireland began work on it in 1915, a year of appalling military disasters and the slaughter of huge numbers of young English men. He must also have been influenced by the deaths of parishioners of St Luke's and very likely also of the ex-choristers. In 1916 the Poet Laureate, Robert Bridges, published an intentionally

Twelve Short Anthems

FOR

Men's Voices (T.T.B.B.)

FOR USE IN

CHURCH, ON DECK, IN CAMP or TRENCH

as Occasion may Require.

COMPOSED FOR AND DEDICATED

TO ALL

Brave Defenders of the Realm of King George V.

WHETHER ON

SEA, LAND or IN THE AIR,

AND

Especially the Men's Choir

OF

H.M.S. "ACHILLES"

" somewhere in the North Sea "

BY

J. STUART ARCHER.	E. STANLEY ROPER.
H. L. BALFOUR.	FRANCIS GEO. SANDERS.
F. W. BELCHAMBER.	FRED. AUG. SEWELL.
HERBERT HODGE.	SYDNEY TOMS.
JOHN IRELAND.	MAURICE VINDEN.
G. O'CONNOR MORRIS.	H. DAVAN WETTON.

Copyright.   Price 1/- net cash

London,

STAINER & BELL, Ltd.

All rights reserved.   58 Berners Street, W.

June 1915.

7.1 The title page of *Twelve Short Anthems*, the volume containing 'An island hymn' uplifting anthology, *The Spirit of Man*, but by the end of the year a deep national despondency prevailed, given the continued military disasters at the Somme. The setting for the Second Violin Sonata was thus a blend of gloom and optimism, and the contrasting sentiments in this work will be revisited in Chapter 8. In 1915, the year in which he began work on this sonata, Ireland also produced a functional anthem for unaccompanied men's voices, 'An island hymn'. This was included in an anthology of anthems to be sung by men away fighting (Figure 7.1).

In November and December 1916, Ireland set three of Major Eric Thirkell Cooper's war poems. These were recent works, published in 1915 in a collection with the title *Soliloquies of a subaltern somewhere in France*. Ireland's settings were originally conceived as a group of three, but only the first two were published at the time. 'Blind', no. I, is a very short, sentimental, Dorian rendering of lines bemoaning the loss of sight in war, its language rather similar to that of the 1918 *Mother and Child* songs. Number III, 'A garrison churchyard', remained unpublished until 1998. This is a reflection on the dead in similar vein. The second song, 'The cost', is a much more impassioned outburst, characterized by driving piano octaves. These were the first examples of obvious musical responses to the war on Ireland's part. Though at this stage rather raw, they contain the kernels of the two types of expression: the anguished and the military.

The first part of the following year was spent completing the Second Violin Sonata, and then, following its public acclaim, Ireland produced a Second Piano Trio, a single-movement work for violin, cello and piano. This is a work of mixed emotions, contrasting passages of stark textures and caustic harmonies with effusive, positive moments and gritty marches. The structure of the work is a succession of episodes exploring different moods, all of which are melodic metamorphoses of the first eighteen bars of the piece. This opening Poco lento is sombre, with a more biting harmonic language than previously used by Ireland. It starts (Example 7.1) with a solo cello line, in which the underlying melancholy is created through a slow linearity containing appoggiaturas and falling, sighing intervals. In bar 4 the cello is joined by the piano, its rising motif adding an element of questioning. The violin joins the texture in bar 12, with bars 13–14 placing great emphasis on a weighted appoggiatura. In bars 17–18 the cello hints at a motif which is to be developed much more fully as the piece progresses.

These eighteen bars are repeated with alterations, the appoggiatura always prevalent, with the section from bar 35 featuring the violin and cello in octaves. At bar 45 a repeating motif in the piano part leads the way to a reiteration of the cello's opening four bars, after which the motif originally heard in bar 17 is swiftly transformed into the basis of a march in the Allegro giusto at bar 60 (Example 7.2). While derived from the modal opening theme, this passage is dominated by the new brisk, staccato slant, and by the pounding piano quavers that are pervasive from bar 72. The driving effect is created through the fact that scale patterns rise, fall, twist and recur.

Example 7.1

Example 7.2

The march gives way to a version of the original idea in bar 120, which is then transformed into an expansive, richer Andante. Here the tone is gentler and much more elegiac, affirmative through the underlying major tonality. The latter part of the piece, from bar 182, consists of a series of further permutations of the main theme, alternating between anguish, elegy and march. From bar 218 an E pedal moves the music definitively into military mode, sealed with the piano's repeating motif at the Allegro in bar 233. The Second Piano Trio is an example of a piece that clearly has many manifestations of the topic of war. The military connotations of the march-derived Allegro giusto, the clipped, accented quavers, and the forceful bass lines, are recurrent features of Ireland's war music. Significantly Ireland was to re-use motifs from this piece in music written at the outbreak of the Second World War.

The Second Piano Trio was followed by settings of three of Rupert Brooke's war poems. Two of these were emotive texts, immensely popular at the time: 'The soldier' and 'Blow out, you bugles'. They were published as a pair, and deploy some of the essential motifs of Ireland's war topic. The first song, 'The soldier', was performed in the same concert as was the Second Piano Trio, in the Wigmore Hall, in June 1917. Here Ireland's solidly tonal language supports a vocal line whose sentimentality derives from the Victorian ballad. The piano accompaniment provides a dependable, chordal base – the security of 'England', highlighting imperialisms which appear at key moments in the text: the introduction of rich chords moving in octaves at the word 'England' in bar 7 is an example of this. Two other motifs in the song are noteworthy: the heavy left-hand octaves, for example in bar 10, and at bars 17–19, and the 'noble' melodic motif which first appears at the 'Con moto' in bar 14 (Example 7.3). This (Example 7.3) has close links both with the Second Violin Sonata, and with the soaring lines of the later *Epic March*. The song is a conscious musical incarnation of 'England': an England that is noble and tranquil, unperturbed by the rumble of a war fought elsewhere.

Example 7.3

Con moto

Gave,___ once, her flow'rs to love,

In January 1918 Ireland wrote 'Blow out, you bugles', the words of which dwell on the subject of dying for one's country as being a noble, glorious action, leading to honour and immortality. To embrace this he employs a march idiom, with descending left-hand octaves, and bugle effects created through a melody that outlines the notes of an E♭ major triad (Example 7.4). Like 'The soldier', 'Blow out, you bugles' is tonally simple. The motif that saturates the song, both in the vocal line and in the piano part, is one which is found throughout Ireland's output, the ^5^3^4^5 motif. It is the driving force behind *These Things Shall Be* (1937), but it is also the melodic basis of 'Chelsea Reach' and of 'Ragamuffin', composed at about the same time as the Brooke songs, in 1917. It seems likely that this motif was associated with England in Ireland's mind, as it is primarily in those works which are concerned with war or which are depictions of an aspect of England, a place or a national character, that the motif appears.

Example 7.4

These Brooke settings form a complementary pair. The first is nostalgic, reviewed as 'manly and dignified' (*MT*, May 1918: 213), the second heroic. They are linked musically by the motif (Example 7.3) which was first heard at the 'Con moto' in 'The soldier' and which reappears in 'Blow out, you bugles' at the words 'And paid his subjects with a royal wage' (bar 44). The two songs contain aspects of Ireland's response to war in general terms, the mood one of sentiment and patriotism.

While Ireland's choice of poetry for his songs written in the years 1916–18 was mainly on account of the obvious war connotations, the appeal of Brooke's verse was not only because of these associations. Given Ireland's propensity for words celebrating pagan, hedonistic aspects of the countryside, Brooke's lyrics were attractive on another level, and the poet's physical beauty and the tragic, romanticized nature of his death may well also have attracted Ireland. His decision to set 'Spring sorrow' in April 1918 (a song which Banfield discusses in some detail in 1985: 165–6 and 170) was because of this mingling of nature, lyricism and personal emotions, all set against the melancholy backdrop of the war. A similar sort of emotional content drew Ireland to Housman, and the 1917 song, 'The heart's desire', was the start of an enduring partnership of words and music. During 1918 Ireland gradually moved away from images of war to romantic nature idylls, as was discussed in Chapter 4. Increasingly his attentions were distracted away from the situation in Europe and back to the pre-war hedonism of 1913. The year 1918 was an incredibly creative year for him, during which he consolidated his position as a songwriter. Shortly after the end of the war, in 1919, Ireland produced another 'practical' work, the hymn tune, 'Fraternity', and then in 1920 returned to Housman.

The post-war work *The Land of Lost Content*, which was also included in Chapter 6, is a bringing together of the sentiments aroused by men, war and a mythical landscape. *A Shropshire Lad*, though published in 1896, became strongly associated with the First World War, and hence an intimate, sometimes fey, manner became part of the war spirit. Paul Fussell's discussion of the concept of 'Soldier Boys' in his book, *The Great War and Modern Memory* (1975: 270–309), looked at the role that Housman's volume of poems played in the establishment of the image of 'beautiful suffering lads' in uniform (ibid.: 282) acting as a licence for homoerotic sentiments. The comradeship of soldier lads was a powerful literary image superimposed on to a current war, and Ireland's *Land of Lost Content* is bound up with these same images. The most obvious song in the set that belongs to the soldier–love–nostalgia theme is 'The encounter', another of Ireland's military marches with pounding bass (Example 7.5). 'Goal and wicket' is more symbolic. The words of this poem set memories of games of football against visions of mortality. Football, at that time a peculiarly British national sport, was adopted as a First World War symbol of national identity (see Fussell, 1975: 27). Ireland's setting clothed the words in unmistakable military garb, once again utilizing repeating bass patterns. This song cycle was the last of Ireland's works for some time to carry any overtones of conflict, and during peacetime his war topic went on hold.

Example 7.5

Ireland's circumstances both before and during the Second World War were quite different from those experienced during the Great War. Before and during the years 1914–18, he had a secure London base, and the prospect of passionate love affairs. In the early 1930s he suffered great personal traumas and lived for long periods in seclusion outside the city. In 1934 he gave up his regular Sussex retreat, and instead periodically began to escape to Deal, Kent, writing from his first residence, the Black Horse Hotel, that the town was 'free from the crushing, tragic weight of ancient times which is so oppressive in the Downs' (HR: Sept. 1934). For a short period, in 1936, he rented a room in a house in Middle Street, Deal. At this time his friend and solicitor, Herbert Brown, was living in Shepherdswell near Dover, and introduced Ireland to the Hulke family, the owners of a large Georgian house, Comarques, in the High Street, Deal. Brown was quite close to Ireland, and was musically knowledgable. The two men evidently met and discussed the composer's attraction to pagan sites, as in 1944 Brown wrote a poem, 'The forsaken altar', to his friend, the subject matter 'nameless rites' (*JIT*, 10). Ireland rented part of the top floor of Comarques between 1936 and 1939. From 1937 he stayed in this flat on an increasingly regular basis, and did much of his writing here. In each of the years 1937, 1938 and 1939 he produced a piece that had connections with the worsening situation in Europe: *These Things Shall Be*, the Third Piano Trio and the *Concertino Pastorale*. The only other works of these years were the three piano pieces that constitute *Green Ways*, and the Five Sixteenth-Century Poems. What is striking about the three big works of 1937–39 is that in them Ireland returns to and rewrites the First World War, rather as Siegfried Sassoon during the Second World War spent the latter part of his life 'plowing and re-plowing the earlier half' (Fussell, 1975: 92). The musical connections between these three works and those of the period *c.* 1912–19 are strong; an undeniable affirmation that Ireland consciously imbued the works with topical, war meaning.

Although officially commissioned for the accession and coronation of King George VI in May 1937, *These Things Shall Be* is a pre-war piece redolent of the spirit of the time. In keeping with the celebratory nature of the commission, Ireland chose to set eight of the fifteen verses of John Addington Symonds' visionary poem, 'A Vista'. Symonds was an ambiguous choice of poet, and appealed to Ireland on several levels. While the uplifting, idealistic words, with their Utopian vision, were apposite to the coronation of a new King, they were in keeping with the late 1930s mood of fraternity, and the desire to seek out a better world. They also had resonances with communist ideals of the day.

Symonds, however, was better known as a writer with an interest in the concept of Platonic love and male beauty. He had experienced a very similar upbringing to that of Ireland. His father was an enlightened Victorian, who introduced the Symonds family to figures such as William Gladstone and Alfred, Lord Tennyson. His mother died when he was just four years old. Like Ireland he married, but his marriage, unlike that of Ireland, lasted, and he had four daughters. Soon after his marriage Symonds became absorbed with the subject of homosexuality, and started to write extensively on the subject. At first his writings were discreet: he discussed the works of Christopher Marlowe, Sidney and Whitman, and studied the Greeks, eulogizing Plato's *Symposium* for its extolling of male comradeship. But Symonds was himself drawn to younger, handsome working-class males, and was very friendly with a number of the Uranian poets, particularly Horatio Forbes Brown, whom he regularly visited in Venice, and who was appointed his literary executor. Privately printed pamphlets, *A Problem in Greek Ethics* and *A Problem in Modern Ethics*, appeared in 1883 and 1891 respectively. These were expressions of his belief that homosexuality was congenital, and that there should be legal reform to allow for homosexual practice. At the time of his death he was working with Havelock Ellis on *Sexual Inversion*. The words of 'A Vista', with references to 'happier men' and 'free comrades' therefore cannot help but carry an undertone of homosexual freedom, while at the same time looking forward to an idealistic state in which the unnecessary barbarity of war no longer exists. An imagined Utopia was something that interested both writer and composer on several levels.

Ireland himself spoke of this text as befitting the war mood. He wrote to Henry Wood (1869–1944) that 'the sentiment of the poem is so particularly applicable to present times' (HW: 8 March 1943). It would seem that what he saw as being appropriate in this text were the references to 'golden days', inhabited by a 'loftier race', halcyon feelings which suited both pre- and post-war sentiments. Ireland had, in fact, set these words previously, supporting evidence that he saw this text as concerned with aspiration for peace and brotherhood. The earlier setting was the 1919 hymn tune, 'Fraternity', which used five rather than eight verses of 'A Vista'. This was produced for the *Motherland Song Book*, the official publication of the League of the Arts for National Civic Ceremony, a compilation of twenty songs and hymns, old and new, intended for use during the 1919 Peace Celebrations. The foreword to the song book speaks of the need to mingle 'national aspiration' with joy and 'a certain solemnity'. The content of this book of songs is intentionally patriotic, reflecting 'the qualities of our national idealism.' While the hymn tune 'Fraternity' has nothing in common with the music of *These Things Shall Be*, save for the choice of key, it is significant that Ireland viewed these words, with some very slight changes, as being suitable for 1919 peace celebrations, for the coronation of a new King and as an expression of Second World War idealism.

Ireland began work on *These Things Shall Be* in 1936, and because of the pressure of time enlisted the help of Alan Bush (1900–95), a former pupil. Bush concentrated on aspects of the orchestration of the work, which was eventually dedicated to him. The piece falls into clearly defined sections, rather akin to the structures of the church anthems. The first of these asks: 'Say, heart, what will the future bring?' by way of parallel octaves outlining an augmented fourth (Example 7.6).

Example 7.6

The orchestral passage that follows develops this motif until the chorus re-enter with the positive proclamation, 'These things shall be!' (Example 7.7), using the ^5^3^4^5 motif of 'The soldier'.

Example 7.7

In addition to the general 'fraternal' nature of the words, this piece was also associated more specifically with left-wing sentiments. During the late 1930s many British composers were involved in left-wing activities. In 1938 Britten set Randall Swingler's poem 'Advance Democracy' (Swingler was at that time on the staff of the Communist *Daily Worker*) and then in 1939 went on to use verse by him in his *Ballad of Heroes*, which honoured Britons who died in the Spanish Civil War. Ireland also had connections with Swingler, though it is unclear exactly when. He set some lines of his as a propagandist part-song with piano, published under the title *Ways of Peace* (Example 7.8 and Figure 7.2). This was written under the auspices of the International Peace Campaign, the aims of which were to strengthen the League of Nations in order to prevent and stop war, to remedy international conditions which might lead to war and to reduce and limit world armaments.

Example 7.8

Alan Bush was something of a figurehead for political music-making in the 1930s. He was a member of the Communist Party, and by 1940 his political affiliations had made him so unpopular with the British musical establishment that his works were banned for a short time by the BBC. With Tippett, he organized the music for the Pageant of Labour at the Crystal Palace in 1934, and in 1935 conducted at the International Workers' Music Olympiad in

7.2 Front cover of *Ways of Peace*, 1930s

Strasbourg. In 1936 the Workers' Music Association was formed, with Bush and Tippett on the executive committee. At the time of writing *These Things Shall Be*, Ireland was a supporter of the Workers' Music Association, as were Bantock, Boughton and Britten. At a late stage in the composition of the piece Ireland decided to incorporate the revolutionary song and at that time national anthem of the Soviet Union, the 'Internationale', into the orchestral parts following the words 'paradise' (Example 7.9).

Example 7.9

Soon after the first performance Ireland removed this tune from the score and rewrote the horn part, justifying his decision on the grounds that it had been rumoured that he was a communist supporter. However, the tune permeates the work too fully for it to be removed without significant revision. The issue of the 'Internationale' continued to trouble him:

> By the way, your reference to the theme 'The Internationale'. Only 4 bars of this are present in 'These Things Shall Be', & I doubt if anyone but a professional musician wd: notice it still ... I regarded it ... as a symbol of the Brotherhood of Man (in no sense a political slogan).
>
> (KT: 20 Feb. 1951)

And again, in 1952:

> You refer to what I told you about an alteration I made in 'These Things Shall Be'. You seem disappointed that I have removed the 'International' [*sic*] tune. Surely the reason must be perfectly obvious. Some musician spotted the tune about two years ago, and I found that rumours were being circulated that I am a communist, and that my use of that tune was a proof of it. In any case, it was not an essential feature of the music, the melodic line being in the upper strings and wood-wind, and what I have put in its place is more appropriate and cannot by any possibility be taken to have any political significance. It was only a subordinate inner part, not meant to be specially heard. The work was written in 1937, and since then things have changed considerably. What was then only mildly 'pink', now stands out as 'bright red'! It is clearly demonstrated, now, that 'communism' will not bring about the Utopian state of affairs suggested by the poem – quite the contrary!! So I think you will agree that it was best to remove anything in the music which could suggest Stalinist aims.
>
> (in Longmire, 1969: 93)

In 1938 Ireland completed a Third Piano Trio in four movements: Allegro moderato, Scherzo, Andante cantabile and Finale (Con moto). The musical material of this work dates from a much earlier period in his career. In April 1912 he had begun work on a Trio in D for clarinet in B flat, cello and piano. This was completed in October 1913 and revised between then and February 1914. In this revised format for clarinet trio the piece was performed in March 1915, at one of Mr de Lara's War Emergency Concerts, in Steinway Hall, but it remained unpublished. At some point, possibly shortly after this, Ireland began to rework the piece as a piano trio, but then abandoned it until 1938, when he returned to the work in earnest, wherever possible using the original manuscript material as a template on which to mark his alterations. In 1943 he wrote:

> It is not really very 'contemporary', as it began to germinate round about 1912 or 1913 … The musical material & the emotional content were all present in the original version, but badly expressed & clumsily managed.
>
> (ARLG: 25 Nov. 1943)

This manner of revisiting material was unusual for Ireland. Although he did return to and revise pieces, this is a unique instance of a comprehensive reworking of an early piece in order to create a new one. The real significance of this is that the 1938 piano trio is linked in the strongest possible way to an earlier war-situated work. The ominous signals in 1938 that another war was approaching may have stimulated Ireland to choose to return to material that originated from before and during the previous conflict.

Of the original trio for clarinet, cello and piano (Version 1), the first and last movements, and two pages of the second movement, survive. Version 2 consists of various workings for piano trio, including a new slow movement. It is therefore possible to trace the evolution from these to the published Version 3, the 1938 Third Piano Trio. The first movement was substantially altered, although the first subject was retained with some small revisions (Examples 7.10a and b).

Example 7.10a   Version 1, first subject

Example 7.10b   Version 3, first subject

The opening piano accompaniment pattern of Version 1 was radically different from the eventual quintuplet/sextuplet figuration (Examples 7.11a and b), and the cello was silent during the presentation of the first subject.

Example 7.11a   Version 1, opening piano accompaniment figure

Example 7.11b   Version 3, opening piano accompaniment figure

Version 2 has only an incomplete presentation of this movement, showing some of the stages between Version 1 and Version 3 – the new piano accompaniment is in place, but the first subject is still in its original format. By 1938 the second subject of Version 1 was abandoned altogether, with major structural, harmonic and melodic changes made to the rest of the movement.

There is no extant second movement for Version 2, but several bars of a section of the Scherzo survive from Version 1. Here the situation is quite different – Ireland has made no really fundamental changes from first to last versions, and the alterations are only in the fine detail. That the top line was originally conceived as a woodwind line does not seem to have affected its transference to the violin. Simply, the original Scherzo was essentially retained for the 1938 version.

No slow movement is extant in Version 1, but there are two sides of manuscript of a slow movement in Version 2. These bars are the first indications that Ireland was reconsidering the work as a piano trio, but they bear no resemblance to the eventual slow movement of Version 3, nor do they appear in any other of Ireland's works. However, it was quite clearly his intention at this time (c. 1915) that these bars should precede the final movement: the fourth movement for Version 2 followed immediately from a further eight bars of workings for this slow movement.

The nature of the changes made to the fourth movement fall somewhere between those made to the first and the second movements: it was not completely rewritten, but the alterations are more significant than those made to the scherzo. The basic melodic material was retained, with the main changes affecting the overall structure of the 1938 finale. The last movement of Version 1 is generally less tightly constructed than Version 3, and contains a section in which Ireland motivically recalls the first movement. Version 2 (which is incomplete in manuscript) is more akin to Version 3, but contains a section in $\frac{4}{4}$ that is missing at the Version 3 stage, and has an extended concluding section.

There are other ways in which the Third Piano Trio has an aura of retrospection. It has four separate movements employing traditional formal structures, and evident French influences that were a feature of Ireland's works around the years 1912–17. It also has motivic connections with yet another earlier work of war, the 1917 Second Piano Trio. The piano's opening bars outline the same melodic pattern as did the first march section of the Second Piano Trio (Example 7.12; and see the cello line in Example 7.2).

Example 7.12

The first movement of the Third Piano Trio uses sonata principle, and is a more lyrical rendering of the contrasting sentiments of the 1917 trio. It is in the second movement that the connections between the piano trios are most recognizable. It uses a traditional format of scherzo and contrasting trio. The scherzo has the buoyant radiance of the finale of the Second Violin Sonata, but also the characteristic march features of the war music.

The slow movement, the only completely new movement in 1938, uses a different harmonic language altogether: it is a sentimental rhapsody, and in places has a contemporary air of cabaret (for example at bars 17–19, as shown in Example 7.13). The brisk finale has thematic links with the first movement.

Example 7.13

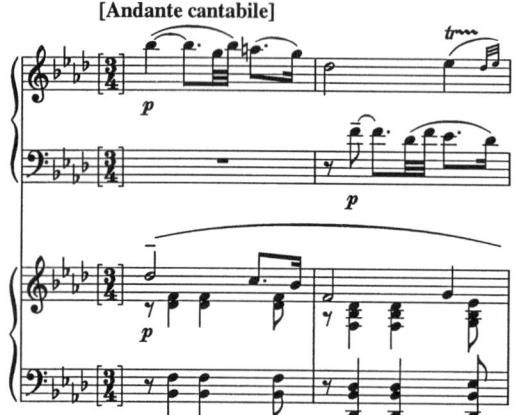

The impetus for both this trio and the one dating from 1912 was impending war, and common to both wars, Ireland's music evinces an awareness of approaching disaster. But whereas the pre-First World War works such as *The Forgotten Rite* focused on nature and pagan elements in a spellbound impressionistic haze, the late 1930s works were more menacing, imbued with a sense of foreboding. One of these was the *Concertino Pastorale*. This is the only work that Ireland conceived originally for string orchestra (the others, including *A Downland Suite*, were all transcriptions and reworkings of other media). It was the result of a commission by the Boyd Neel String Orchestra, for a performance in the 1939 Canterbury Festival, written while Ireland was living in Deal, completed in May and performed in June, shortly before he left the county. In 1951 Ireland described the way in which the work was influenced by his responses to the impending war:

> Whatever I had in mind is expressed in the music, and cannot (quite) be put into words. At that particular time, the menace of Hitler hung rather heavily on any thinking person, and it is to be noticed, perhaps, that the first movement opens with a distorted and 'nightmarish' treatment of the spring-like theme which is the real basis of the movement. The Threnody perhaps expresses in some way the transitoriness and poignancy of the beautiful. After the seriousness of the two preceding movements, the Toccata gives some sense of liberation, and musically is a change in texture and form from the closely-packed Eclogue and the emotion of the Threnody.
>
> (HRawlinson: 9 June 1951)

There are some parallels with the Second Violin Sonata in terms of the musical organization of the piece. The backdrop is war, though this time potential rather than actual. Like the Second Violin Sonata, the three movements explore a gamut of shifting emotions. The opening Eclogue deploys some of Ireland's 'conflict' motifs: a pulsing pedal, the underlying sense of grimness and starkness emphasized by chromatic melodies and prominent semitones. He uses the same unaccompanied meandering melody lines found in the Second Violin Sonata and later in the Fantasy-Sonata. After the sombre opening the piece settles into the 'eclogue' proper, its lyricism and tonal stability placing it firmly within Ireland's 'country'. Perhaps here the composer was consciously conveying his image of rural countryside in the same way that J.B. Priestley's book, *Our Nation's Heritage* (1939) and Hugh Massingham's *The English Countryside* (1939) evoked features and experiences of rural England in order to locate and establish a distinctly British identity at a time of crisis.

The Threnody which follows is like a number of Ireland's 'middle' movements. It is in a flat major key, and is a lyrical, contemplative rhapsody. What is significant about this movement is the very strong reference to *The Forgotten Rite* (see Example 3.1) in bars 59–60 (Example 7.14)

Example 7.14

The work as a whole is both nostalgic and premonitory: while the second movement is a reminiscence of the loveliness of Jersey before the First World War and a contemporary attempt to recall pastoral England, the concluding toccata has an unrelenting ferocity unusual in Ireland's output.

In June 1939 Ireland decided to shut Gunter Grove, vacate the Deal rooms and leave England for Guernsey. On 3 July, along with John Longmire, he travelled from Southampton to St Peter Port. According to Longmire (1969: 40), this was a project which had been discussed for some time, and was certainly being mooted during 1938. Rather as Ireland's works just before the First World War are sensuous and escapist, so too was this brief period before the outbreak and during the first few months of the Second World War. Although Britain was officially at war from 3 September, the 'Phoney War' appeared to have little, if any, impact on the Channel Islands. Though there is evidence that Ireland expressed some concern that Guernsey was considered vulnerable, in comparison with London the island appeared to be a positively safe haven. Ireland wrote in September 1939 that he intended to stay on indefinitely, 'as apart from "blackout" and the usual A.R.P. precautions, Guernsey is quite peaceful, and I suppose comparatively safe, although the aerodrome has been taken over by a detachment of the R.A.F. with some men and 4 or 5 warplanes which I believe are for spotting submarines, and patrol work' (PW: 23 Sept. 1939).

Whereas some of his musician contemporaries who had remained in England professed an inability to compose, the war acting as an artistic block, Ireland was far enough removed from the political and social instability to be able to continue to produce music. His letters from the months in Guernsey, right up until his departure in 1940, are more concerned with the general state of his own intoxication induced by his experiences on the island. Unlike some of his colleagues in England, he suffered none of the material discomforts of the first months of the war: from October 1939 he lived in a marvellous, spacious house, Fort Saumarez. In 1940 Ireland was still primarily occupied with the enjoyment of life on Guernsey. Longmire, with whom he was living in Fort Saumarez, recalled that:

> The days passed pleasantly. In that remote spot, one day was much like another. The coast and headland were a constant joy to us, and our rambles interspersed with visits to the L'Erée Hotel and our chats with the local fishermen became part of our daily routine.
> We visited the fascinating town of St Peter Port twice a week to do our shopping. Ireland revelled in the fine granite-built market, with its stalls of fruit, vegetables and fruit in profusion. He enjoyed making various purchases, always choosing with the eye of a connoisseur.
>
> (Longmire, 1969: 53)

For Ireland, it truly was a time of profusion and well-being, enhanced still further on his move from Fort Saumarez to the Birnam Court Hotel, home of Michael Rayson and inspiration for 'In a May morning'. There was no sign of a musical response to the early years of the war, and the only works produced were the Missa *Sancti Stephani* and the first movement of *Sarnia*, neither of which has any demonstrable associations with the international situation.

The rosy idyll did not last for long. The Channel Islands were at risk of invasion, and after France's armistice with Germany in June 1940 the situation became pressing. On 19 June the Channel Islands were demilitarized, and evacuation was soon under way. By 21 June many of Guernsey's children had left. Ireland was still there on 22 June, waiting for transport off the island. Boult and the BBC became involved in urging the War Office to secure a passage for him, and he was on one of the last boats to leave Guernsey, the SS *Antwerp*, along with Longmire and Percy Turnbull, the latter a composer friend who had been visiting. On his arrival in Weymouth later that day, Ireland wrote to Thompson, describing his ordeal. Guernsey was bombed by the *Luftwaffe* on 28 June, and invaded on 30 June. Jersey surrendered the next day, followed by Alderney on 2 July and Sark on 3 July. Many hotels were commandeered, as was Fort Saumarez. This became a German headquarters, and a concrete observation tower was built on the site of the Martello Tower in order to defend L'Erée headland. As had been feared, many Channel Islanders were eventually deported to Germany. These included Ireland's friend from St Saviour's Church, the Reverend Wood and his wife, who were taken to the Biberach internment camp in September 1942. Reverend Hartley Jackson from St Stephen's was also interned, but all returned to the island in 1945. On 22 June 1950, exactly ten years after the escape, Ireland recalled:

> In case it has not occurred to you, today is the 10th anniversary of our forced exit from Guernsey, in 1940.
>
> Cast your mind back to that day in all its details – remember how you, Turnbull and myself went early to the gathering-place at the bottom of St Julian's Avenue – and how we gradually made our way to the boat after some three hours' waiting and gradual progress, step by step – being quite uncertain whether we should really be able to make our escape after all.
>
> Remember the large numbers of people and the many boats crossing to the mainland with their loads of refugees – and the absolutely miraculous fact that the <u>Germans did not know of it</u> – and how, if they had known, they would have exalted in bombing the defenceless procession of ships and their packed human cargoes.
>
> Remember how, in mid-channel, our boat was pursued by a submarine? How the future was dark and hidden from us?
>
> (JL: 22 June 1950, in Longmire, 1969: 62)

Ireland's circumstances on his return to England were in great contrast to his situation on Guernsey. He could not return to Gunter Grove, and his Deal flat was in a hazardous spot on the exposed and vulnerable south coast of England. Thenceforth Ireland spent the war years relying on the hospitality of friends. He went first to Alan Bush's home in Radlett, a town which was itself heavily bombed, and from there to Banbury, where he completed *Sarnia*.

From this period a substantial correspondence survives, in which Ireland expresses his aversion to the situation. Shortly after his return, in July 1940, when Britain was threatened with invasion, he wrote to Kenneth Thompson:

> I do not agree with you at all when you try to pretend we are living through bracing times. The whole thing is hellish and disgusting, and life is quite impossible except for those who are taking an active part in the conflict. Everything that made life worth living is at a standstill. All values are perverted – for instance, a person with my particular capabilities is useless in the present régime, which is simply a game being played between statesmen – a game involving the lives & happiness of many millions of mere pawns.
>
> (KT: 24 July 1940)

During 1941 Ireland also wrote of his struggle with the composing process, saying that 'a sort of nausea has come over me' (KT: 25 Nov. 1941). In that he was not living his own house, and for some months had no access to a piano, his circumstances were not terribly conducive to working. The year was the start of a series of personal losses, the first of which was the destruction of

Chelsea Old Church in a raid on London in April 1941, this church one of Ireland's loved landmarks. Queen's Hall was also destroyed in 1941. But despite his expressions of difficulty, during the years 1940–45 Ireland was surprisingly productive, and this period in his life occasioned a varied and sizeable output, including several important works. 1941 was primarily a year of wistful backward glances at life on Guernsey: *Sarnia* was completed in March, and there followed a number of short church works and a series of unison songs and piano miniatures. These are retrospective, both in thought and in musical content. There are dedications to Guernsey choristers, and there are rewritings of early works, such as the first two of the *Three Pastels*. The interest in Eleanor Farjeon's poems for children, specifically poems concerned with boys, which emerged in 1941, continued through 1942.

During this period, Ireland was commissioned to write works of a functional, public nature, but at the same time he produced introspective, personal pieces. There is a dramatic contrast between the works that reflect a particular moment in time, and those which are either retrospective or timeless. The public spirit of the Second World War was very different from that of the First World War, and soon after Ireland's departure for Guernsey, Herbert Brown had written to him, describing the early sirens of September 1939 and the changed attitude to war:

> The sirens went off for the first time at 11 o'clock on Sunday, before we knew anything of the declaration of war, and I assumed that this was the promised opening of the 'blitzenkrieg' and that we were in for hell's delight, but to our relief the all clear blew soon afterwards ...
>
> People in the town seem pretty calm, but there is a notable lack of any enthusiasm for war and of the 'Land of hope and glory' spirit of August 1914. The fact is that all, except perhaps the very youthful or the irredeemably militant, have lost all illusions about this war business, and see its infinite folly and wickedness all too clearly.

(HB to JI: 7 Sept. 1939)

For many it was felt that the only solution to the latest war was to create a new world order, and to purge Europe of its rotten core. J.B. Priestley talked of this need in one of his 1940 broadcasts, saying that the war demanded a collective effort, a turning away from traditional British interests in property and power to a new emphasis on community and creation:

> I tell you, there is stirring in us now, a desire which could soon become a controlled but passionate determination to remodel and recreate this world of ours, to make it the glorious beginning of a new world order, so that we might soon be so fully and happily engrossed in our great task that if Hitler and his gang suddenly disappeared we'd hardly notice that they'd gone. We're even now the hope of free men everywhere but soon we could be the hope and lovely dawn of the whole wide world.

(Priestley: 21 July 1940, in Giles and Middleton, 1995: 127)

These stirring words summed up the spirit of the time, a spirit created and cultivated to a certain extent by the Ministry of Information. The image of a collective toil and sweat permeated popular thought for some years. Writer Rollo Myers commented on musical activity in Britain during the war, stating that 'in spite of the material dangers and difficulties to which this country was exposed during six long years, spiritual and artistic values were never lost sight of or allowed to be submerged in the heat and dust of the struggle' (Myers, 1947: 43).

Several pieces were commissioned from Ireland to be overtly stirring in spirit in accordance with national sentiments. The first of these, in 1941, was a song for voice and piano, 'O happy land', a setting of a poem by W.J. Linton, which Ireland felt was 'particularly suitable to the present time' (GP: 13 Nov. 1941). With its repeating stanzas and noble tone, it is more hymn than song. Motivically it has connections with the 'noble' tune that was used in 'The soldier' and 'Blow out, you bugles' (Example 7.15, and see Example 7.3).

Example 7.15

'O happy land' takes up the sentiments of *These Things Shall Be*, and pre-empts those of *Epic March*, an orchestral work commissioned by the Ministry of Information. The ministry's aim was to construct a 'People's War', a war which relied on community spirit and a national, democratic aspiration for peace. In 1940 the Ministry of Information had prescribed that feature films, documentaries and cartoons should actively aim to promote British life and character, ideas and institutions. London's survival of the Blitz became a symbol of British fortitude, and the film, *London (Britain) Can Take It*, directed by Humphrey Jennings, made much of the fact that German bombing had been unable to quash British spirit and courage. In conjunction with Boult and the BBC, the Ministry of Information also commissioned a number of musical works for propaganda purposes. In September 1940 Boult approached Vaughan Williams to produce a song or hymn on a patriotic theme, the outcome of which was *England, my England*, and in November of that year he proposed to Ireland that he should write a patriotic march. Ireland was obviously attracted to the commission, as he discussed the proposed march with Herbert Brown, who wrote that 'bearing in mind the tremendous rhythmic zest and vitality with which you can write, I do not for one moment doubt your capacity, given the mood, to compose a thoroughly stirring and effective one' (HB to JI: 8 Dec. 1940). Ireland worked on the piece in 1941, in June writing that he was developing 'stern & purposeful' ideas (KT: 26 June 1941). It was completed in March 1942.

Before deciding on the title *Epic March*, Ireland considered several options (see Craggs, 1993: 108), including 'Grim and Gay' (a quotation from one of Churchill's speeches), 'The Liberators', 'Calling all Shirkers' (presumably a wry reference to Coates' 'Calling all Workers'), 'Ussia (USSR) v. Prussia', 'Heroic March' and 'March in C minor'. He eventually added a definition of the word 'epic' to the front of the score: 'Concerning some heroic action or series of actions and events of deep and lasting significance in the history of a nation or race'.

Epic March was a continuation, but a somewhat different presentation, of the sentiments expressed in *These Things Shall Be*. Ireland said that the work was 'meant to be anti-fascist music' (NB: 20 June 1942) and initially considered using a tune from *These Things Shall Be* as the central section of the march, a suggestion that came from Boult:

> In sounding you out we have very much in mind your glorious London Overture and the big broad tune in 'These Things Shall Be'. With a blend of the spirit and essence of these two – (in fact, wouldn't an adaptation, in measure, of the latter tune make a splendid trio in the March?) – the appeal is guaranteed straight away.

(AB to JI: 28 Nov. 1940)

Herbert Brown advised against this, on the grounds that the sentiments of *These Things Shall Be* were not at all jingoistic, but rather 'pacific and idealistic', and suggested instead that Ireland might reuse one of his 'last war tunes (something from "The Soldier" perhaps)' (HB to JI: 8 Dec. 1940). Ireland's decision to agree to the commission at all was partly due to his loathing of the world situation, but also because it happened to coincide with a time of interest in writing for the orchestra. The work is a tonal march with two clearly defined musical ideas. The first, in C minor (Example 7.16a), is a grim, driving theme, dominated by brass.

Example 7.16a

[Allegro energico]

Its forward momentum is created by the rhythmic figure from which it is derived and which contributes to the deliberately stoic feel. A second, rather more ponderous theme in C major arises from this. The central section introduces a new melody in E flat major (Example 7.16b), its broad lyricism in contrast to the brittle opening. This is the section where Ireland considered using the tune from *These Things Shall be*, and indeed the new material he eventually produced has strong similarities both with this work and with 'O happy land', not least the symbolic choice of key. Once again the 'noble' downward scale used in 'The soldier' is present. The deliberate contrast between driving movement and positive lyricism also has parallels with Elgar's Pomp and Circumstance marches, and with *Mai-Dun*, itself an expression of war and repose.

Example 7.16b

Largamente

p ma sonore ed espress.

After the central section the C minor motif reappears, followed by a brief reference to the second theme, this time in C major, complete with bells and organ. The march ends with its opening music now transformed into C major. In his use of the full orchestra, his creation of several climactic moments and in his calculated juxtaposition of grim and noble determinations, Ireland pre-empted his single foray into film music.

In July 1942 Ireland moved to Little Sampford Rectory, in a village near Saffron Walden, Essex, to stay with his old friend Paul Walde. Soon after this move he was commissioned to write incidental music for a BBC production of *Julius Caesar*, which appropriately required battle music. In terms of work, 1943 began as a lean year. Ireland wrote that he had 'got out of the habit of writing music – whether it is sheer indolence or lack of stimulus, I don't know … Before the war I was teaching, examining and composing – now I am doing absolutely nothing except making a few reports on BBC programmes and sitting once a month on the Advisory Music Panel' (KT: 16 Feb. 1943). But later that year inspiration must have been renewed, as he started work on his Fantasy-Sonata for clarinet and piano.

Living outside London, Ireland was able to view the effect of the war on the city from a distance, a war that continued to inflict personal destruction. The rooms in Deal in which he had worked on *These Things Shall Be*, the Third Piano Trio and the *Concertino Pastorale*, were devastated when the house, Comarques, was badly damaged by a shell from German guns on the French coast on 4 December 1943 (Figure 7.3). In 1944 he wrote of a particularly appalling air-raid:

> … the raid that evening was one of the worst since 1941. 175 planes came over and 100 reached London! It started about midnight, and I watched it from here [Sampford]. I really never saw anything like it, and I was thankful I was not there. It must have been awful. It went on for nearly one-and-a-half hours, and one could see the fires from here – all around the horizon.
>
> (JL: 22 Feb. 1944, in Longmire, 1969: 101)

7.3 Shell damage to Comarques, 1943

In 1944 Gunter Grove suffered bomb damage. Later this year Ireland moved to The White House, Great Sampford, to stay with the Hutcheson family, friends from some years earlier. Gunter Grove was then repaired, and in 1945 he was moving between London and the Sampford addresses. There were two major projects in the years 1944–46. These were the orchestral overture, *Satyricon*, and the film score for *The Overlanders*. During the war a number of British composers had become involved in writing film music. At the request of the Ministry of Labour and National Service, William Walton (1902–83) worked primarily on films, including such patriotic offerings as *Next of Kin* (1941) and *The First of the Few* (1942). Bax, too, wrote film music at this time, as did Vaughan Williams. Ireland initially had reservations about writing for film. However, in 1946 he was asked to provide the music for *The Overlanders* (see Plate 17), and he became engrossed in the project. Some years earlier, in 1943, Jack Beddington, then controller of film-making for the Ministry of Information, had asked producer Michael Balcon of Ealing Studios to consider making a film on the subject of the Australian national response to the war. Director Harry Watt (who had directed the 1936 Britten–Auden collaboration, *Night Mail*) was sent to Australia to research a subject, and on a visit to the Australian Ministry of Food heard about a remarkable achievement of 1942. In this year tens of thousands of cattle were overlanded from the Northern Territory to Cairns in order to save them from Japanese aerial attack or invasion. The film that ensued was as much documentary as fiction, the emphasis placed firmly on the dramatic Australian landscape, shown on film for the first time, with superb photography supervised by Osmond Borradaile.

Ireland was asked by the music director of Ealing Studios, Ernest Irving (1878–1953), to write a series of short musical episodes to accompany key moments in the film. He wrote that:

> Tho' terribly hard, *cruel* work, this film is very interesting and exciting. It is to do with Australia – all about 1000 cattle, horses and drovers, and the obstacles met, in moving the cattle South, when a Jap invasion was expected. It needs a lot of heavy, symphonic music, and what I have done is extremely good and will make an excellent concert suite – but the amount of work is fantastic. I get up at 6 every morning – and work till 1 or 2 a.m. – *every* day !

(MW: 1946, in Searle, 1979: 120)

Both the film, starring popular Australian actor Chips Rafferty, and the music were extremely well received. Irving himself wrote:

> This film, as I predicted, is having a great success and John Ireland's forceful and honest-to-God music has certainly helped to 'put it over'. The music for the river crossing, the two stampedes, and the mountain crossing holds up long action scenes without dialogue and adds greatly to the tension and excitement of the Homeric episodes in the 1,500 mile cattle-trek from the Australian Northern territory to 'Queensland'.

(Irving, 1946: 27)

And Scott Goddard, an admirer of Ireland's music, commented:

> Artistic intent can be found in John Ireland's music for *The Overlanders*, and I can imagine Dreyer agreeing that it both supports and deepens a mood already prepared in the action. I am told that some Australians feel otherwise ; that the mood of the bush country has in the first place not been understood. As a foreigner I cannot judge that, though I can realize that any music with a slight tang of English folk-song would sound out of place to an Australian. And I seem to recall that one sequence has that flavour. But for the average English listener Ireland's music is like a freshening wind. From the very start the fanfares of the title music have an individuality unmistakably his own, a turn of harmonic design never before heard in the cinema.

> (Goddard, 1947: 66)

The Overlanders is a film that relies heavily on the impact of dramatic landscape shots. Because of this there are long sections of dialogue without music, and natural sounds such as the night cries of cockatoos play an important role. But in addition there are a number of clearly defined passages of music which contribute to the action. Ireland had to provide the music for the opening and end titles, and for a sequence of dramatic episodes within the film. Many of these were orchestrated by Irving, who also conducted the Philharmonia Orchestra on the original film track, and some by Alan Rawsthorne (1905–71). In order to create these sections of music Ireland drew on his long-established methods of response to different situations, and in this film he can be seen using his topics to match particular scenes.

The music for the opening title plunges the viewer (and listener) into the war. Like *Mai-Dun*, which began *in medias res*, the film opens with driving rhythms and busy semiquavers. As a local family set fire to their property to deny its use by potential invaders, Ireland's 'Scorched Earth' has the two types of musical response to war that have been seen throughout this chapter: swiftly moving, repetitive patterns and slow, mournful melodies. However, as a ship carrying local inhabitants leaves the Northern Territory to take its passengers to join up, the emphasis of the film, and thus the music, changes. The transition from fixed place to cattle-droving is effected rather appropriately, through another of Ireland's *ranz-des-vaches* melodies, whose outline is very similar to that of the horn introduction to *Legend*.

As the drovers leave to overland the cattle, there is a new section of music. This is one that returns periodically, and which is used to symbolize the cattle in the landscape. To this end Ireland returned to his 'pastoral', and this music has all the established characteristics: a $\frac{6}{8}$ time signature, a major tonality, gently rocking motion and always a pleasant and undisturbed character. As the trek overland progresses, there are a number of dramatic incidents which have accompanying music. The first of these is a river crossing, during which cattle and horses have to be swum across a crocodile-infested river. Here the pastoral music is retained, but transformed into a more striving version, the final chord a postive major one as the last successful crossing takes place.

The incident with the most striking music is that involving wild horses. After the domestic working horses die from eating poisoned weed, the drovers have to catch wild horses, or 'brumbies', and Ireland provided two sequences of music associated with this event. The first was 'Catching the Brumbies', a brilliant whirl, with the same ferocity as the finale of the *Concertino Pastorale*. For the short sequence, 'Breaking the Brumbies', a 'wild and wayward' clarinet solo over spiky staccato is eventually 'tamed' back to the opening 'Scorched Earth' music.

There is one brief 'love' interlude in the film, for which Ireland wrote an unrestrained melody, assured in the manner of the slow movement of the Piano Concerto and the second subject of *A London Overture*, though much less expansive. In the film this was interrupted by a cattle stampede, an opportunity for demonstrations of horsemanship and more spectacular camera work. Ireland's music for this was essentially war music – man in conflict with the cattle. He produced another perverted version of the pastoral passages, major turned minor, marked rhythms prominent and the overall effect again similar to that of the opening of *Mai-Dun*. (The links between this last with *Legend* and *The Overlanders* perhaps hint at some part of Ireland's mind that interpreted the vast expanse of the Australian outback as having pagan qualities.) Here again the successful domination of the cattle provoked a rousing major conclusion.

The last two scenes in the film were accompanied by overtly pictorial music. The first, 'Mountain Crossing', was another moment of conflict, this time man against the mountain. And here again Ireland used the inexorable rhythms of his war topic, contained within a fugue. The last, 'Water Stampede', used such basic techniques as trills to evoke the wind shaking the reeds and disturbing the water's surface, the tempo increasing with the cattle stampede. This section surely shows the influences of Stravinsky's *Sacre du printemps*.

While Ireland never professed to have any particular skill or interest in this area, his single film score demonstrated that he was extremely adept at working to images, and that he could well have produced other successful examples. What is interesting is that here he produced a succession of short pieces that accord with the different topics discussed in this book. There are other works in which this mixing of topics can be seen, and in a much more discursive manner.

Chapter 8

Songs and sonatas, sacred and profane: knowing Ireland

The intention of this book has been to concentrate on the expressive and extramusical qualities of Ireland's music. Many of his works are clearly situated within a particular topical field, and it can been seen that 'expressive considerations motivate compositional choices' (Hatten, 1994: 1). Often the meaning of a piece is implicit in its title as well as in its internal musical characteristics. To revisit the six main topics of the book, Ireland was a practising Anglo-Catholic, who wrote functional church music, intended primarily for amateur performance. There are two main musical responses, the one prophetic, the other sweetly transcendent, and there is little sign of musical development from early to late pieces. He deploys a conscious 'church' style, one inherited from the Victorians, using a harmonic language that is a mixture of diatonicism and modality. Chords are in root position, melodic lines are simple, and word-setting syllabic. There is a fascination with Christ's Passion, which inspired three anthems that have similar structures, with motivically related subsections. There is also a light music element in the organ music. The pagan Ireland was attracted to the work of writers, particularly Machen, who shared his interest in an indefinable 'other-worldliness'. There are works that are musical evocations of Pan, using ternary structures in which a mood is established, a new world entered and the old one re-entered, now subtly altered. There are also narrative structures and gestural signals in the music. Common harmonic and melodic features include hovering second inversion chords and sliding parallel perfect fourths. There are aspects shared with the 'country' Ireland, notably bare fifths, though in the pagan topic there are added chromaticisms.

Ireland's country is embedded in single mood miniatures without narrative structures. There are subtopics, or 'types' within his country: the pastoral works that draw on an inherited tradition, pieces depending on lyrical figuration, trills and cross-rhythms, impressionistic responses to Symbolist poetry and ballads, both vigorous and tender. There are significant literary influences that are shared with the city, notably the poetry of Symons. Ireland's London is a mixture of past and present. There are representations of place, and character pieces that embody the composer's vernacular style, with clear-cut phrases, joky melodies and offbeat rhythms. There are also more complex narrative structures that mix people and places.

Love for Ireland is concentrated in songs and piano music. There are manifestations of different types of love. Ecstatic, fulfilled experiences are found mainly in works from *c.* 1913–26. In contrast there are expressions of repression and denial, found in modal, speech-like musings and explored in angular melodies. There is the symbolic Passion motif and motivic links between the pieces that fall into this topic, such as the Piano Concerto and 'Spring will not wait'. There are recurring literary influences, for example the work of Housman, whose poetry also has strong connections with Ireland's war topic. As in the church music, there are two main types of response to war, the one striving, the other mourning. Recurring motifs feature in the war music, especially the ^5^4^3^2^1 pattern, and there are strong links between the pieces of the two wars. Marches, incisive rhythms, pedals and propelling upbeats all feature in this topic.

Some pieces are easy to define by a single topic, some are more complex, and hover between worlds, as was seen, for example, in nature-ecstasy works such as 'Earth's call'. In others, and especially the chamber works that bear no programmatic title, topics mingle and create a narrative structure. Sometimes one particular topical area is prevalent, sometimes no single topic is foregrounded, but areas of feeling come and go as the piece progresses. Some of the song-cycles fit into this category, in that they explore different states within a whole that is integrated by motif or by literary connections: the best example of this is *Songs Sacred and Profane*, which will be discussed later in this chapter. But it is in the three-movement piano and chamber works that this can be seen most clearly, and which was hinted at in the discussion of the Piano Concerto in Chapter 6. This includes the two Violin Sonatas, the Piano Sonata and the Sonatina, the Cello Sonata, and to a lesser extent the three Piano Trios. It also includes some of the extended one-movement works, most notably the late Fantasy-Sonata for clarinet and piano.

Throughout his life, Ireland's favoured strategy for producing a large-scale work or suite, most often in three movements, was to write three contrasting, but connected movements. The connections might be thematic, as in the Second Violin Sonata; literary, as was seen in *Decorations*; topical (*London Pieces*); or a mixture of motivic, literary and autobiographical, as in *Sarnia*. Where works have three movements these serve clearly defined functions, and carry distinct meanings. Thus the middle movement is nearly always a love song, whether or not this is made explicit in the title or caption.

The four *Preludes* for piano, written between December 1913 and April 1915, showed Ireland beginning to mix topics within a set of pieces, and the early reviews of this set picked this up. The *Musical Times* described the first piece, 'The undertone', as 'significant, though brief' and 'a piece of quite singular appeal' (*MT*, June 1918: 258). This short prelude is a rumination on a two-bar (ten-note) ostinato, the pitches of which remain constant for the duration of the piece. Ireland imbues the different presentations of the ostinato figure with changing textures, harmonies and melodies, and contains the whole within an arch structure. The prelude builds up to an impassioned climax in bar 31 and then dies back to end with a simple, unadorned version of the ten notes. The prelude that follows is called 'Obsession', its earlier tentative title 'Mandrake'. This was described in the same *Musical Times* feature as 'a difficult and at first somewhat repellent movement'; perhaps repellent in that it is a much more neurotic version of the angular, sparse Symbolist types such as 'Moon-glade'. This is countered by the simplicity of 'The holy boy', and the set ends with 'Fire of spring', a short, but extravagant nature piece drawing on the cross-rhythms and ecstatic coruscations (bars 35–6 and 48–50) of Ireland's country. Evans, in 1919, commented on contrasts within the collection, writing of 'Obsession' that it 'might have been suggested by Edgar Allan Poe, or by the counsels of a witch's familiar' (1919a: 218), and of 'Fire of spring' that it was a 'rhapsodical outburst' (ibid.: 219). While this set of pieces contains examples of Ireland's different topics, there is no real sense of continuity or narrative, and the preludes are essentially simply a collection of short piano pieces which explore diverse moods, in the manner of the Debussy sets of preludes for the piano. The same is true of *Decorations*, though the three pieces that make up this group have stronger topical connections.

The first piece in which Ireland began to experiment with an extended formal structure within which he mixed topics was the one-movement Rhapsody for piano (1915). This was Ireland's largest piece for solo piano at this time, and stands as a link between the loosely related suites and the tightly integrated works of 1917–20, such as the Piano Sonata and *London Pieces*. Its structural predecessor was the Phantasie Trio, which was a one-movement work with two main themes. The Rhapsody is a more complex, less restrained version of the same idea, and like the earlier work is influenced by Brahms in terms of its melodic development. It is a pianistic rhapsody in that there are two main themes, the second derived from the first, which evolve freely through different states of harmony and quixotic changes of tempo. The changing states, however, are not abstract ones, and are always redolent with meaning as Ireland moves around his world. A 1917 review of the piece noted these two opposing states without giving a specific reading: 'There are pleasing themes – notably that in F major – which contrast admirably with the marked rhythmic figures mostly in evidence' (*MT*, May 1917: 211).

The music that opens the Rhapsody belongs to Ireland's expressions of conflict, with its driving upbeat and initial bare octaves (Example 8.1a). This has strong parallels with the first bars of the Second Violin Sonata and 'the rugged character of the opening' is also a 'pre-echo of *Mai-Dun*' (Palmer, 1992: 4) (this latter a manifestation of war in a pagan landscape).

Example 8.1a

This topic soon gives way to another, the composer's country. The second main theme, starting at the upbeat to bar 39, is part of Ireland's pastoral, in that its compound time is combined with drones, consonant harmonies and a simple, stepwise melody (Example 8.1b).

Example 8.1b

The Symbolist aspect of Ireland's country is also present in the piece, particularly from bar 119, with the section marked 'in a chime-like sonority' and the use of *una corda* from bar 127 being references to 'The island spell'. Similarly, the figurative cadenza that constitutes bar 197, and the sometimes thinner textures and markedly delicate melodies, all belong to facets of this topic in Ireland's music. The shifting parallel chords that recur across Ireland's output as a symbol of ecstasy are present, for example in bars 70–72, as are the short passages of chordal repose that also seem to be associated with a spiritual aspect of Ireland's country. The most striking example of this is at bar 198, where the brilliant figuration of the cadenza gives way to a Tranquillo, an eight-bar section of slow-moving chords. The landscape of the Rhapsody can also be a pagan one, through its unresolved, expectant harmonies and emphasized augmented fourths. As Palmer suggested, the piece 'despite its non-comittal title, is ... charged with the legendary atmosphere of *The Forgotten Rite*' (1992: 4). There is even a direct quote of the notes of the flute call of *The Forgotten Rite* (bar 196). The piece is therefore a juxtaposition of the currency of war with the rural and historic aspects of Ireland's country. Sometimes, as in the transition from first to second subject, the juxtapositions are dramatic. Here driving war suddenly accedes to overt pastoral. Sometimes the moves are more subtle.

The large-scale work that followed the Rhapsody was the Second Violin Sonata. This was introduced in Chapter 1 as a work that was strongly influenced by its date of composition, and concerned with 'stormy times' (EC: 5 March 1948). The descriptive terms used by Edwin Evans in 1919 defined the first movement as having 'rugged vigour', the second as being 'concerned with lyrical solace', and the third as 'a relaxation of the prevailing tension' and humour (Evans, 1919c: 458). What has become evident from looking at Ireland's output in terms of its meanings and associations, as expressed through an identifiable topic system, is that Evans' interpretations have credence, and that the work cannot be viewed in purely abstract terms.

The single overpowering consideration that filled 'the minds of all thinking men' (Evans, 1919c: 457) was the war. Going off to fight for one's country was the one thing of importance at this time, and in a sense the only thing to write about. As was discussed in the previous chapter, Ireland was at home at the time of writing the piece. In the original call to arms in 1914, he was deemed too old and physically unsuitable. But though his working life continued as usual, in London the war was a constant presence, visible everywhere in temporary street shrines, in the reports of the horrific death toll in the early battles of Mons, Aisne and Loos, in the news of the Gallipoli campaign and the much-publicized and romanticized death of Rupert Brooke in April 1915. These events were the backdrop to the commencement of work on the Second Violin Sonata in October 1915. The public mood in the first part of the war was largely one of optimism, fuelled by stirring propaganda, but in 1916 there were more appalling battles, and increasing signs of revolt and protest, expressed in anti-war prose and in works such as Siegfried Sassoon's 'In the Pink' and H.G. Wells' novel, *Mr Britling Sees It Through*.

Set against these happenings, and through its juxtaposition and integration of topics, this sonata tells a story. It is a narrative of war; its actuality, its consequences and the potential for rebirth and redemption. What it is not is an account of battle, and there is never a point at which fighting takes place. The interpretation that follows is a hermeneutic reading of the piece. It is an interpretation, but it is grounded in the topics that have been established in this book.

As was discussed in Chapter 1, the first movement uses sonata form, with a clear exposition, development and recapitulation. In narrative terms, the situation is war, juxtaposed against rural visions. The exposition is just that: a presentation of characters within a location and a time. The setting is Chelsea, Ireland's home at the time of writing. And the movement opens directly on to the war, in the manner of *Mai-Dun* and *The Overlanders*. The piano's first upbeat, forward momentum and clipped military melody (see Example 1.11) plunges us into the conflict, the violin's entry in bar 4 an indication that the protagonist is involved in this conflict. The opening is not a march, but some other martial activity, perhaps the digging of trenches. The backdrop is not only a war that is already taking place in Europe, but also the home city, London, and very soon a reference to the chords of 'Chelsea Reach' in bars 15–17 (perhaps a passing glimpse of the river from one of the roads that lead off the Kings Road) remind us of this. These bars drag the hero away from thoughts of war back to London, and a new tune in bar 18 has the hero on home territory, strolling in the French manner of the 'Soho forenoons' perambulation. This melody is modal, against which the bass moves in contrary motion, and the accompaniment offbeats are lighthearted. War again rears its ugly head in bar 31, but is swiftly swept away in a sea of coruscations, most strikingly in bars 38–9. Perhaps these are memories of countryside idylls, perhaps the hero has stopped to admire some paintings in a shop window (as Ireland did), and is temporarily transported to rural ecstasies. Then in bar 46 the jaunty offbeats reappear, this time as the second subject proper, now in F major, as the hero strolls onward. Again the driving upbeats return (bar 52), but are again banished, this time in a big, affirmative, F major tune (from the upbeat to bar 57). This is a pastoral theme, with strong tonic-dominant movements. Another glimpse of the Thames follows at bar 61. There are glimmerings of the anguish that is to follow, in a wistful version of the F major tune (bar 67), and in bar 76 it is transformed again, this time appearing in country mode, with cross-rhythms, trills and clearcut major tonality. Bar 87, with its piano tremolo, signals that something is about to happen, and the exposition closes with a definitive return to war.

The development section comes to rest for a while – perhaps the soldier has paused in a café, or for a beer, his mind wandering. This section is devoted to the first subject, and here the mood is entirely sombre, the contemplation of the future reality of war. The tune is now supported by a tolling pedal (see Example 1.12). Between presentations of this transformation of the war theme, there are tiny allusions to the lyrical part of Ireland's country, in bars 116–18 and 127–30. A striking rhythmic transformation of this section is at bar 113, whose gentle dotted notes are to become an essential part of the finale. The Tranquillo at bar 131 has the war theme now muted, and marked 'con tristezza' at bar 135. But even more significant is the fact that the original, 'digging' $\frac{3}{4}$ has turned into a march in bars 133–5. These images of the anguish of the war are blown away as the pace quickens (the protagonist moves on) and the military rhythms propel the movement to the recapitulation.

The recapitulation (the walk back down the Kings Road) returns to war, the approaching actuality now bigger by way of the fact that the piano's clipped upbeats here appear in both hands, and the runs that separate these are more elaborate. The protagonist returns via the same glimpses of Chelsea Reach, and the jaunty strolling theme recurs, as do the coruscations. But the big tune starting at the upbeat to bar 201 is now in A major, pastoral F major subsumed to war. But how does this part of the story end? With the protagonist joining up in the coda. And is his mood wistful or bold? From bar 231 the war theme (the first subject) takes over completely, passed between violin and piano, the mood one of grief. The clipped nature of the theme has turned legato, the semiquaver rests removed, and the piano's tolling falling bass from bar 237 indicative of loss. The motif that dominates from bar 244 is one of the most wistful, anguished of the sonata, and had already been hinted at in the development section, in bar 137. But in bars 251–2 there is new resolve: 'stiff upper lip, do one's duty, patriotic fervour', and the concluding version of the war theme, from the upbeat to bar 253, returns to the clipped rhythms as the protagonist, now turned soldier, departs.

There is no battle scene, and instead the second movement moves straight to the aftermath of slaughter. This is one of Ireland's love-nature pieces, an expression of grief for people, places, ways of life lost. There is no clue that it is in memory of a particular person, though ex-colleagues from the RCM and St Luke's are very likely part of this grief. Its sentiments have much in common with Housman's lyrics of loss, and the poem 'On the idle hill of summer', from *A Shropshire Lad*, is the best example of this, with its distant drumming, soldier lads and prospect of rebirth:

On the idle hill of summer,
    Sleepy with the flow of streams,
Far I hear the steady drummer
    Drumming like a noise in dreams.

Far and near and low and louder
    On the roads of earth go by,
Dear to friends and food for powder,
    Soldiers marching, all to die.

East and west on fields forgotten
    Bleach the bones of comrades slain,
Lovely lads and dead and rotten;
    None that go return again.

Far the calling bugles hollo,
    High the screaming fife replies,
Gay the files of scarlet follow:
    Woman bore me, I will rise.

(Housman, 1990: 24)

The opening bars of this movement, in which two melodies interweave (see Example 1.13) are a succession of sighs. The weight of the movement is carried in the main E flat major theme that appears at bar 15. The immediate impact of this tune is made greater by the fact that the first fourteen bars have been of an introductory nature, and end with a minim of silence before this tune starts. It is one of Ireland's most passionate, most expressive moments.

Below the violin's melody the piano mourns in the repeating quavers of the composer's war topic, and in a chiming, descending motif in the right hand (Example 8.2). The E flat major serenity belongs to Ireland's church music – it is the key of 'Love unknown', the *Meditation on John Keble's Rogationtide hymn*, the setting of Psalm 23 and *Ex ore innocentium*. This passage is an expression of bereavement, but there is a feeling that all will be well.

Example 8.2

The repeat of the tune hints that all will *not* be well, however, in the chromatic wanderings that disturb the serenity in bars 26 and 27. The tolling idea is developed further from bar 33, where the piano has repeating E♭s, perhaps the rumble of distant guns, under the violin's winding, descending line. This is a moment of pause for thought, of solemnity and reflection.

The central part of the slow movement, from bar 40, belongs to Ireland's pastoral, with its new 12/8 time signature (see Example 1.15), rocking patterns and diatonic sections in G flat major, G major and A major. The little trills which were introduced into the development section of the first movement are now much more prominent, their rustic dance-like quality a hint at rural ways destroyed. Within this section there is another link to 'Chelsea Reach', as pastoral becomes swaying barcarolle at the upbeat to bar 52. This is the most passionate moment of the movement, and the heart of the sonata as a whole, the crisis point coming at the end of bar 62, as a laden cycle of fifths, and the rumbling guns, move back towards the sighing music of the opening, the 'frame' for the grief and rural escape. In bar 82 there is a second appearance of the main theme, pianissimo, shared between violin and piano. In bar 90 it becomes an impassioned outpouring for the violin, but now the questioning of Christian redemption is stronger, in the clashing, twisting piano chords beneath this serene melody. The movement ends with the wandering melodies and tolling Eʙs.

The last movement returns to war, but here too there is a sense of questioning, with the dramatic juxtapositions of clipped rhythms and driving piano octaves, and, from bar 7, poignant falling intervals (Example 8.3).

Example 8.3

But this movement is the jubilant antidote to the first, and at bar 30, the Con brio, there is a sudden decisive change of mood, with a deliciously effervescent new melody in A major (see Example 1.16) and a bouncing accompaniment. The tune is a ditty, akin to the popular songs of the day, and once again the flavour is French. The mood is not always optimistic, and at bar 62 the shift to B flat minor adds a note of menace. The march aspect of the first movement is heard in bar 82, and there are more religious connotations, with the sentimental E flat melody and churchy chords in bar 111. These are swept away in another march in bar 140, and glimpses at the rural and drumming aspects of the second movement. The war dialectic returns in bar 155, but is banished at the return of the Con brio in bar 178. This time the menacing B flat minor is swept away in rural, and rather pagan revelry. The 'alla burla' at bar 228, the droning burlesque element in bar 289, the jaunty little tune in bar 332 (Example 8.4) all signal life, youth, character, rebirth, the concluding bars a joyous A major rout.

Example 8.4

The musical and popular success of the Second Violin Sonata, as discussed in Chapter 1, was partly because of the nature of its first performance, but surely also for its sentiments, which would have been keenly felt and recognized. Its reception must have encouraged Ireland to think about further large-scale sonatas, as the year after its première, he began work on a three-movement Piano Sonata. The Second Violin Sonata, within which Ireland mixes topics, and at the same time creates real unity of construction within a large-scale chamber work, is the model for the Piano Sonata, which was organized in a similar manner. Here there is external as well as internal evidence to support a programmatic reading.

Many writers on Ireland's music have tended to view the Piano Sonata as a landmark in his output. Townshend called it 'perhaps the most satisfactory embodiment of his talent' (1943: 70), Hill a 'remarkable work ... full of intensity of expression' (1946: 103). In the 1950s the piece continued to be reviewed as one of Ireland's masterpieces, Crossley-Holland, in *Grove 5*, describing it as 'the most impressive of all his piano works' (1954: 536), and Ireland himself called it 'one of the finest, if not the finest modern piano sonata' (KTaylor: 4 July 1951). All these writers have viewed the sonata as a major work in which Ireland's mature style can be seen, but since the 1950s it has been little discussed. Despite its widespread acclaim, it is a less convincing piece than the Second Violin Sonata, and it was in the works that involved two players that Ireland's narratives were most successful.

The Piano Sonata was written during the period October 1918 to January 1920, while Ireland was based in Chelsea, and over the same years in which he was writing the *London Pieces* (the third of which was completed in February

1920). Because of this there are motivic links between the Piano Sonata and the *London Pieces*. This was one of Ireland's most fertile times, seeing the composition of several remarkable songs and some short piano pieces. Like the Second Violin Sonata, the piano sonata is in three closely related movements. Ireland described the work as 'condensed' and 'closely packed' (KTaylor: 4 June 1943), and talked about it in the same way that he talked about the Rhapsody and *Sarnia*, feeling that all three of these works were difficult for the listener on account of their compression of ideas.

Like the Second Violin Sonata, the Piano Sonata is both a sonata in the abstract sense of the word and a resource book of ideas. Little motifs redolent of meaning abound, and add up to a larger whole. Although written in London, the work resonates with the impact of visits to other places. There is internal evidence to support this in the many musical links with some of Ireland's pagan pieces, both earlier and later ones. But there is also one particular documentary source that gives us some idea of the background to the work. From 1919 Ireland had a composition pupil called Horace Randerson (1892–1992). There are letters from Ireland to Randerson from 1925–43, mainly short, but being almost exclusively confined to musical matters, they are quite revealing. There is also a surviving diary belonging to Randerson, which he kept during his time as Ireland's pupil. His entry for June 1920, referring to the

8.1 Chanctonbury Ring, West Sussex

Piano Sonata, reads: 'Tremendous music – 1st movement Life(?) 2nd more sublime – the first two bars were conceived at Pangbourne while very happy with a friend, more ecstatic. 3rd movement tremendous – rolling forces of Nature, inspired by a rough autumnal day on Chanctonbury Ring & old British Encampment ...' (*JIT*, 11). There seems to be no reason why this description should not have come from Ireland himself. He was staying in Pangbourne in 1918, and the 'friend' was possibly Charlie Markes, who was close to him at this time, and to whom he wrote from Berkshire. Equally, we know that West Sussex was a strong influence on his music.

The first movement uses modified sonata form, with the first subject group dominant. There are four main melodic ideas in this movement, two in each of the subject groups (Examples 8.5a–d).

Example 8.5a

Example 8.5b

Example 8.5c

Example 8.5d

[Allegro moderato]

The movement opens in E minor, though with the melodic material modal, the second subject groups are in B flat major and the movement closes in E major. The sharp minor/flat major (or flat minor/sharp major) opposition is typical of Ireland, and not only serves as the backbone of the whole movement, but is also an intermittent feature, for example the combining of an F minor chord with an implied B major chord in bar 20.

Randerson's recording of the word 'Life' in conjunction with the first movement seems apt, as it is a real mixing of topics. It opens in London, and the first section, from bar 1 to bar 35, is again akin to the perambulations of 'Soho forenoons', because of the similar folk melody, contrary motion and constant bass that constitute Ia^1 (Example 8.5a). The second subject group not only produces a key contrast, but also a shift of sensibilities. The two themes that comprise this group belong to Ireland's vernacular, as characters emerge in the London streets. Ib^1 (Example 8.5c) is a general type by way of its staccato and jovial melodic outline, while Ib^2 (Example 8.5d) is more specific. With its offbeats and melody in the inner part, this is a character theme similar to those used as the basis of 'Ragamuffin' and 'Puck's birthday', and in particular is akin to the second subject of 'The boy bishop'.

The main function of the development section is to transform Ia^1. Thus the addition of ornaments and the removal of the pedal from bar 62 create a more lyrical, 'country' nuance, and from this Ireland moves off into his nature coruscations in bar 75. From bar 84 there is another change of scene, as the heavy pedal, one of Ireland's symbols of war, gives the motif menacing connotations. Bar 90 has an embryonic version of the Passion motif, and in bar 95 we are back in London. There are military rhythms in bar 110. The recapitulation moves towards E major and attainment, passing again through different topical fields. It ends with the same type of positive upward flourish that closed 'Ragamuffin'. The second movement of the sonata both looks backwards and heralds new developments in Ireland's writing. In its construction it is a logical continuation of the second movements of the two violin sonatas. At the same time it pre-empts the mood which pervades Ireland's works written in the 1920s, in that it explores aspects of sexuality and nature. The movement stems from a single phrase (Example 8.6a).

Example 8.6a

Non troppo lento

This melody is used as the basis of the outer sections of the movement, presented in increasingly complex versions (in a manner similar to that of nature pieces such as 'April' and elegies of love such as 'In a May morning'). Version 1 comprises the first 7 bars. The melody is an example of Ireland's stoical modality, here liturgical in its measured stateliness and reliance on a limited number of pitches oscillating round a central note. There are some similarities with the opening of 'A Grecian lad', and also with the song 'Penumbra'. From the outset the movement is therefore a mixture of topics, essentially an expression of personal stoicism in a landscape. The second presentation of the theme that immediately follows extends the phrase and doubles the melody in octaves, and the third (from bar 25) is contrapuntally more complex. A fourth rendering of the melody starts in bar 38, but fades into a version of the Passion motif (bar 41). The first part of this movement ends with a passage of shifting parallel chords reminiscent both of the slow movement of the First Violin Sonata and of the tolling reflection of the Second Violin Sonata.

Example 8.6b

[Non troppo lento]

The central section shifts from barren stoicism to a richer, more expansive meditation on a theme derived from the first movement (Example 8.6b). This section depends heavily on the nature coruscations (Ireland was also working on 'Earth's call' at this time, and the similarities are obvious). The section ends with a moment of harmonic stasis and then silence. The return of the opening theme leads swiftly to a climax containing Ireland's Passion motif in its original format, as used in 'Youth's spring-tribute' (see Example 6.1a). The ending of the movement is almost identical to that of the slow movement of the Second Violin Sonata. The overall passage of the central movement is therefore again a real mixing of topics – love, country and the mourning aspect of Ireland's war.

The epic third movement has strong musical connections with other pagan places. In a letter to Edwin Evans, Ireland spoke of this, linking several pagan works: 'you might with justice have added that my little-known "Legend" for piano and orchestra comes within the same category, as perhaps also do "Mai-Dun" and the finale of my piano sonata' (EE: 1 Dec. 1941). It is constructed from three main melodic ideas (Examples 8.7a–c), by far the most important of which is the first, which dominates the movement, and which is derived from the opening of *The Forgotten Rite* (see Example 3.1).

Example 8.7a

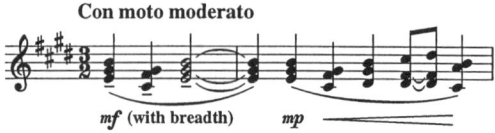

Example 8.7b   Bar 22

Example 8.7c   Bar 58

This opening places the music firmly within a pagan landscape. On to this Ireland superimposes fleeting references to other pieces and to the first movement of the sonata – bar 11 is derived from Ia^1 and bar 21 from Ia^2, for example, and bar 14 is closely related to the first subject of the first movement of the Third Piano Trio. The second melodic idea is related to 'Song of the springtides', and there are also brief references to the chords of the First Violin Sonata and to Ireland's military driving themes (bar 71). The movement is firmly rooted in E major, with movement through other, primarily major, keys.

Crossley-Holland spoke of the three movements as serving different functions, the first having 'rugged energy', the second 'aspiring beauty' and the third 'successfully resolving' the moods of the first two (1954: 536). There is a real mixing of topics, and movement in and out of different worlds. The work is a clear precursor of *Sarnia*, as was mentioned in Chapter 3, and the structural and harmonic similarities between these two works make it possible to assign meaning to the Piano Sonata. It is an expression of a pagan place, but an unnamed pagan place, against which a personal experience is hinted at, but not unveiled. (*Sarnia* might also be regarded as a later, explicit version of the implicit sentiments of the Piano Sonata; an unnamed pagan place named.)

The first movement of *Sarnia*, 'Le Catioroc', is paganism named, a Pan visitation with contrast between pagan place and pagan revelry, and A minor/A flat major oppositions. The first movement of the Piano Sonata is also about place and person, with contrasting yearning and vernacular subjects, and E minor/B flat major oppositions. The concerns of the slow movements of both works are love and landscape, named in *Sarnia*. They both have the same structure, which is a ternary form, in which the opening A section subjects a single melody to development, while the B section is a nature eulogy. The last movements of the Piano Sonata and *Sarnia* are pantheistic rhapsodies, again located and made overt in 'Song of the springtides' with the Swinburne quotation and the Guernsey backdrop. Both quote from previous movements, and the pagan qualities of the final of the Piano Sonata are made explicit from the outset, with the opening bars that derive from *The Forgotten Rite*. Both movements have a similar harmonic structure, moving though a series of major keys: the Piano Sonata uses E major, E flat major, A major, A flat major, B flat major and E major. 'Song of the springtides' travels through D major, A flat major, D major, A flat major, E flat major and D major.

Ireland himself considered the Piano Sonata to be one of his most important pieces, and had strong views on how it should be performed. He admired the playing of Frederic Lamond (1868–1948), who gave the first performance of the sonata, and some years later, in 1943, expressed his appreciation of the playing of this work by Kendall Taylor (1909–2000):

> I was immensely impressed by your masterly performance of my sonata last evening. It was not only incomparably the finest performance it has ever had, but in comparison with yours all the previous performances except Lamond's have been merely trifling & childish ... It is a sobering thought that the sonata, perhaps my very best work, has had to wait 23 years before receiving one wholly satisfying performance!

(KTaylor: 4 June 1943)

After the completion of the Piano Sonata, Ireland moved away from the three-movement sonata to concentrate mainly on songs and piano music. He also produced the orchestral piece, *Mai-Dun*, in 1921. In 1923 he returned to the sonata, this time a work for cello and piano in G minor:

> The chief feature of Miss Beatrice Harrison's 'cello recital at the Æolian Hall on April 4th was a new sonata for 'cello and piano by John Ireland, the piano part being played by Mr. Evlyn Howard-Jones. If the work impressed at a first hearing, it was because of its austere clarity and the beautiful balance maintained between the instruments. One was left aware, however, that the power and impulse were the fruit of hard mental labour, and that the executants were called upon to wrestle with technical difficulties as formidable as those which must have originally beset the composer: perhaps it was because of its obvious intellectual labouring, so to speak, that we much preferred the slow movement which had a very eloquent kind of folk melody.
>
> (*MO*, May 1924: 789)

Ireland must have spent most of the year engaged on this project, as there are no other pieces dating from 1923. The sonata is a stunning work, with brilliant writing for both instruments, and received reviews praising it as 'the most remarkable British work of the kind which has appeared for some time' (*MT*, Aug. 1924: 716). Like the Piano Sonata, it bears no programmatic title or associated literary quotations, but like its predecessor it has undeniable associations and meanings. It has the same motivic links between movements as the Second Violin Sonata, but here they are even more tightly integrated. And in its harmonic language it shows advances on the earlier works. It deploys a sparer, more biting style than did its predecessors, and the mid-1920s saw Ireland writing in a more modernist style, the melodic lines angular and obsessively repeating, as the opening cello melody demonstrates (Example 8.8a).

Example 8.8a

If the first movement of the Piano Sonata was 'Life', this movement is a more frenzied, turbulent presentation of some of the same ideas. It is less a walk in London than an expression of turmoil (and 1923 was a year of close involvement with Arthur Miller, as seen in Plate 12). Although the first movement has two subjects, the second, at bar 48, a more lyrical tune in B flat major, it is dominated by the opening melody above. There are two moments of dramatic reference inserted into the movement. The first comes at bar 102. Here a new Tranquillo quotes from the song 'The trellis'. The passage that Ireland initially wrote to the words 'None but the flow'rs have seen / Our white caresses' is here transformed for cello and piano, marked 'secreto'. In other words, the passage is an allusion to the 'secret', hidden love of 'The trellis'. The second reference is at bar 137, where the busy, repetitive cello figuration is played out over a version of the Passion motif (Example 8.8b).

Example 8.8b

The second movement is closely linked to the slow movements of both the Piano Concerto and *Sarnia*. After a brief, but impassioned introduction, it settles into being one of Ireland's sentimental slow movements, here in E flat major, the emphasis on the drawn-out melody. An unaccompanied cello line leads the way to the final Con moto e marcato. According to a number of writers on Ireland's music, including John Longmire (1969: 141), this work was another of Ireland's Sussex-inspired works with pagan associations, and it is in the last movement that this is most evident. Jocelyn Brooke wrote of this work in both 1949 and 1950, in his semi-autobiographical *A Mine of Serpents* and *The Goose Cathedral*. He viewed the work as being imbued with pantheistic feelings, and for him it was 'inextricably associated with winter evenings by the sea: the sunset flaming yellow in the west, the last rainy light gleaming in the puddles on the cliff-paths, and the sullen thudding of the waves on the beach below' (Brooke, 1981b: 349). Brooke then went on to say that he found this quality in other works by Ireland, specifically *Month's Mind*, *Soliloquy* and Ballade: 'a bracing, "open-airish" feeling combined with a rather austere note of nostalgia, an awareness of 'old, unhappy, far-off things' (ibid.). Brooke wrote this in 1950, some years before he met Ireland in person. He situates the Cello Sonata as a piece of pagan landscapes, where the wind's song has 'a wilder note – a bardic rhapsody of successive, violent statements, abrupt as the lashes of a whip: the opening of the third movement of Ireland's Sonata for 'cello and piano' (Brooke, 1981a: 156–7). Longmire's account wrote more specifically of the work's associations with the Devil's Jumps, a set of Bronze Age round barrows at a remote and inaccessible spot on Treyford Hill, near Uppark in West Sussex. Though there is no extant evidence to support this, the finale demonstrates a wilder and more violent aspect of Ireland, with its succession of upward leaps and brusque marked opening (Example 8.8c).

Example 8.8c

The more overtly demoniac aspect of the composer was developed in the Fantasy-Sonata in 1943, but before that in the Sonatina for piano in 1926, whose last movement, as was discussed in Chapter 3, was linked to Townsend Warner's sabbath in *Lolly Willowes* (and which, incidentally, was a test piece for the *Daily Express* Piano-Playing Contest of that year). The Sonatina took the spare lines of the Cello Sonata a stage further, and the piece is the most concentrated of all of Ireland's three-movement works. Its opening Moderato derives from one main theme, which features a melody line with the same angularity as that of the Cello Sonata, and lean piano textures (Example 8.9a).

Example 8.9a

In the short second movement the spare textures are even more extreme, and pre-empt the desolation of 'We'll to the woods no more'. The thirds that open and dominate this movement (Example 8.9b) were taken up as an integral part of the following year's song, and are part of the progress from ecstasy to personal angst that occurred in the 1920s.

Example 8.9b

The work was very well received, and after hearing it Peter Warlock wrote:

> It is quite one of the best things you have done, and your performance came off magnificently. You are one of the very few living composers in whose work one can discern a steady development along wholly personal lines, through a number of years; and in these days when so many musicians leap from one style to its opposite extreme in two successive works in the hope of achieving a factitious semblance of originality, it is more than ever pleasing to encounter a work such as the Sonatina which, for all its very real originality and newness, is clearly the logical development of a style that was already very individual fifteen years ago, or more.

(in Hill, 1946: 104)

This logical development, refining and paring down of the more expansive Piano Sonata, was continued in the Fantasy-Sonata, but in the interim period Ireland produced a song-cycle which is itself a bringing together of musical topics.

Between 1929 and 1931 Ireland wrote six songs that were published as *Songs Sacred and Profane*, featuring poems by Alice Meynell, Townsend Warner and Yeats. In 1934 the composer wrote that these songs 'form a very personal document, & a very comprehensive one, as you will see' (GP: 24 Oct. 1934). The title of the cycle was a perfect choice, and as a group they embody different aspects of his life and musical language. They span years of personal crisis, and Ireland's transference of infatuation from Arthur Miller to Helen Perkin. But they are also linked motivically, and have a real coherence as a cycle. The first song, 'The advent' was, like 'The holy boy', composed at Christmas. Ireland described the song as 'churchy' (GP: 7 Feb. 1932), and influenced by the Roman Catholic atmosphere of the poem. What makes this song 'churchy' is Ireland's use of the harmonic language and textures of his church music. The opening chords embody this, with the simple, unladen Dorian modality and chordal piano writing (Example 8.10a).

Example 8.10a

This passage has its roots in another, earlier song, which was itself an imbuing of words for secular performance with sacred music. This was the setting of Dowson's 'The adoration', which opened with similarly weighted chords, and deployed a similar modality (Example 8.10b).

Example 8.10b

But 'The advent' is not exclusively sacred. After a short passage of Ireland's parallel, 'solemn' chords (bar 29), the chordal assurance gives way to first, a few bars of oppositions in several senses, which begins in bar 31. At bar 33 the right hand has repeated legato F major chords, while the left hand has marked, *pesante* augmented fourths. This swiftly gives way to a staccato motif that is developed later in the cycle, before the renewal of the 'churchy' music. Thus, although this opening song is the 'sacred' part of the cycle, other topics are hinted at.

The second song, 'Hymn for a child', was dedicated to Helen Perkin. It picks up the tenuto chords of 'The advent', and is a wonderfully lyrical dance-like song. A new motif introduced in bar 12 is a descending run, which becomes an essential element of the third song, 'My fair', which Ireland regarded as one of his best: 'I think it is perhaps the most important song I have written, & the best technically. However, it can be only for the very few' (GP: 7 Feb. 1935). Although it carries no dedication, it clearly belongs to Arthur Miller. It was composed in July 1929, Ireland's time of great personal crisis, and the month in which he wrote 'If we must part'. The manuscript has an inscription that has been heavily deleted. Within the British Library collection of Ireland's manuscripts, it is only the Miller pieces that carry these frenzied obliterations. The song is a fervent declaration of love, a love that lasts even though time moves on and beauty fades. At the central moment of the song, when 'all the dear tones pass away', there is a version of Ireland's Passion motif, but here it has changed shape, and has become a sequence of unfulfilled rising octaves (Example 8.10c).

Example 8.10c

The fourth song, 'The Salley Gardens', breaks the tension, with the resumption of the chordal accompaniment. This is one of Ireland's static modal ballads. The fifth song, 'The soldier's return', described in 1938 as a 'macabre little ballad' (*The Times*, 5 Nov. 1938: 8), is a short 'war' piece in that it uses the composer's march genre and military rhythms. It also reintroduces the melodic lines of 'Hymn to a child'. The final song, 'The scapegoat', is a humorous conclusion. It develops the dance-like aspects of the second song of the cycle, and its clearcut phrases and jaunty accompaniment belong to Ireland's vernacular style (Example 8.10d).

Example 8.10d

The work as a whole is a collection of topics and a motivically unified cycle.

During the period after the Cello Sonata Ireland did produce one other large-scale three-movement work, this being the Piano Concerto, but twenty years elapsed between the work for cello and piano and the next work for a solo instrument with piano. In 1943 he wrote what was both his final fantasy, and his final sonata. This was the Fantasy-Sonata for Clarinet and Piano, Ireland's sole work of this year. Work began on the piece in April 1943, and it was completed in December. The first performance took place shortly after this, in February 1944.

The Fantasy-Sonata stands within Ireland's output as a late flowering, a summational work that draws together the musical topics and structural techniques exercised by Ireland throughout his composing career. It is a work that makes no compromise to either the listener or the performer, a '*tour de force* of compactness' (Crossley-Holland, 1954: 538). Structurally, the Fantasy-Sonata can be seen as the culmination of Ireland's melody-driven, monothematic approach. It was a return to the one-movement fantasy genre used in the first of Ireland's chamber works, the Phantasie in A minor for piano trio, but it was also a final paring down of the earlier three-movement sonatas. Where the Phantasie was in essence a sonata form movement, with conventional tonal relationships and two subjects, the later piece has the rhapsodic quality of a fantasy and is tightly constructed from restricted melodic material. But while the piece is in one movement, there are three clear musical sections, and these are the equivalents of the first, second and third movements of his earlier sonatas. Within these sections there are formal frameworks which follow the tendencies of the violin sonatas. Thus there is a 'first movement' (bars 1–149) with first and second subjects, a 'slow movement' with a ternary structure (bars 150–221) and a fast finale (bars 220–72). In this sense the work is not only the logical successor to the Phantasie, but also the 1943 answer to the 1917 Second Violin Sonata. What was then a thirty-minute sonata for violin and piano, in three separate, but thematically and tonally related movements, becomes a tightly condensed fifteen-minute single movement work for clarinet and piano, in which melodic fragments emerge, are transformed and integrated into the texture.

The work can also be regarded as a 'culmination' in another sense. That is, in terms of a drawing together of topics. And the *MMR* review of the score noted that:

> There never was a more *consistent* composer than John Ireland. This is not an oblique way of saying there has been no development but rather that the development issues from a more and more detailed discovery of a musical country charted by the composer thirty years ago. This finely-made and effective new work reveals no addition to the composer's vocabulary, but is a mature summing-up of modes and tendencies revealed in all his work.
>
> (*MMR*, Jan. 1946: 17)

In this late flowering Ireland touches on many different areas, returning to melodic motifs which had not been revisited for some thirteen years, mixing meanings in a complex, but inobtrusive combining of topics. Melodic and motivic aspects of Ireland's paganism, country, love and war are present, structures and connotations closely entwined. The fact that the work was written during the Second World War inevitably coloured Ireland's musical vocabulary, notably in the driving rhythms that dominate the last section of the work. There are also some clues to hidden meanings in a letter to Arthur Lee Gardner of August 1943, in which Ireland wrote: 'it is really about some aspects of Gito – the boy in the "Satyricon" – I should like to call it "The Song of Gito" – but, of course, I dare not!' (ARLG: 5 Aug. 1943).

At this time Ireland was interested in Petronius' writings, and specifically in the boy Giton featured in the *Satyricon*. There are three works of the early 1940s that have associations with things Roman: the incidental music for *Julius Caesar* (1942), the Fantasy-Sonata and the orchestral overture, *Satyricon* (1946). Ireland had borrowed Gardner's copy of Petronius, in a seventeenth- or eighteenth-century translation, and also had access to an English rendition by Burnaby. This fascination will be discussed further in Chapter 9.

The clarinet's opening five-bar phrase (Example 8.11a), which is the 'first subject' of the 'first movement', contains the kernels of the whole piece, notably a falling perfect fourth, the falling perfect fifth which follows, and the grace note.

Example 8.11a

The evocative power of this opening owes much to the chord-spacing of the first bar, with its doubled major third and high, distant clarinet Eb–Bb, but also to the shift from E flat major to an Eb minor⁷ chord in bar 2, this twist a harmonic feature common to Ireland's pagan pieces. These five bars alone embody Ireland's personal style: there is a sense of brooding and stillness, and the prevalent falling fifth has always been a crucial element in much of his music. The bare octaves of the piano part in bars 5–8, with the occasional added chords and the overall descending movement, refer directly to the first extended passage for solo piano in *Legend*, a further clue that we are in Ireland's pagan country. The clarinet's next entrance in bar 9 features an appoggiatura pattern (Example 8.11b) that is another essential part of Ireland's melodic language. The first fifteen bars are thus both a straightforward presentation of melodic material and a locating of the music in a pagan landscape.

Example 8.11b

Bars 16–20 are based primarily on another Ireland hallmark, the four-note descending scale pattern which was so prominent in the Piano Concerto and *A London Overture*. Bar 21 introduces a motif which at this point seems innocuous and fleeting, but which re-emerges transformed into a demonic pounding to become one of the main features of the concluding Giusto. This section is followed by a second presentation (bars 28–35) of the opening theme, this time in B flat. Bar 36 is the start of a rhapsodic development. The piano establishes a one-bar ostinato, a technique already used by Ireland as a means of developing material in 'Song of the springtides'. Above this the clarinet line muses on elements of its opening phrase, figurations becoming more complex, the falling fourth prominent, and the harmony moving away from the flat side from here until bar 59. Bar 60 is the start of the 'second subject' of the 'first movement'. The new key is A major, its tritonic relationship with the opening Eb typical of Ireland's approach to the sonata as a genre. The new material is harmonically ambiguous, the left hand firmly rooted in A, while the right hand D#s contribute a modal yearning (Example 8.11c). This new material belongs to Ireland's country, its lyricism and left hand piano figuration in the same vein as 'April' and 'Amberley Wild Brooks'.

Example 8.11c

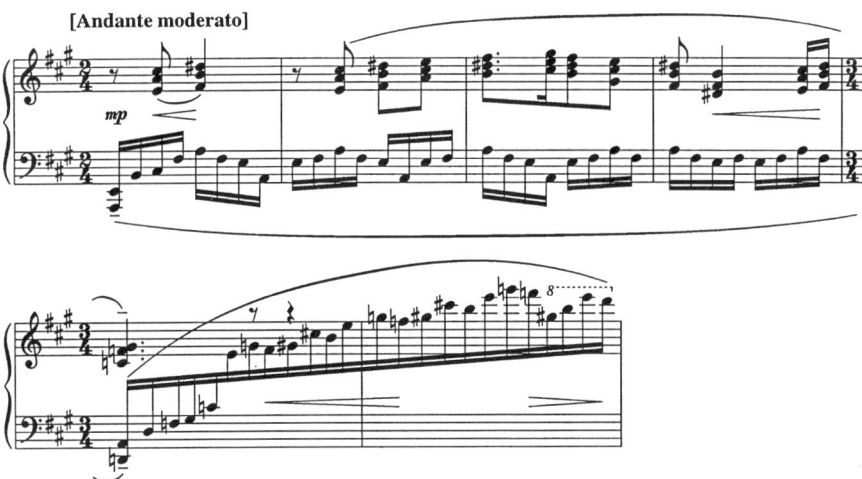

The shift to a D minor^7 chord in bar 64 again emphasizes the pagan location of this section. This is also the most reflective part of the Fantasy-Sonata, where Ireland's nature-ecstasy music is apparent in the shimmering coruscations and parallel chords creating this second theme. The way in which propulsion is achieved via dotted rhythms from bar 72 has similarities with the way in which the tempo and rhythmic pace intensify in 'Le Catioroc', after which the twisting solo line of bars 64 and 65 is picked up and developed in bar 77 (and later in bar 98). The second subject is taken up by the clarinet in bar 84, with increasingly brilliant runs and trills until reaching a moment of stasis at bar 100. Bar 103 maintains the stasis, but also hints at a reiteration of the first subject. The sonata's most striking quotation then follows, in bar 106, where an overt version of the Passion motif appears in the piano part (Example 8.11d).

Example 8.11d

It was the first time that Ireland had used this Passion motif since 1930. While it is often difficult to ascertain whether Ireland is self-quoting, or whether little patterns and turns of phrase are just an integral part of his style, the sudden appearance of this motif, and the fact that it had not been used for so long, do imply that this is a deliberate reference. And in December Ireland had written again of the piece to Gardner:

> The music is inspired by some experiences you will understand – in one place I hope you may be conscious that the brass is being very well polished !... it is now christened with the sober title of 'Fantasy-Sonata' – with no clues given. 'He that hath ears to hear, let him hear'!

> (ARLG: 18 Dec. 1943)

In other words, it has definite associations with some aspect of love, Ireland's reference presumably once again to the boy Giton in the *Satyricon* and from its terminology to masturbatory fantasies.

The Tranquillo that follows, from bars 109–49, is a type of recapitulation, in that the 'first subject' reappears and dominates this section, though in a much gentler, subdued presentation, in which the falling fourth is accentuated over a continuous piano ostinato in the manner of Ireland's impressionistic nature pieces (Example 8.11e).

Example 8.11e

This first part of the sonata is thus akin to a first movement. Two distinct melodic ideas in different, in this case opposing, keys, are featured, though the music is dominated by the motifs of the first subject. There is some sense of development, and some sort of recapitulation. And at the same time different topics emerge and disappear.

The central section of the work uses a ternary structure, within which a contemplative Più lento contrasts with a Poco più moto. The outer sections, with their lyrical melodies and frequent ornaments belong to Ireland's country. The opening of this 'movement', at bar 150, presents a new melodic idea (Example 8.11f), though this is derived from the opening of the work in that it depends on falling fifths and grace notes.

Example 8.11f

Più lento

The section from 150 to 178 is dominated by this melodic idea, passed repeatedly between piano and clarinet. The Poco più moto at bar 179 is a sudden, brilliant diversion, triadic oscillations in the piano below clarinet figurations. The rapid movement between parallel major chords recalls Ireland's early, impressionistic, French-influenced piano writing, and in particular 'The scarlet ceremonies'. The Calmato at bar 191 returns to the ostinato of 101, this section harmonically static. The brief, slightly altered return of 8.11f at the Commodo in bar 200 is in B flat, thus taking the work back towards the flat side. It soon erupts into dazzling runs, motifs appearing from bar 216 that herald the concluding Giusto.

The final section of the piece is shockingly demonic, powerful, after the tranquil meditations that have gone before, but is derived entirely from motifs used earlier in the sonata. The piano figuration that opens this section, at bar 220, makes use of the interval of a fourth (Example 8.11g). This passage is both pagan in the sense of the frenzied finales of the Cello Sonata and the Sonatina, and also reflective of the turmoils of the current war, with its pounding bass. At bar 224 parallel chords in the right hand of the piano part transform the 'second subject' of the first part of the piece. When the clarinet enters in bar 231, it is with a return to the opening theme of the Fantasy-Sonata, before picking up the second subject, now marked 'grottesco' (Example 8.11h).

Example 8.11g

Example 8.11h

The inexorable movement towards a conclusion in this latter part of the piece is enhanced by a repeating pattern that starts at bar 263, and which was first heard in bar 21. The final six bars (Example 8.11i) maintain the repeating pattern in the piano part, while the clarinet's melodic line steadily rises to the final flourish and E flat major chord.

Example 8.11i

In terms of its structure and its mingling of meanings and associations, the Fantasy-Sonata stands as a culminational work. It is also of particular interest for the relationship between composer and performer involved in the preparation of the work. It was written for the renowned clarinettist Frederick Thurston (1901–53), a figure who had a significant impact on the work of a number of British composers, inspiring many works for the clarinet. Thurston was principal clarinet with the BBC Symphony Orchestra from 1930 until 1946. As far as Ireland was concerned, this was a very fruitful partnership, and the prominence of the clarinet part in both *Satyricon* and *The Overlanders* was a direct result of his work with Thurston on the Fantasy-Sonata. Thus it could be said that Thurston stands to Ireland rather as Mühlfeld stood to Brahms – a performer who inspired great writing for his instrument in the latter years of the composer's life.

Thurston studied with Charles Draper (1869–1952), and was influential in establishing a style of clarinet playing which was far removed from the heavy vibrato style of another important contemporary, Reginald Kell (1906–?). Thurston's sound was more focused and cleaner. Ireland worked closely with him on the composition of the piece, as is evinced by the letters written to Thurston in 1943 and 1944. In these letters Ireland asks specific questions about technical aspects of the instrument, and there is clear evidence of his having accepted and incorporated the player's comments and alterations. Some of the extremely difficult passages must also have been written with Thurston specifically in mind, and with his approval.

The characteristics of Thurston's own style which find their way into the music include the taxing and sustained use of the upper register of the instrument, Thurston being renowned for his ease of production in this register. The long, legato phrases are typical of Ireland's writing, but are also in keeping with Thurston's style, as can be deduced from the clarinettist's editorial work. The correspondence that survives dates from August 1943, when Ireland wrote describing the forthcoming work as

> a very free & rhapsodic piece, I think I shall call it Fantasy-Sonata – it will be in 1 movement – 12–15 minutes, perhaps – I am v. pleased with what I have done so far, & can only hope it will be worthy of your playing, & that you will feel in sympathy with the music, which is in no way 'contemporary'!!
>
> (FT: 13 Aug. 1943)

In the same letter he questioned Thurston on the practicalities of a trill, saying 'I believe I have written an impracticable trill (according to Forsyth) C♯ & D♯ but I hope his views are out of date!' (ibid.). No such trill appears in the piece, so presumably Ireland must have been advised against this. In this same letter he mentioned that he was adding phrasing marks in pencil only, in order that Thurston could have some input into this aspect of the piece. Composer and performer worked closely together on the first, slow part of the sonata, Ireland writing in November that he had 'had to reconsider and alter parts of the section you already have' (FT: 21 Nov. 1943). The final section was only completed in December, Ireland describing it as 'by no means easy, but I hope it is all right, & effective' (FT: 16 Dec. 1943).

In January Ireland wrote to Thurston:

> If you find you really like the work, I shall be happy to dedicate it to you, as it is your playing which led me to write for your instrument. And I have heard some good clarinet playing – Mühlfeld in my early days made a sensation here, & in his time Charlie Draper was remarkable. So I am in a position to appreciate your playing & what it means to music.
>
> (FT: 15 Jan. 1944)

The first performance, with Kendall Taylor at the piano, was a success, and was swiftly followed by a broadcast with Ireland as accompanist. Even once the work had been performed, Ireland continued to make small changes in preparation for publication. The opening phrase must have troubled him, as he wrote: 'By the way, I have put the opening clt. phrase down an octave, & if you think any other alterations are needed you might let me know ... It is no use publishing it in a form which can only be played by yourself!' (FT: 16 April 1944). In the end, the published edition contained alternatives at this point, the higher register for the opening retained, with the player offered the option of the lower register. Still later that year Ireland wrote that he had 'altered one passage in the clt. part – as I must have that high Bb, somehow' (FT: 3 Oct. 1944). In 1947 and 1948 Thurston gave a number of performance of the work, now accompanied by the pianist Ernest Lush (*b.* 1908).

This close collaboration between composer and performer was in a sense the ultimate outcome of Ireland's previous associations with performers. While aspects of the Piano Concerto were influenced by Helen Perkin's playing style and technical abilities, here Ireland consulted the player closely during the process of composition. Thus in every sense it can be viewed as a summational work, though it was not the last piece in which Ireland quoted from his earlier music.

Chapter 9

Conclusion

Ireland wrote only a few pieces after the Fantasy-Sonata, though these did include the score for *The Overlanders*. The other substantial work following the clarinet sonata was the orchestral overture, *Satyricon*. In the Fantasy-Sonata Ireland had been working with Petronius' *Satyricon* as inspiration. The following year (1944) he began work on an orchestral work with the material of this book at its heart. The work was completed in 1946, and performed in that year's Promenade season. It is a continuation, and a bigger version, of the sentiments of a number of works of the 1940s, including the *Three Pastels* for piano. The entwined themes of historical subject matter and beautiful youths were an obsession for Ireland at this time. In 1941 he completed these piano miniatures, and in 1942 produced the incidental music for a BBC radio production of *Julius Caesar*. As with *The Overlanders*, Ireland had to construct a sequence of short numbers, among them battle music, several marches, 'Lupercalia Music' and 'Lucius' Song', the latter for the boy servant to Brutus. This was the number that he found most congenial:

> Compared with writing the music for 'Julius Caesar', penal servitude would have been a recreation. The only number I enjoyed was a setting of 'Come live with me and be my love' written for a boy, impersonating Lucius. And it was sung by a boy, too, with an execrably played *lute* accompaniment ...
>
> (GB: Feast of St Michael and All Angels, 1942, in Foreman, 1987: 253)

The fascination with Roman servant boys continued in the overture, *Satyricon*. When first asked for a new overture, Ireland wrote: 'I have not a single idea in my head, at present' (KT: 27 Feb. 1944). By June 1946 ideas had returned to him, and he continued: 'About 2 years ago I began an Overture based on the "Satyricon" of Petronius – a rather naughty book, the spiciest parts of which are in Latin ...' (KT: 22 June 1946). He had asked Thompson to translate some passages for him, and then responded: 'The kind of material you translated for me is not suggested in my music – only the rather ... vagabondish life of the 3 young Romans – & the generally 18th century atmosphere of the translation ...' (KT: 20 Aug. 1946).

The word 'satyricon' means 'a recital of lecherous happenings'. The score is prefaced with a quotation from the book:

> I ... am resolved to be as good as my Word, being so met to our Desires; not only to improve our Learning, but to be merry, and put life in our Discourse with pleasanter Tales.

OVERTURE "SATYRICON"

9.1 The opening bars of the overture, *Satyricon*

The overture is very similar in construction and mood to *A London Overture*. It has seven main sections, containing three principal ideas. The first, the A material, which has two melodic subjects, is the joyous side of the *Satyricon*, with bouncy rhythms, prominent brass and percussion, the latter picking out fragments of melodies. But most striking is the use of the whip, surely a witty reference on the composer's part to the whipping scenes in Petronius. The second section has a big, affirmative tune, characterized by falling intervals and brass proclaiming that all is well. Then follows a shortened recapitulation of the A material, this time with jingles, but minus the whip. The centre of the work has a third new tune, a rhapsodic clarinet solo – a reference to the boy Giton, perhaps – over shimmering strings and rippling harp. The swooning melody is taken up first by the flute, and then by the strings, before the A material returns, though this time starting from the second subject. As might be expected, there is a second hearing of the B material, and the overture closes with the vivacious A material, the whip reinstated, the tone entirely joyous. This is Ireland saying, 'Yes, life is wonderful. *Carpe diem*'.

After this point Ireland composed very little music, and what he did write is insubstantial, and was produced to commission only. In his latter years the composer increasingly suffered from health problems, including arteriosclerosis and worsening eyesight, which had been deteriorating from about 1946. Nevertheless, during this period Ireland continued to read extensively, and to write regularly to friends and colleagues. Much of his time in 1947 was taken up with the appointment of Norah Kirby to be his housekeeper, but there were also two short pieces in this year. These included a work for SATB and brass band, 'Man in his labour rejoiceth'. This was commissioned by the *Daily Herald* in co-operation with The National Coal Board, and was a last burst of socialist sympathies on Ireland's part. Dedicated to 'the Mineworkers of Britain', it is in a similar vein to *Ways of Peace*. The other was the hymn tune, 'Sampford'. At this time Ireland was toying with the idea of returning to Guernsey, and had tentatively rented some unfurnished rooms from December 1947, but this plan did not come to fruition. Instead, a holiday in West Sussex in September 1948, and then another visit in November, reawakened his love for this county:

> ... it was a great pleasure renewing contact with the old places such as Chanctonbury & other downland haunts of mine – though of course I could do no climbing up hills on foot. Foreign scenes are grander and more spectacular, but give me the South Downs & I am content ...

> (KT: 8 Nov. 1948)

In 1949 Ireland turned seventy. This was marked with an impressive autograph book (*JIT*, 12) presented to the composer, which had been signed with greetings from many important figures, among them Moeran, Alan Rawsthorne, Malcolm Sargent, Thurston, Vaughan Williams and Townsend

Warner. Ireland had written a short piano waltz, *Columbine*, earlier in the year, and this was to be his final foray into light music conventions. In June of the following year, though still primarily based in London, he took a flat at The Old Rectory, Ashington, which had 'an uninterrupted view of Chanctonbury Ring' (KT: 25 June 1950). Although Ireland was writing nothing at this time, he continued to work as a pianist, and in 1951 accompanied Peter Pears in *The Land of Lost Content*, and also maintained his interest in new music, going to the first performance of Britten's *Billy Budd*.

There was no further new composition until June 1953, when Ireland produced 'The hills', for SATB, to mark the occasion of the coronation of HM Queen Elizabeth II. This is an unexciting piece, and by far the most interesting event of this year was the move from Gunter Grove to settle in Sussex. This had been prompted partly by the fact that Ireland's situation in Ashington had become very difficult. In the autumn of 1953 he purchased Rock Mill, and wrote to Longmire:

> Well, John, at last after 38 years, I am definitely leaving this house, and, of course, London, where I have lived for 60 years – since I was 14. It has all come about in a curiously inevitable sort of way, during these Summer months – as a culmination of accumulated circumstances. The constant heavy traffic in this street has become absolutely *unbearable*. During the last 12 or 18 months there has been an increase of at least 100% – this, together with the constant poisonous fumes have become really a menace to one's health ... But until July this year I did not see any way of escape – and it all seemed too drastic for me to undertake. However, late last June, I was driving in Sussex, near Ashington (with Norah) and thought I would go past a place (a house) that I have had an eye on for about 30 years – and always felt attracted to it in some strange way, though from the road there is practically nothing to be seen of the place except the *top of a windmill*. I said to Norah that morning, 'Let's go past the windmill' – as we passed it, Norah said, 'Stop! There is a "For Sale" board up here!' ...
>
> Well, John, to cut a long story short, leaving out all the details of the progress of the matter ... I signed the contract, and actually am to move there ... It is in a superb situation, with a direct uninterrupted view of Chanctonbury Ring (about a mile-and-a-half distant in a straight line) and the neighbouring downs, stretching from Steyning to Amberley. There is no other house in sight. It stands about 350 to 400 feet above sea level. The soil is sandy, *not* clay. There is a delightful but *manageable* garden and some wild, uncultivated land, in all about one-and-three-quarter acres ...
>
> (JL: 27 Sept. 1953, in Longmire, 1969: 131–2)

The early months at the mill seemed to bring a tranquillity of spirit to the composer, and although he found the winter of 1954 extremely cold, and the mill difficult to heat, the tone of his letters of these first few months is quite mellow. By April 1954 Ireland was suffering 'a period of <u>hideous</u> depression' (KT: 27 April 1954), brought about by the fact that Rock Mill was bounded by sand-quarrying activites that he found increasingly irksome. But things had picked up again by August, and on his seventy-fifth birthday Ireland was pleased to hear from old friends, among them St Luke's clergy, Peacey and McNeill Shelford. This birthday was also celebrated at the Proms with performances of *A London Overture*, *The Forgotten Rite*, the Piano Concerto and *These Things Shall Be*. The tribute in *The Times* observed the problems in placing Ireland that were discussed in the Introduction to the current study:

> In one sense Ireland has been born out of his time: he is indubitably a twentieth-century composer – without Debussy, without Stravinsky, he could not have achieved his mature individuality, even though it is of the young Brahms that we are reminded by his finest piano pieces, in their exuberance and their natural command of the instrument's resources. But also he is a composer for the home, one whose music is loved in musical drawing rooms, but whose popularity would have been a hundredfold increased in a country that had not neglected the delights of home music making.
>
> *(The Times*, 13 Aug. 1954: 9)

In 1956 Ireland wrote the carol, 'Adam lay ybounden'. There was no work forthcoming in 1957, but in 1958 there were two slight, but remarkable pieces. Their content suggests that Ireland was contemplating his own mortality, as both are reflective pieces with a religious slant. The first was in March of this year, a setting of Psalm 23 (Figure 9.2). Ireland wrote to George Parker of the piece:

> It is not a SONG – really it is only <u>inflected</u> <u>speech</u> – the time is free & the note-values only an <u>indication</u>, as in plainchant, which it somewhat resembles – in the Mixolydian mode, more or less.
>
> (GP: 22 March 1958)

This extraordinary piece, coming to rest in E flat, is a musing on death and the afterlife, its unaccompanied status and opportunity for flexible delivery giving it an air of mental wandering, silent thought.

On 29 May 1958 Ireland completed his final composition. Rather fittingly, this was an organ piece, a return to the years of his youth. In this work Ireland chose to quote unequivocally from his earlier music, the work thus serving as valedictory autobiography. The *Meditation on John Keble's Rogationtide Hymn* was the result of a commission from a firm in New York, something that would not have appealed to Ireland at one time, and certainly not at this stage in his life, when his eyesight problems were making it almost impossible for him to use manuscript paper. However, the commission must have held some sort of personal appeal, and evidently offered sufficient financial incentive for Ireland to accept it, as he wrote that he 'would have refused the commission but was implored for something by the H.W. Gray Co. of N. York and they are paying a reasonable sum for the job' (CM: 10 June 1958).

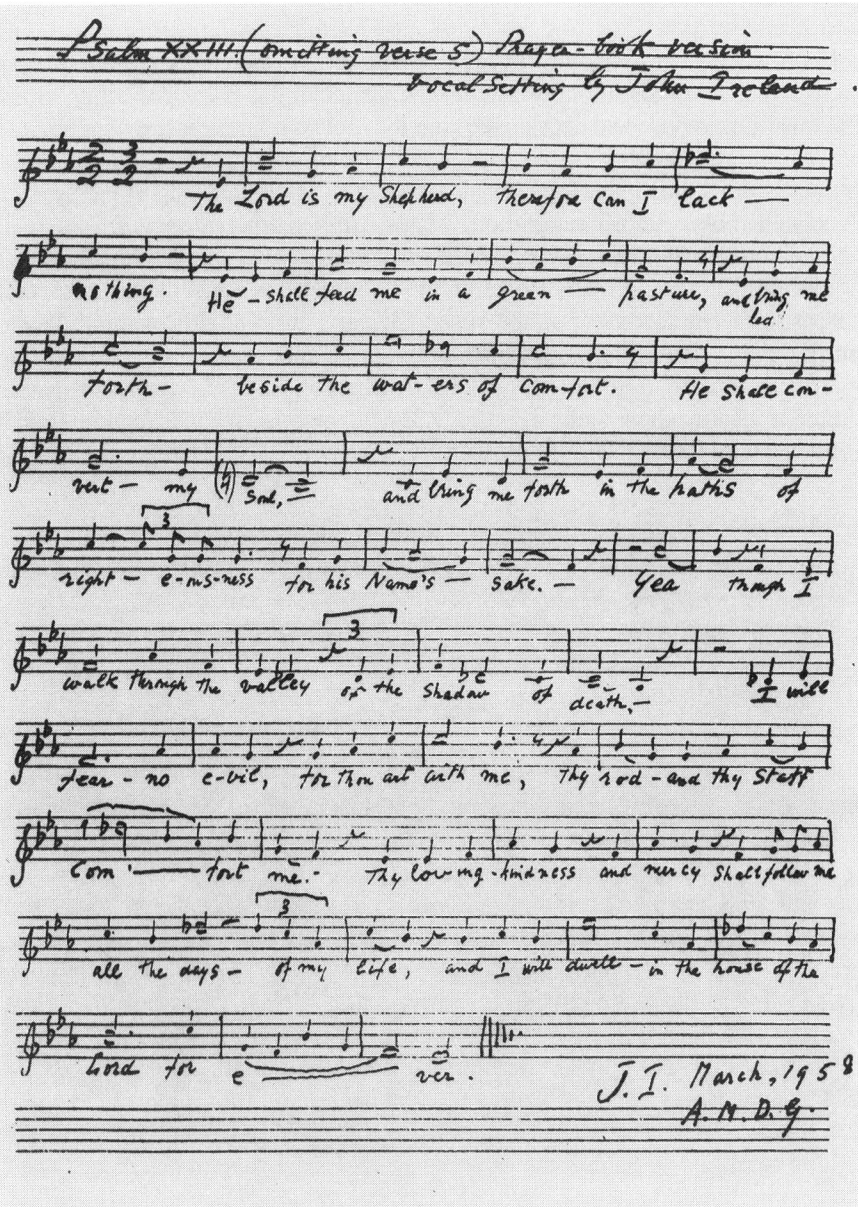

9.2 Psalm 23

The *Meditation* is fundamentally tonal, with a basic ternary structure and a six-bar coda. But a closer look inevitably reveals layers of messages at work, and this tiny piece, despite its simplicity, is a last mixing of topics. The difference between this and the sonatas and song-cycles is that whereas they were a real synthesis of opposing musical symbols, this has a prevailing mood of constraint, repose and acceptance, and the topical references are quotations.

The title of the piece itself carries all sorts of connotations. Like many of Ireland's titles, this underwent considerable discussion, most significantly with Jocelyn Brooke, whose suggestion was *Meditation at Ambervalia*. The final choice was *Meditation on John Keble's Rogationtide Hymn*. Why meditation? Why John Keble? And why Rogationtide? The piece is a meditation in several senses: on Keble's verses, on the observance and customs of Rogationtide and on Ireland's own life. The choice of John Keble was surely a nostalgic backward glance both at Holy Trinity Church, with its statue of Keble dominating the choir stalls (Figure 9.3) and at St Luke's, a church much influenced by Keble's Oxford Movement.

9.3 Relief of John Keble above the choir stalls, Holy Trinity Church

Rogationtide is a religious festival that would have appealed to Ireland on account of its pagan roots. Standing between the Resurrection and the Ascension, the three Rogation days, or 'gang-days', are days of prayer for the crops and their workers, during which time it was customary for the clergy and choirboys to perambulate the parish, singing hymns and asking for blessing on the fruits of the earth. The origins of Rogationtide were ancient and pagan, dating from Roman times, when the May Feast of Ambervalia celebrated the earth and its riches. Rogation and its pagan foundations were included in Brand's *Observations on Antiquities*, the book that had already instigated the titles of *Month's Mind* and 'The boy bishop'. The suggestion from Brooke stemmed from discussion of this book.

There are few hymns for Rogation. The only two that are regularly included in hymnals are those by Keble and Bishop How. Keble's verses, 'Lord, in thy name thy servants plead', are an expression of faith, an unambiguous, poetic offering of homage for 'green ear' and 'golden grain', thanks for 'precious things brought forth / By sun and moon below'.

Thus in one sense the *Meditation* is a clear manifestation of Ireland's own faith and long-standing associations with the Anglican church, and the outer parts of the piece are appropriately hymn-like, serene and tonally secure, in the religious key of E flat major. However, things are not so simple, and even here a secular motif permeates the music. This is the four-note pattern, ^1^7^2^1, that is a hallmark of Ireland's music, used prominently in the slow movement of the Piano Concerto and the *Concertino Pastorale*.

The central section moves away from the secure E flat major to murkier harmonic waters. There is a repeating A, and the E♭–A opposition is a return to the tritonic opposition that had been a feature of so many works. The chromatically shifting parallel triads that dominate this section, notably in bars 40–43 (Example 9.1), are a reference to the sinuous triads that were also a feature of *Satyricon* (from bar 41), and which were heard in a different format in 'We'll to the woods no more' (bar 17).

Example 9.1

The climax of the piece is reached in bar 58, with the final appearance of Ireland's Passion motif (Example 9.2), some forty years after he had first created and used this pattern.

Example 9.2

After this a single melodic line leads the way back to the E flat major music. It seems as though the music will end as it started, but Ireland adds a six-bar coda that tips things in a different direction. This is a quotation of the opening bars of *The Forgotten Rite* (Example 9.3, and see Example 3.1), a pagan ritual inserted into a piece for use in Christian worship, coming to rest ultimately in E flat.

Example 9.3

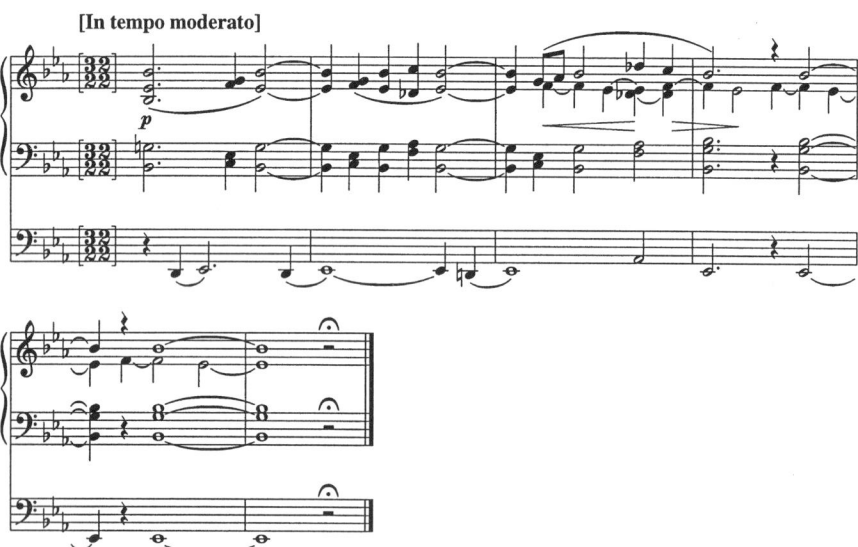

During the years that followed, Ireland wrote nothing, but continued to attend concerts which included his music. August 1959 saw him celebrate another big birthday, his eightieth. He again received congratulations from old friends, including Alfred Sebire and Andrew White, both from Guernsey. This birthday was celebrated at the Proms with performances of the Piano

Concerto, *The Forgotten Rite* and *Satyricon*, and *The Times* review commented on their reflection of the different aspects of the composer, and wrote of *The Forgotten Rite* that it took refuge 'from harsh contemporary reality in the world of nature and its mystical links with the past' (*The Times*, 15 Aug. 1959: 3). Later in the year the MacNaghten Concerts series began its season with a programme devoted to Ireland's music, and the composer was present to hear his Third Piano Trio, the First Violin Sonata, *Decorations* and songs sung by George Parker.

In 1960 there was a new impetus to Ireland's music, with the formation of the John Ireland Society. Its chairman was Harold Rutland, music critic and long-time friend of the composer, and Lawrence Norcross, a teacher and former sailor serving alongside Kenneth Thompson, was secretary to the society. Its inaugural concert included *Sarnia*, the First Violin Sonata, the Fantasy-Sonata, *The Land of Lost Content* and other songs, and *London Pieces*. The performers were pianists Alan Rowlands and Eric Parkin, tenor John Steel, clarinettist Thea King and violinist Vyvyan Yendoll. The society was active not only in promoting Ireland's better-known works, but also in procuring first performances of early and unpublished material: the Sextet had its first public airing in March 1960, and in October 1961 *In Those Days* was premièred, as was the part-song 'Cupid'.

9.4 St Mary the Virgin, Shipley, West Sussex

Ireland died on 12 June 1962 at the age of 82. His funeral took place on Saturday 16 June. He was buried in the church of St Mary the Virgin, Shipley, West Sussex (Figure 9.4). The choice of burial place was symbolic and appropriate. It is a small church in an idyllic setting, surrounded by the Sussex countryside, with Hilaire Belloc's windmill in the background. Inside the church is a commemorative plaque, while Ireland lies buried outside, his grave marked by pagan sarsen stones brought from Dorset to West Sussex. Kenneth Thompson officiated at the service, and the attenders included nephew Anthony, Norah Kirby, Charlie Markes, Arthur Miller, Alan Bush, Peter Crossley-Holland, John Longmire, Alan Rowlands, Ernest Chapman, Eric Parkin, Scott Goddard, Percy Turnbull, Horace Randerson and Lawrence Norcross.

A further memorial to the composer took place two years later, with the unveiling of a stained glass window dedicated to Ireland, in the Musicians' Chapel of the Church of the Holy Sepulchre, Holborn Viaduct. This window shows different aspects of John Ireland. The opening bars of *Greater Love Hath No Man* are there, as are the closing bars of 'Sea fever', along with visual representations of London, Jersey, Maiden Castle, West Sussex and the cattle of *The Overlanders*. The unveiling took place as part of a memorial service on 22 November 1964. As the final farewell to the composer George Parker fittingly sang the unaccompanied setting of Psalm 23.

List of works

1890s	'The peaceful western wind' (Campion)	SATB
1895 (rev. 1941)	*In Those Days*: 'Daydream'; 'Meridian'	Piano
1896	Communion Service in A flat major: Responses to the Commandments; Nicene Creed; Sanctus; Benedictus; Agnus Dei; Gloria	Boys' voices and organ
	Pastoral	Piano
1897	First String Quartet in D minor: Allegro; Molto allegro; Andante moderato; Finale (Vivace)	String quartet
	Second String Quartet in C minor: Allegro moderato; Nocturne (Andante); Scherzo (Presto); Poco allegro	String quartet
1898	Sextet: Allegro non troppo; Andante con moto; Intermezzo (Allegretto con grazia); In tempo moderato	Clarinet, horn and string quartet
	Vexilla Regis A hymn for Passion Sunday	Soli SATB or semi-chorus, SATB chorus, 2 trpts in B♭, 3 trbns and organ
1899	Symphonic Prelude: *Tritons*	Orchestra: 2 flts (2 doubling piccolo), 2 obs, 2 clts in B♭, bass clt in B♭, 2 bsns, 4 hns in F, 2 trpts in F, 3 trbns, tba, timpani, side drum, cymbals, strings
1899–1900	*A Sea Idyll*	Piano
1902	Berceuse	Violin and piano
	Elegiac Romance	Organ
c. 1903–11	*Songs of a Wayfarer*: 'Memory' (W. Blake), 'When daffodils begin to peer' (Shakespeare), 'English May' (D.G. Rossetti), 'I was not sorrowful' (Dowson), 'I will walk on the earth' (J.V. Blake)	Voice and piano

1904	Orchestral Poem in A minor	Orchestra: 2 flts (2 doubling piccolo), 2 obs, 2 clts in A, 2 bsns, 4 hns in F, 2 trpts in F, 3 trbns, tba, timpani, cymbals, strings
	Cavatina	Violin and piano
c. 1904	*Marcia popolare*	Organ
c. 1904 (publ. 1912, rev. 1944)	Intrada	Organ
	Villanella	Organ
	Menuetto-Impromptu	Organ
1905	'Eastergate'	Hymn tune
	Evening Service in A major: 'Magnificat', 'Nunc Dimittis'	SATB and organ
1905–06	First Rhapsody in C sharp minor	Piano
1906	Phantasie in A minor	Violin, cello and piano
1907	Te Deum in F major	SATB and organ
1908	Psalm 42	SATB soli, SATB chorus and string orchestra
	'Full fathom five' (Shakespeare)	SA and piano
	'Spring, the sweet spring' (Nashe)	SATB
	'There is a garden in her face' (Alison)	SA and piano
1908–09 (rev.1917 and 1944)	First Violin Sonata in D minor: Allegro leggiadro; Romance (In tempo sostenuto, quasi adagio); Rondo (Allegro sciolto assai)	Violin and piano
c. 1909	'The frog and the crab' (early sixteenth century)	Unison voices and piano
	'In praise of May' (Morley)	SA and piano
c. 1910	'Annabel Lee' (Poe)	Recitation for voice and piano
	'A laughing song' (W. Blake)	SATB
	'Cupid' (W. Blake)	SATB
1911	Bagatelle	Violin and piano

	Alla Marcia	Organ
	Sursum Corda	Organ
	Capriccio	Organ
	'Hope the Hornblower' (Newbolt)	Voice and piano
	'Hymn to light' (J.V. Blake)	Voice and organ ad lib.
	'When lights go rolling round the sky' (J.V. Blake)	Voice and piano
	'Billee Bowline' (Weatherly), as Turlay Royce	Voice and piano
	'Love's window' (Banning), as Turlay Royce	Voice and piano
	'Alpine song' (J.V. Blake)	Unison voices and piano
	'At early dawn' (J.V. Blake) (also publ. as 'We hardly see the sunbeam yet')	SA and piano
	'Hillo, my bonny' (J.V. Blake), as Turlay Royce	Voice and piano
	'In summer woods' (J.V. Blake) (also publ. as 'How jubilant the summer sky')	SA and piano
	'In praise of Neptune' (Campion)	Unison voices and piano
	'Vesper hymn'	Hymn tune
	'Slumber song' (J.V. Blake)	SA and piano
	'Spring' (J.V. Blake)	SA and piano
1912	*Greater Love Hath No Man* (text selected from the scriptures) A motet for Passiontide and other seasons	Treble and baritone soli, SATB chorus and organ
	'A cradle song' (W. Blake)	SATB
	'Aubade' (Dobell)	SA and piano
	Benedictus in F major	SATB and organ
	'Here's to the ships!' (P.J. O'Reilly)	Voice and piano
	'Evening song' (J.V. Blake)	SA and piano
	'See how the morning smiles' (Campion)	SA and piano
1912–13	*Decorations*: 'The island spell'; 'Moon-glade'; 'The scarlet ceremonies'	Piano
	Trio in D major	Clarinet in B♭, cello and piano

	'Bed in summer' (Stevenson)	Unison voices and piano (also arr. voice and piano)
1913	*The Almond Tree*	Piano
	'Child's song' (Moore)	Unison voices and piano
	Communion Service in C major: Responses to the Commandments; Responses before and after the Gospel; Credo; Sanctus; Benedictus; Agnus Dei; Pater Noster; Gloria	SATB and organ
	Marigold: 'Youth's spring-tribute' (D.G. Rossetti); 'Penumbra' (D.G. Rossetti); 'Spleen' (Dowson) Impression for voice and piano	Voice and piano
	The Forgotten Rite	Orchestra: 3 flts (3 doubling piccolo), 2 obs, ca, 2 clts in B♭, bass clt in B♭, 2 bsns, 4 hns in F, 2 trpts in B♭, 3 trbns, timpani, celesta, harp, strings
	'The echoing green' (W. Blake)	SA and piano
	'Nurses' song' (W. Blake) (also publ. as 'Sunset play')	Unison voices and piano
	'Sea fever' (Masefield)	Voice and piano
	'Song from o'er the hill' (P.J. O'Reilly)	Voice and piano
	Three Dances: 'Gypsy dance'; 'Country dance'; 'Reapers' dance'	Piano
	'Porto Rico' (Weatherly) (as Turlay Royce)	Voice and piano
1913–15	*Preludes*: 'The undertone'; 'Obsession'; 'The holy boy'; 'Fire of spring'	Piano ('The holy boy' arr. violin and piano; cello and piano; organ (1919); voice and piano or strings (1938); SATB; string orchestra (1941))
1914	Jubilate Deo in F major	SATB and organ
1915	Evening Service in F major: Magnificat; Nunc Dimittis	SATB and organ
	Rhapsody	Piano

(rev. 1955 as 'Island praise')	'An island hymn' (Isaiah 42:10, 12)	TTBB
1915–17	Second Violin Sonata in A minor: Allegro; Poco lento quasi adagio; In tempo moderato-Con brio	Violin and piano
1916	*Two Songs* (Thirkell Cooper): 'Blind'; 'The cost'	Voice and piano
	'A garrison churchyard' (Thirkell Cooper)	Voice and piano
1917	Second Piano Trio	Violin, cello and piano
	'The heart's desire' (Housman)	Voice and piano
1917–18	*Two Songs* (Brooke): 'The soldier'; 'Blow out, you bugles'	Voice and piano
1917–20	*London Pieces*: 'Chelsea Reach'; 'Ragamuffin'; 'Soho forenoons'	Piano
1918	'Earth's call' (Monro) A Sylvan Rhapsody	Voice and piano
	'Spring sorrow' (Brooke)	Voice and piano
	'The bells of San Marie' (Masefield)	Voice and piano
	'I have twelve oxen' (anon.)	Voice and piano
	'If there were dreams to sell' (Beddoes)	Voice and piano
	'The sacred flame' (Mary Coleridge)	Voice and piano
	Leaves from a Child's Sketchbook: 'By the mere'; 'In the meadow'; 'The hunt's up'	Piano
	Merry Andrew	Piano
	Mother and Child (C. Rossetti): 'Newborn'; 'The only child'; 'Hope'; 'Skylark and nightingale'; 'The blind boy'; 'Baby'; 'Death-Parting'; 'The garland'	Voice and piano
	'Remember' (Mary Coleridge)	Voice and piano
	'A song of March' (J.V. Blake)	Unison voices and piano
	The Towing Path	Piano
	'(Three) Variations on "Cadet Rousselle" ' (anon.)	Voice and piano (folk song arrangement)
	'Irene'	Hymn tune

1918–19	*Three Songs* (Symons): 'The adoration'; 'Rest'; 'The rat'	Voice and piano
1918–20	Piano Sonata: Allegro moderato; Non troppo lento; Con moto moderato	Piano
1919	'May flowers' (C. Rossetti)	SA and piano
	Benedicite in F major	SATB and organ
	'Love unknown'	Hymn tune
	'Hawthorn time' (Housman)	Voice and piano
	'Mighty Father'	Hymn tune
	Summer Evening	Piano
	'Fraternity'	Hymn tune
1920	*Two Songs*: 'The trellis' (Huxley); 'My true love hath my heart' (Sidney)	Voice and piano
	The Darkened Valley	Piano
	'When May is in his prime' (Edwardes)	SATB
	'The East Riding' (Chilman)	Voice and piano
	'The journey' (Ernest Blake)	Voice and piano
	'The three ravens' (anon.)	Voice and piano (folk song arrangement)
c. 1920s	'When I am old' (Dowson)	Voice and piano
1920–21	*The Land of Lost Content* (Housman): 'The Lent lily'; 'Ladslove'; 'Goal and wicket'; 'The vain desire'; 'The encounter'; 'Epilogue'	Voice and piano
	Mai-Dun	Orchestra: 3 flts (3 doubling piccolo), 2 obs, ca, 2 clts in A, bass clt in A, 2 bsns, 4 hns in F, 3 trpts in C, 3 trbns, tba, timpani, side drum, cymbals, triangle, tambourine, glockenspiel, strings
1921	*Two Pieces*: 'For remembrance'; 'Amberley Wild Brooks'	Piano
	'Love is a sickness full of woes' (Daniel)	Voice and piano
	'The merry month of May' (Dekker)	Voice and piano

	'The ferry' (C. Rossetti)	Unison voices and piano
	'Fain would I change that note' (Hume)	SATB
1922	*On a Birthday Morning*	Piano
	'The vagabond' (Masefield)	Voice and piano
	Soliloquy	Piano
	'Twilight night' (C. Rossetti)	SATB
	Equinox	Piano
1923	Cello Sonata in G minor: Moderato e sostenuto; Poco largamente-Non troppo lento; Con moto e marcato	Cello and piano
1924	Prelude	Piano
	'When I am dead, my dearest' (C. Rossetti)	Voice and piano
	'What are you thinking of?' (C. Rossetti)	Voice and piano
	'They told me, Heraclitus' (Cory)	TTBB
	'Chelsea'	Hymn tune
1925	*Two Pieces*: 'April'; 'Bergomask'	Piano
	'Great things' (Hardy)	Voice and piano
	'Santa Chiara (Palm Sunday; Naples)' (Symons)	Voice and piano
	Three Songs to Poems by Thomas Hardy: 'Summer schemes'; 'Her song'; 'Weathers'	Voice and piano
1926	*Five Poems by Thomas Hardy*: 'Beckon to me to come'; 'In my sage moments'; 'It was what you bore with you, woman'; 'The tragedy of that moment'; 'Dear, think not that they will forget you'	Voice and piano
	'A graduation song' (Drinkwater)	Unison voices and piano
	Three Songs: 'Love and friendship' (E. Brontë); 'Friendship in misfortune' (anon.); 'The one hope' (D.G. Rossetti)	Voice and piano
1926–27	Sonatina: Moderato; Quasi lento; Rondo (Ritmico, non troppo allegro)	Piano
1927	*We'll to the Woods no more*: 'We'll to the woods no more' (Housman); 'In boyhood' (Housman); 'Spring will not wait'	Voice and piano ('Spring will not wait' for piano solo)

	'New prince, new pomp' (Southwell)	SATB
1928	*Two Songs*: 'Tryst' (Symons); 'During music' (D.G. Rossetti)	Voice and piano
1929	'If we must part' (Dowson) A valediction for voice and piano	Voice and piano
	Ballade	Piano
1929–30	*Two Pieces*: 'February's child'; 'Aubade'	Piano
1929–31	*Songs Sacred and Profane*: 'The advent' (A. Meynell); 'Hymn for a child' (Townsend Warner); 'My fair' (A. Meynell); 'The Salley Gardens' (Yeats); 'The soldier's return' (Townsend Warner); 'The scapegoat' (Townsend Warner)	Voice and piano
1930	Piano Concerto in E flat: In tempo moderato; Lento espressivo; Allegretto giocoso	Piano and orchestra: 2 flts (2 doubling piccolo), 2 obs, 2 clts in B♭, 2 bsns, 4 hns in F, 2 trpts in C, 3 trbns, bass tba, timpani, side drum, cymbals, triangle, tambourine, Chinese block, strings
c. 1930	*Ballade of London Nights*	Piano
1930s	*Ways of Peace*	SATB and piano
1931	'Meine Seele erhebt der Herren'	Transcription for piano of J.S. Bach
1932	*Indian Summer*	Piano
	'Tutto e sciolto' (Joyce)	Voice and piano
	A Downland Suite: Prelude; Elegy; Minuet; Round	Brass band
1933	*Month's Mind*	Piano
	Legend	Piano and orchestra: 2 flts, ob, ca, 2 clts in A, 2 bsns, 4 hns in F, 2 trbns, timpani, bass drum, cymbals, gong, triangle, tambourine, strings
1934	*Comedy Overture*	Brass band

1936	*A London Overture*	Orchestra: 2 flts (2 doubling piccolo), 2 obs, 2 clts in B♭, 2 bsns, 4 hns in F, 3 trpts in B♭, 3 trbns, tba, timpani, side drum, bass drum, cymbals, gong, triangle, tambourine, jingles, glockenspiel, xylophone, strings
1937	*These Things Shall Be* (Symonds)	Baritone or tenor solo, SATB chorus and orchestra: 3 flts, 2 obs , ca, E♭ clt, 2 clts in B♭, 2 bsns, contra bsn, 4 hns in F, 3 trpts in C, 3 trbns, tba, timpani, side drum, bass drum, cymbals, gong, triangle, glockenspiel, xylophone, tubular bells, celesta, organ, strings
	Green Ways: Three Lyric Pieces: 'The cherry tree'; 'Cypress'; 'The palm and may'	Piano
1938	Third Piano Trio in E minor: Allegro moderato; Scherzo; Andante cantabile; Finale (Con moto)	Violin, cello and piano
	Five Sixteenth-Century Poems: 'A thanksgiving' (Cornish); 'All in a garden green' (Howell or Edwardes); 'An aside' (anon.); 'A report song' (Breton); 'The sweet season' (Edwardes)	Voice and piano
1939	*Concertino Pastorale*: Eclogue; Threnody; Toccata	String orchestra
1940	Missa *Sancti Stephani*: Kyrie; Responses to the Commandments; Sanctus; Benedictus; Agnus Dei; Gloria	SATB
1940–41	*Sarnia: An Island Sequence*: 'Le Catioroc'; 'In a May morning'; 'Song of the springtides'	Piano
1941	Morning Service in C major: Te Deum Laudamus; Benedictus; Jubilate Deo	SATB and organ

	'Ride a cock-horse' (anon.)	Unison voices and piano
	Evening Service in C major: Magnificat; Nunc Dimittis	SATB and organ
	Ninefold Kyrie in A minor	SATB
	'O happy land' (Linton)	Voice and piano
	'Boys' names' (Farjeon)	Unison voices and piano
	'Here be naked boys' (Farjeon)	Unison voices and piano
	Three Pastels: 'A Grecian lad'; 'The boy bishop'; 'Puck's birthday'	Piano
	'A New Year carol' (anon.)	SATB
1941–42	*Epic March*	Orchestra: 2 flts (2 doubling picc), 2 obs, 2 clts in B♭, 2 bsns, 4 hns in F, 2 trpts in C, 3 trbns, tba, timpani, side drum, bass drum, cymbals, gong, triangle, xylophone, tubular bells, organ, strings
1942	'The boy' (Farjeon) (also publ. as 'Looking on')	Unison voices and piano
	'The bell in the leaves' (Farjeon)	Unison voices and piano
	'Joseph fell a-dreaming' (Farjeon)	Unison voices and piano
	'Immortality' (Crompton)	SATB
	Julius Caesar (Music for the play by Shakespeare)	Orchestra: 2 flts (2 doubling piccolo), 2 obs (2 doubling ca), 2 clts in B♭ (2 doubling clt in E♭), 2 bsns, 3 hns in F, 3 trpts in B♭, 3 trbns, tba, bass tba, timpani, side drum, bass drum, cymbals, triangle, tambourine, piano, lute, 3 double bass
1943	Fantasy-Sonata	Clarinet in B♭ and piano
1944	*Ex ore innocentium* (Bishop W.W. How)	SA and piano or organ

1944–46	*Satyricon*	Orchestra: 2 flts (2 doubling picc), 2 obs, 2 clts in A, 2 bsns, 4 hns in F, 2 trpts in C, 3 trbns, tba, timpani, cymbals, tambourine, glockenspiel, xylophone, whip, harp, strings
1946	*The Overlanders* (Music for the film)	Orchestra: 2 flts and piccolo, 2 obs, ca, 2 clts in B♭ and A, bass clt in B♭, 2 bsns, 4 hns in F, 2 trpts in B♭ and A, cornet, 3 trbns, tba, timpani, tenor drum, side drum, bass drum, cymbals, triangle, glockenspiel, xylophone, piano, harp, strings
1947	'Man in his labour rejoiceth' (Bridges)	SATB and brass band or piano
	'Sampford'	Hymn tune
1949 (rev. 1951)	*Columbine*	Piano
1953	'The hills' (Kirkup)	SATB
1956	'Adam lay ybounden' (anon.)	SATB
1958	Psalm 23	Baritone solo
	Meditation on John Keble's Rogationtide Hymn	Organ

Select bibliography

Abbate, C., *Unsung Voices: Opera and Musical Narrative in the Nineteenth Century* (Princeton, 1991)

Alcorn, J., *The Nature Novel from Hardy to Lawrence* (London, 1977)

Allcroft, A.H., *Downland Pathways* (London, 1924)

Anderton, H.O., 'Cameo Portraits: No.22 – Ariel Enmeshed', *Musical Opinion*, 45 (Aug. 1922), 953–5

d'Arch Smith, T., *Love in Earnest: Some Notes on the Lives and Writings of English 'Uranian' Poets from 1889 to 1930* (London, 1970)

Armstrong, M.D., *Exodus and Other Poems* (London, 1912)

Arnell, R., 'John Ireland (1879–1962)', *Tempo*, 61–2 (Spring–Summer 1962), 39–40

Austin, E., 'About Two "Things of Beauty"', *Musical Times*, 59 (Oct. 1918), 444–5

Avallaunius, the journal of the Arthur Machen Society

Bacharach, A.L. (ed.), *British Music of Our Time* (London, 1946)

Baker, D.Z., *Mythic Masks in Self-Reflexive Poetry: A Study of Pan and Orpheus* (North Carolina, 1986)

Banfield, S., *Sensibility and English Song* (Cambridge, 1985)

Banfield, S., 'Forgotten Rites', *Figures in the Margin* IV, BBC Radio 3, 20 Jan. 1994

Barr-Hamilton, A., 'The Excavation of Two Bronze Age Barrows at Friday's Church, Barpham Hill', *Sussex Archaeological Collections*, 118 (1980), 171–82

Barthes, R., *Image Music Text* (London, 1977)

Bartlett, J., *Familiar Quotations* (London, 1968, first edn 1855)

Bax, A., *Farewell, My Youth and other writings*, ed. L. Foreman (Aldershot, 1992)

Beckett, A., *The Spirit of the Downs* (London, 1924)

Beckson, K., *Arthur Symons: A Life* (Oxford, 1987)

Benson, E.F., *The Inheritor* (Brighton, 1992a, first edn 1930)

Benson, E.F., *The Collected Ghost Stories*, ed. R. Dalby (London, 1992b)

Bergonzi, B., *Wartime and Aftermath: English Literature and its Background 1939–60* (Oxford, 1993)

Birmingham Daily Post

Blake, J.V., *Poems* (Boston, 1887)

Bliss, R.C., *From the Green Book of the Bards* (London, 1903)

Blom, E., 'Ireland's Piano Concerto', *Monthly Musical Record*, 61 (Jan. 1931), 9–11

Blom, E., *Music in England* (London, 1942)

Blom, E., 'Some New Ireland Works', *Tempo*, 8 (Sept. 1944), 2–3, 12

Blom, E. (ed.), *Grove's Dictionary of Music and Musicians*, fifth edn, 10 vols (London, 1954)

Blunt, R., *Red Anchor Pieces* (London, 1928)

Boardman, J., *The Great God Pan: The Survival of an Image* (London, 1997)

Boult, A., Letters to John Ireland, in *JIT*

Bourdillon, F.W., *A Lost God* (London, 1891)

Brand, J., *Observations on Popular Antiquities* (London, 1913)

Bradbury, M. and McFarlane, J. (eds), *Modernism: A Guide to European Literature 1890–1930* (London, 1991, first edn 1976)

Brown, H., Letters to John Ireland, in *JIT*

Browning, E.B., 'A Musical Instrument', in Pritchard (1990)

Brook, D., *Violinists of Today* (London, 1948)

Brooke, J., 'Far Off Things', *Time and Tide* (9 June 1951), 546–7

Brooke, J., 'The Music of John Ireland: An Appreciation', *Musical Times*, 99 (Nov. 1958), 600–602

Brooke, J., *The Birth of a Legend: A Reminiscence of Arthur Machen and John Ireland* (London, 1964)

Brooke, J., 'John Ireland: A Reminiscence', *London Magazine* (April 1965), 75–80

Brooke, J., *A Mine of Serpents* (London, 1981a, first edn 1949)

Brooke, J., *The Goose Cathedral* (London, 1981b, first edn 1950)

Brooke, J., *The Image of a Drawn Sword* (London, 1983, first edn 1950)

Brooke, J., *The Dog at Clambercrown* (London, 1990, first edn 1955)

Brooke, R., *The Poetical Works* (London, 1970, first edn 1946)

Burke, J., *Musical Landscapes* (Exeter, 1983)

Burton, H.M. (ed.), *Selections from Swinburne* (Cambridge, 1927)

Bush, G., *Left, Right and Centre: Reflections on Composers and Composing* (London, 1983)

Bush, G., Introduction to Craggs (1993), ix-xii

Bushaway, B.,'Name upon name: the Great War and Remembrance', in Porter (1993), 136–67

Byfield, D., 'Musical Reflections', *Musical Opinion*, 104 (April 1981), 246–8

Carpenter, E., *Iolaus, An Anthology of Friendship* (London, 1902)

Carpenter, H., *Benjamin Britten: A Biography* (London, 1992)

Carpenter, R., 'Baines and Britten: Some Affinities', *Musical Times*, 97 (April 1956), 185–7

Chapman, E., *John Ireland: A Catalogue of Published Works and Recordings* (London, 1968)

Chilman, E., *Sixty Lyrics and One* (London, 1945)

Clark, K., *The Best of Aubrey Beardsley* (London, 1979)

Coburn, C., 'The Man Who Broke the Bank': Memories of the Stage and Music Hall (London, 1928)

Cohan, S. and Shires, L., Telling Stories (New York and London, 1988)

Colmer, J., E.M. Forster: The Personal Voice (London, 1975)

Cook, N. and Everist, M. (eds), Rethinking Music (Oxford, 1999)

Craggs, S., John Ireland: A Catalogue, Discography, and Bibliography (Oxford, 1993)

Cross, T., Artists and Bohemians: 100 Years with the Chelsea Arts Club (London, 1992)

Crossley-Holland, P., 'John Ireland', in Blom (1954), IV: 533–44

Crowther, M.A., 'The Tramp', in Porter (1993), 91–113

Daily Telegraph

Das, G.K. and Beer, J. (eds), E.M. Forster: A Human Exploration (London, 1979)

DeGaris, M., Folklore of Guernsey (Guernsey, 1975)

Demuth, N., 'John Ireland', Musical Opinion, 81 (Oct. 1957), 21

Dentith, S., Bakhtinian Thought: An Introductory Reader (London, 1995)

Dickens, C., Oliver Twist (London, 1975, first edn 1837–39)

Dickinson, A.E.F., 'The Progress of John Ireland', Music Review, 1/4 (Nov. 1940), 343–53

Dickson, A. (ed.), Art and Literature, vol. 14, The Pelican Freud Library (London, 1988, first edn 1985)

Ditchfield, P.H., Old English Customs Extant at the Present Time: An Account of Local Observances, Festival Customs and Ancient Ceremonies yet Surviving in Great Britain (London, 1901)

Dobson, R., Brangham, G. and Gilbert, R.A. (eds), Arthur Machen: Selected Letters (Wellingborough, 1988)

Docherty, B., 'The Murdered Self: John Ireland and English Song 1903–13', Tempo, 171 (Dec. 1989), 18–26

Dunhill, D., Thomas Dunhill: Maker of Music (London, 1997)

Dunhill, T., 'The R.C.M. Literary and Debating Society', RCM Magazine, 5/1 (1908–09), 17–21

Eco, U., Interpretation and Overinterpretation (Cambridge, 1992)

Ellmann, R., Oscar Wilde (London, 1987)

Empson, W., Some Versions of Pastoral (London, 1995, first edn 1935)

Evans, E., 'John Ireland', Music Quarterly, 5 (1919a), 213–20

Evans, E., 'John Ireland', Musical Times, 60 (Aug. 1919b), 394–6 and (Sept. 1919c), 457–62

Evening Post, Jersey

Farjeon, E., Over the Garden Wall (London, 1933)

Faunus, the journal of the friends of Arthur Machen

Ferguson, N., The Pity of War (London, 1998)

Field, N.H. and Bugler, J., *The Ancient Monuments of Dorset* (Dorchester, 1972)

Firbank, R., *Valmouth and Other Stories* (London, 1996)

Foreman, L. (ed.), *From Parry to Britten: British Music in Letters 1900–1945* (London, 1987)

Foreman, L., Sleeve notes to choral and orchestral works by John Ireland (Chandos, 1990)

Forster, E.M., *Collected Stories* (London, 1947)

Forster, E.M., *Two Cheers for Democracy* (London, 1972, first edn 1951)

Forster, E.M., *Aspects of the Novel* (London, 1990, first edn 1927)

Foss, H., 'John Ireland', *Musical Times*, 103 (Aug. 1962), 536–7

Frazer, J., *The Golden Bough* (Ware, 1993, first edn 1922)

Fussell, P., *The Great War and Modern Memory* (London and New York, 1975)

GD, 1: George Dannatt's account of the relationship between Charles Markes and John Ireland, GB-Cu (Add. MS 9473)

Giles, J., and Middleton, T. (eds), *Writing Englishness 1900–1950* (London and New York, 1995)

Gillie, J., *A Preface to Forster* (Essex, 1983)

Goddard, S., 'John Ireland's Fantasy-Sonata for Clarinet and Pianoforte', *Tempo*, 8 (Sept. 1944), 6–9

Goddard, S., 'Music of the film', *Penguin Music Magazine*, III (Sept. 1947), 64–6

Gower, R., 'John Ireland's Organ Music', *Musical Times*, 120 (Aug. 1979), 682–3

Grahame, K., *Pagan Papers* (London, 1898)

Grainger, P., Letters to John Ireland, in *JIT*

Grant, J., *Harold Monro and the Poetry Bookshop* (London, 1967)

Grinsell, L.V., 'Sussex Barrows', *Sussex Archaelogical Collections*, 75 (1934), 217–75

Halperin, D.M., *One Hundred Years of Homosexuality* (London, 1990)

Hanson. E., *Decadence and Catholicism* (Cambridge, Mass., 1997)

Hardy, T., *A Changed Man and Other Stories* (Stroud, 1997)

Harman, C., *Sylvia Townsend Warner: A Biography* (London, 1989)

Harman, C. (ed.), *The Diaries of Sylvia Townsend Warner* (London, 1995, first edn 1994)

Hatten, R., *Musical Meaning in Beethoven: Markedness, Correlation, and Interpretation* (Indiana, 1994)

Henderson, P., *Swinburne: The Portrait of a Poet* (London, 1974)

Henley, W.E., *London Voluntaries* (Edinburgh, 1892)

Herbage, J. and Instone, A. (eds), *Music Magazine* (London, 1953)

Hill, R., 'John Ireland', in Bacharach (1946), 99–112

Hillsdon, S., *Jersey: Witches, Ghosts and Traditions* (Norwich, 1987)

Hillsdon, S., *Jersey* (Ashbourne, 1997)

Holdsworth, R. (ed.), *Arthur Symons: Selected Writings* (Manchester, 1989, first edn 1974)

Holland, A.K., 'John Ireland at 75 – an appreciation', *Tempo*, 32 (Summer 1954), 7–8

Holme, T., *Chelsea* (London, 1972)

Housman, A.E., *Last Poems* (London, 1922)

Housman, A.E., *A Shropshire Lad* (London and Toronto, 1990, first edn 1896)

Howes, F., *The English Musical Renaissance* (London, 1966)

Hugo, V., *The Toilers of the Sea* (transl. of *Les Travailleurs de la Mer*) (Boston, 1888)

Hull, A.E. 'A Modern English Classicist', *Musical Opinion*, 42 (Feb. 1919a), 281–2

Hull, A.E., 'John Ireland's Songs', *Musical Opinion*, 42 (March 1919b), 350–1

Hull, A.E., 'The Instrumental Music of John Ireland', *Musical Opinion*, 42 (April 1919c), 415–17

Hunt, P., *The Dolmens of Jersey* (Jersey, 1998)

Hunter, J., *Edwardian Fiction* (Cambridge, Mass., 1982)

Huxley, A., *Limbo* (London, 1920)

Ireland, Alexander, *Cheap Literature and the Love of Reading* (Manchester, 1882)

Ireland, A., *The Book-Lover's Enchiridion: Thoughts on the Solace and Companionship of Books* (London, 1883)

Ireland, Alleyne, *Briton and Boer in South Africa* (Boston, 1899)

Ireland, A., *Joseph Pulitzer: Reminiscences of a Secretary* (New York, 1914)

Ireland, A., *The New Korea* (New York, 1924)

Ireland, Anthony, *Byron in Piccadilly* (London, 1945)

Ireland, A.E.N. – see Nicholson, A.E.

Ireland, E., Letters to John Ireland, in *JIT*

Ireland, E., *Some new letters by Leigh Hunt and Stevenson* (Boston, 1898)

Ireland, J., Letter to Mary Bentley, in *JIT*

Ireland, J., Letters to Adrian Boult, in GB-Cu (Add. MS 9473), in *JIT* and in GB-Lbl (Add. MS 60498)

Ireland, J., Letters to Jocelyn Brooke, in Harry Ransom Research Center, University of Texas at Austin

Ireland, J., Letters to Nancy Bush, in GB-Cu (Add. MS 9473)

Ireland, J., Letters to Ernest Chapman, in GB-Lbl (Add. MS 61884)

Ireland, J., Letters to Edward Clark, in GB-Lbl (Add. MS 52256)

Ireland, J., Letters to Cramer, in GB-Lbl (Add. MS 68943)

Ireland, J., Letters to Clifford Curzon, in *JIT*

Ireland, J., Letters to Thomas Dunhill, in *JIT*

Ireland, J., Letters to Edwin Evans, in *JIT*

Ireland, J., Letters to Arthur Robert Lee Gardner, in *JIT*

Ireland, J., Letters to Percy Grainger, in *JIT*

Ireland, J., Letters to Cecil Gray, in GB-Lbl (Add. MS 57785)

Ireland, J., Letters to Ethel Ireland, in *JIT*

Ireland, J., Letters to Silvio Ireland, in *JIT*

Ireland, J., Letters to John Longmire, in *JIT*

Ireland, J., Letters to Elizabeth Lutyens, in GB-Lbl (Add. MS 71144)

Ireland, J., Letters to Charlie Markes, in *JIT* and in GB-Cu (Add. MS 9473)

Ireland, J., Letters to Sydney Nicholson, in *JIT*

Ireland, J., Letters to George Parker, in *JIT*

Ireland, J., Letters to Helen Perkin, in *JIT*

Ireland, J., Letters to Horace Randerson, in *JIT*

Ireland, J., Letters to Harold Rawlinson, in *JIT*

Ireland, J., Letters to Aidan Reynolds, in *Faunus*

Ireland, J., Letters to Harold Rutland, in *JIT*

Ireland, J., Letters to Linton Shields, in *JIT*

Ireland, J., Letters to Herbert Sumsion, in Gloucester City Library

Ireland, J., Letters to Kendall Taylor, private collection

Ireland, J., Letters to Revd Kenneth Thompson, in GB-Lbl (Add. MSS 60535–6)

Ireland, J., Letters to Frederick Thurston, in the private collection of Thea King

Ireland, J., Letters to Majorie Walde, in *JIT*, and quoted in Longmire (1969)

Ireland, J., Letters to Paul Walde, in *JIT*

Ireland, J., Letters to Henry Wood, in GB-Lbl (Add. MS 56420)

Ireland, J., Letters to Kenneth Wright, quoted in Longmire (1969)

Ireland, J., 'Stanford', *Music and Letters*, 5/3 (July 1924), 195

Ireland, J., 'A Speech for the Opposition', *Music and Letters*, 8/2 (April 1927), 109–10

Ireland, J., 'My Introduction to Beethoven', in Herbage and Instone (1953), 26–31

Ireland, J., 'Albert Sammons: A Tribute', *Musical Times*, 98 (Oct. 1957), 548

Ireland, J., 'Tribute to Vaughan Williams', *Musical Times*, 99 (Oct. 1958), 535–6

Irving, E., 'The Overlanders', *Tempo*, 2 (1946), 27

Jacobs, A., *Henry J. Wood: Maker of the Proms* (London, 1994)

Jebb, K., *A.E. Housman* (Bridgend, 1992)

Jenkyns, R., *The Victorians and Ancient Greece* (Southampton, 1984)

JIT, 1: Ireland's notes on his early training and on the Second Violin Sonata

JIT, 2: Ireland's notes on the Phantasie for Piano Trio

JIT, 3: Ireland's tribute to Albert Sammons

JIT, 4: Ireland's tribute to Sir Walter Alcock

JIT, 5: Ireland's comments on performances of Brahms and Stravinsky

JIT, 6: A set of holiday photographs from 1922 to 1923

JIT, 7: Material relating to Helen Perkin

JIT, 8: Material relating to Arthur Miller

JIT, 9: Material relating to Herbert Brown

JIT, 10: Herbert Brown, poem, 'The forsaken altar'

JIT, 11: Horace Randerson's diary, and letters from Ireland to Randerson

JIT, 12: Autograph book presented to Ireland in 1949

Johnston, C., *A Guide to St Luke's Church Chelsea* (London, 1999)

Keats, J., *Selected Poems* (London and Glasgow, 1978)

Kemal, S. and Gaskell, I. (eds), *Landscape, Natural Beauty and the Arts* (Cambridge, 1993)

Kinnes, I., *The Dolmens of Jersey* (Jersey, 1988)

Kirby, N., Letters to George Dannatt, in GB-Cu (Add. MS 9473)

Kivy, P., *Sound and Semblance* (Princeton, 1984)

Lambert, H., Letters to Gerald Finzi

Lambert, H., 'John Ireland's Piano Concerto', *Sackbut* (Jan. 1931), 168–9

Lamond, F., 'Some Remarks on John Ireland's New Sonata', *Monthly Musical Record*, 50 (Aug. 1920), 170–72

Lanser, S., *The Narrative Act* (Princeton, 1981)

Laroon, M., see Shesgreen (1990)

Lawrence, D.H., *St Mawr* (London, 1925)

Lawrence, D.H., *Phoenix: The Posthumous Papers of D.H. Lawrence* (New York, 1936)

Lee, E.M., 'The Amateur's Repertoire', *Musical Opinion*, 52 (July 1929), 908–9

Lee, E.M., 'John Ireland's "Sarnia"', *Musical Opinion*, 65 (April 1942), 231–2

Legg, R., *Cerne's Giant and Village Guide* (Wincanton, 1990)

Lemprière, R., *Jersey in Old Photographs: A Third Selection* (Stroud, 1993)

Lenoir, H., Autobiographical notes, in *JIT*

Lewis, C.S., *Prince Caspian* (London, 1974, first edn 1951)

Leyshon, A., Matless, D. and Revill, G. (eds), *The Place of Music* (New York, 1998)

Longmire, J., 'Obituary', *Musical Opinion*, 85 (July 1962), 599

Longmire, J., *John Ireland: Portrait of a Friend* (London, 1969)

Longmire, J., Introduction to *The Land of Lost Content and Other Songs* (London, 1976)

Lovecraft, H.P., *Supernatural Horror in Literature* (New York, 1945)

Lyle, W., 'The Songs of John Ireland', *Sackbut* (July 1922), 27–30

Macdonald, L., *1914–1918: Voices and Images of the Great War* (London, 1988)

Machen, A., Letters to John Ireland, in *JIT*

Machen, A., *The Great God Pan* (London, 1894)

Machen, A., *The House of Souls* (London, 1906)

Machen, A., *The Secret Glory* (London, 1922)

Machen, A., *The London Adventure* (London and New York, 1924)

Machen, A., *The Three Imposters* (London, 1926, first edn 1895)

Machen, A., *The Hill of Dreams*, in Palmer (1988a)

Machen, A., *The Great God Pan* (London, 1993, first edn 1894)

Machen, A., *Precious Balms* (Horam, 1999, first edn 1924)

Manchester Examiner

Manchester Guardian

Mann, W., 'John Ireland's New Appeal', *The Times* (15 Aug. 1969), 9

Mann, W., Sleeve notes to song sets by John Ireland (Lyrita Records, 1975)

Markes, C., Letters to George Dannatt, in GB-Cu (Add. MS 9473) and in *JIT*

Martin, C., *The Edwardians* (London, 1974)

Massingham, H., *The English Countryside: A Survey of its Chief Features* (London, 1939)

Matless, D., *Landscape and Englishness* (London, 1998)

Merivale, P., *Pan the Goat-God: His Myth in Modern Times* (Cambridge, Mass., 1969)

Meyer, L., *Emotion and Meaning in Music* (Chicago, 1965)

Meyer, M. (ed.), *The Politics and Poetics of Camp* (London and New York, 1994)

Mitchell, D. and Reed, P. (eds), *Letters from a Life: The Selected Letters and Diaries of Benjamin Britten 1913–1976* (London, 1998)

Moeran, E.J., 'John Ireland as Teacher', *Monthly Musical Record*, 61 (March 1931), 67–8

Money, J., *Aspects of War: The German Occupation of the Channel Islands 1940–1945* (Guernsey, 1995)

Monthly Musical Record

Monro, H., *Children of Love* (London, 1914)

Monro, H., *Strange Meetings* (London, 1917)

Moore, J.N. (ed.), *Music and Friends: Seven Decades of Letters to Adrian Boult* (London, 1979)

Moore, T.S., *Pan's Prophecy* (London, 1904)

Musical Opinion

Musical Quarterly

Musical Times

Music and Letters

Music and Musicians

Music Review

Myers, R., *Music Since 1939* (London, 1947)

Nicholson, A.E., *The Life Story of Jane Welsh Carlyle* (New York, 1891)

Nicholson, A.E., *Longer Flights* (London, 1898, posth.)

Nicholson, J.G., *A Chaplet of Southernwood* (private publication, 1896)

Nicholson, S., Letters to John Ireland, in *JIT*

Noolas, R. (P. Warlock), *Merry-Go-Down: A Gallery of Gorgeous Drunkards Through the Ages* (London, 1929)

Observer

Orledge, R., *Charles Koechlin (1867–1950): His Life and Works* (Switzerland, 1989)

Ottaway, H., 'The Piano Music of John Ireland', *Monthly Musical Record*, 84 (Dec. 1954), 258–66

Ottaway, H., 'Ireland's Shorter Piano Pieces', *Tempo*, 52 (Autumn 1959), 3–6, 17

Ottaway, H., 'John Nicholson Ireland', in Sadie (1980), IX: 325–7

Palmer, C., *Impressionism in Music* (London, 1973)

Palmer, C. (ed.), *The Collected Arthur Machen* (London, 1988a)

Palmer, C., Sleeve notes to music by John Ireland (Chandos, 1988b and 1992)

Pauwels, L. and Bergier, J., *The Dawn of Magic*, transl. R. Myers (Paris and London, 1960)

Pears, P., Sleeve notes to *The Land of Lost Content* (Argo, 1964)

Penguin Music Magazine

Perkin, H., Letters to John Ireland, in *JIT*

Perkin, H., Letters to John Longmire, in *JIT*

Petronius, *The Satyricon* (Oxford, 1999)

Pevsner, N., *The Englishness of English Art* (1993, first edn 1956)

Pilkington, M., *Gurney, Ireland, Quilter and Warlock* (London, 1989)

Pirie, P., *The English Musical Renaissance* (London, 1979a)

Pirie, P., 'A Vision Dimly Seen', *Music and Musicians*, 27 (Aug. 1979b), 18–20

Plato, *The Symposium* (London, 1999)

Porter, R. (ed.), *Myths of the English* (Oxford, 1993)

Priestley, J.B., *Our Nation's Heritage* (London, 1939)

Pritchard, R.E. (ed.), *Poetry by English Women – Elizabethan and Victorian* (Manchester, 1990)

RCM students' registers and teaching registers

Read, B.A., *No Cause for Panic: Channel Islands Refugees, 1940–45* (Jersey, 1995)

Reid, F., *The Garden God* (London, 1986, first edn 1905)

Reid, F., *Uncle Stephen* (London, 1988, first edn 1931)

Reynolds, A. and W. Charlton, *Arthur Machen: A Short Account of his Life and Work* (London, 1963)

Rowlands, A., 'John Ireland 1879–1962', *RCM Magazine*, 58/3 (1962), 70–71

Rowlands, A., 'John Ireland: A Significant Composer?', *RCM Magazine* (Summer 1992), 18 and *RCM Magazine* (Spring 1993), 13–19

Rutland, H., 'The Achievement of John Ireland', *Musical Times*, 100 (Aug. 1959), 421–2

Rutland, H., 'John Ireland', *Recorded Sound*, 50–51 (April–July 1973), 190–98

Sadie, S. (ed.), *Grove's Dictionary of Music and Musicians*, sixth edn, 20 vols (London, 1980)

Schafer, R.M., *British Composers in Interview* (London, 1963)

Schama, S., *Landscape and Memory* (London, 1995)

Schneller, H.M. and Peters, R.L. (eds), *The Letters of John Addington Symonds* (Detroit, 1967)

Schur, O., *Victorian Pastoral: Tennyson, Hardy, and the Subversion of Forms* (Ohio, 1989)

Scott-Sutherland, C., 'Nationalism and John Ireland', *Music Review*, 22/3 (1961), 195–7

Scott-Sutherland, C., *John Ireland* (Rickmansworth, 1980)

Scott-Sutherland, C., *Edward Thomas and John Ireland* (British Music Society, 1993)

Searle, M., *John Ireland: The Man and His Music* (Tunbridge Wells, 1979)

Self, G., *The Music of E.J. Moeran* (London, 1986)

Sheldrake, R., *The Rebirth of Nature* (London and New York, 1993, first edn 1990)

Sheldrake, R., *The Presence of the Past* (London, 1994, first edn 1988)

Shesgreen, S. (ed.), *The Criers and Hawkers of London: Engravings and Drawings by Marcellus Laroon* (Aldershot, 1990)

Smith, B., *Peter Warlock: The Life of Philip Heseltine* (Oxford, 1994)

Smith, E., *A Dictionary of Classical Reference in English Poetry* (Cambridge, 1984)

Spalding, F., *Whistler* (London, 1994, first edn 1979)

Spicer, P., *Herbert Howells* (Bridgend, 1998)

St Luke's: parish magazines, 1904–23, and parish minutes

Stanford, C.V., *Musical Composition: A Short Treatise for Students* (London, 1949, first edn 1911)

Starrett, V., *Arthur Machen: A Novelist of Ecstasy and Sin* (Horam, 1996, first edn 1918)

Stephens, J., *Collected Poems* (London, 1954)

Stevenson, R.L., *Virginibus Puerisque* (Edinburgh, 1898)

Stone, W., *The Cave and the Mountain: A Study of E.M. Forster* (California, 1966)

Stradling, R. and M. Hughes, *The English Musical Renaissance 1860–1940: Construction and Deconstruction* (London and New York, 1993)

Summers, J., *Soho: A History of London's Most Colourful Neighbourhood* (London, 1989)

Sunday Times

Symons, A., *Days and Nights* (London, 1889)

Symons, A., *London Nights* (London, 1895)

Symons, A., *London: A Book of Aspects* (London, 1909)

Thirkell Cooper, E., *Soliloquies of a Subaltern Somewhere in France* (London, 1915)

Thomas, E., 'The Glory', in *The Oxford Book of Twentieth Century English Verse* (Oxford, 1975), 131

Thompson, K., Letters to John Ireland, in *JIT*

Thompson, K., Letters to Colin Scott-Sutherland, in *JIT*

The Times

Todorov, T., *The Poetics of Prose*, transl. R. Harvard (Cornell, 1977)

Townsend Warner, S., *The Espalier* (London, 1925)

Townsend Warner, S., *Mr Fortune's Maggot* (London, 1927)

Townsend Warner, S., *Selected Poems* (Manchester, 1985)

Townsend Warner, S., *Lolly Willowes* (London, 1993, first edn 1926)

Townshend, N., 'The Achievement of John Ireland', *Music and Letters*, 24/2 (April 1943), 65–74

Updike, J., 'Get a Life', *Daily Telegraph* (6 Feb. 1999), A1 and A10

Viinikka, A., *From Persephone to Pan: D.H. Lawrence's Mythopoeic Vision of the Integrated Personality* (Turkey, 1988)

Vinci, L., *Pan: Great God of Nature* (London, 1993)

Wellek, R. and Warren, A., *Theory of Literature* (London, 1993, first edn 1949)

Wheeler, M., *Maiden Castle* (London, 1972)

Whitman, W., *Leaves of Grass* (Oxford, 1990, first edn 1855)

Williams, C., *All Hallows' Eve* (Michigan, 1991, first edn 1948)

Williams, R., *The Country and the City* (London, 1973)

Wilson, A.N. (ed.), *The Faber Book of London* (London, 1993)

Wilson, E., *Axel's Castle: A Study in the Imaginative Literature of 1870–1930* (London, 1993, first edn New York, 1931)

Woodring, C., *Nature into Art: Cultural Transformations in Nineteenth-Century Britain* (Cambridge, Mass., 1989)

Index of works

Index